Encyclopaedia of Indian Theatre — 4

# Dictionary of Music, Dance and Drama

**Encyclopaedia of Indian Theatre - Series**

1. Bhasa
2. Major Sanskrit Dramatists
3. Kalidasa
4. Dictionary of Music, Dance and Drama
5. Rabindranath Tagore

Encyclopaedia of Indian Theatre — 4

# Dictionary of Music, Dance and Drama

Biswajit Sinha

Raj Publications
Delhi-110009

*First Published in 2003*

ISBN 81-86208-18-6 (Series)
**ISBN 81-86208-** 24-0

Illustration : Sukanta Deb (Machpota)



*Published by* : Mrs. Poonam Goel
**Raj Publications**
**R-115/2, Model Town - III,**
**Delhi - 110009**

**Tel. : 7143321**

**E-mail : rajpub@now-india.net.in**

*Laser Typesetting by* : Aarati Computers, Delhi-110 009

*Printed at* : Chawla Offset Printers, Delhi-110 052

In

Fond Memory of My Sister

**Deepali Bose**

# Preface

Gestating in mind, my dream project, in the form of an extensive and all inclusive 'Visva-Natya Kosha' to explore all possible fields of study, Sanskrit Drama, Folk Theatre, History of Regional Theatres, Schools, Repertories, Troupes, Personalities, Dramatic literature, Techniques, Trends, Movements etc. with which would be appended a summary of World Theatre for the benefit of the Indian students and researchers. In last fifteen years, I have collected immense materials on Indian drama for this purpose.

However, in the meantime, under the series **'Encyclopaedia of Indian Theatre,'** already appeared in print three theme-based volumes. The present dictionary is the fourth in the process. All such independent volumes under the series took shape from my personal collections which I bring into the orbit of the present generation of students and researchers to cater to their immediate need. The production of such volumes have also been motivated my another factor, i.e. my huge, and variegated stuff (once published in printed formats) get restored and organized topic-wise that can be interlinked in later stage, when I shall take up a cumulative encyclopaedia. Presently I don't possess a computer, an indigent circumstance.

A select dictionary, the present book extracts important terminologies from the treasure house of classical sanskrit literature, Vedas, Natyashastra, Dasarupaka, Abhinayadarpana, Bhavaprakashanam, Sahityadarpanam, Sangitaratnakara, Sangitasamayasara, Sangitamakaranda etc.

A concise lexicography of this kind which covers an essential vocabulary of music, dance and dramatic words, as found in the traditional doctrines in simplified manner is perhaps the first effort of its kind which, I hope would help the students and art enthusiasts alike.

**— Biswajit Sinha**

# A

**Abharaṇakrit**

The *Natyashastra* refers to some Acharyas who are expert in preparing materials for the stage. There are many types of artisans seem to have been necessary in the presentation of plays. The 'Abharanakrit' is one who prepares ornaments for the characters as prescribed in the traditional dramatic doctrines.

**Abhigita**

Passing from Dvitiya to Prathama is called 'Abhigita', one of the eight Gīti-upāyas employed in the recitation of the Samaveda.

**Abhiluptārtha** **see Dosas**

**Abhinaya**

This is 'Histrionics' in Indian concept.

The term is used for Actor's art of communication.

Though it refers to 'Acting', but Bharata in his *Natya Shastra*, mentions it is not just acting, but various other things which go to make up the medium of expression. Bharata explains the word etymologically from the root '*nī*' to "*carry*", with the preposition '*abhi*' meaning "*towards*", that which carries the meaning (lit. the performance) to the audience is called *Abhinaya*. In broadest term, Abhinaya is the art of expressing the mood and nature of a dance or drama composition or convey ideas.

*Natyashastra* states that '*Abhinaya*' is of four types, ie,

(1) *Angika*

(2) *Vāchika*

(3) *Sattvika* (*Samanya*)

The word 'Angika' comes from the '*Anga*' or the '*body*' and therefore denotes '*Bodily Acting*'. This comprises of many modes from simple gestures to deliberate postures and artistic movements.

The 'Vacika, ie, literally belonging to '*speech*'.

**Aharya Abhinaya**

Aharya Abhinaya is which is produced through Nepathya. It covers painting, make-up, costume properties, ornaments etc.

*Sattvika Abhinaya* seems to be expression in a graceful or charming manner the various *Bhavas*, ie, feelings. Grace or charm excludes impropes looks, gestures, movements.

Thus, there are four modes of Abhinaya, the ideas and emotions of an actor. are reflected. As said, the modes of expression are purely physical (*Angika*), song and speech (*Vachika*), ornamental (*Aharya*) involving the use of costumes, make-up or stage sets and emotional (*Sattvika*).

Abhinaya in drama assumes great importance for it is through this mode that human feelings are expressed. It helps in expressing the emotions and creates the intended ambiance. Even internal conflict experienced by a character can be understood through Abhinaya. According to Natyashastra, Abhinaya is so called because in the performance together with gestures and speech it explains the meaning of different things.

In one of the verses in Chapter VI of *Natyashastra*, Bharata has furnished eleven elements of Drama which can be collectively called the '*Digest of Natyashastra*. There significant dramatic components are :-

Rasa (Sentiment)

Bhava (Emotion)

Abhinaya (Acting)

Dharmi (Modes of representation)

Vritti (Styles of expression)

Pravritti (Local usages)

Siddhi (Success of production)

Svara (Note)

Atodya (Musical instruments)

Gana (Song)

Ranga (Theatre)

Abhinaya is the one of the most essential elements in it.

Bharata in this treatise (XXV, 125) states "The behaviour of the people is of various kinds; conveying that by acting and bodily movements in called drama (acting)". He further says "It is not possible to form rules (or give directions) for acting or conveying the (unbelievable) various actions and objects of the world. (XXV, 128). Acting is therefore left to the talent of actors/actresses.

Abhinaya is conveyed through *Natyadharmi* (stylised) and *Lokadharmi* (realistic) representation.

**Abhinaya see also Chitra - Abhinaya**

**Abhineta**

Means an actor

**Abhinetavya**

To be acted or dramatically represented.

**Abhinetri**

Denotes an actress.

**Abhineya**

To be acted or dramatically represented.

**[see also Itivritta]**

**Abhinit**

Means "Performed, represented dramatically".

**Abhipraya, (Fancy) see Vagyabhinaya.**

**Abhiri**

This is one of the sub-dialects of Prakrita and is not available in any extant dramas, but is mentioned in dramatic treatises. Abhiri or Shabari was prescribed for those who lived in places where elelphants, horses, goats, sheeps, camels or cows were kept.

**Abhisarika Nayika**

Bharata's treatise on dramatics furnishes eight varities of Heroine-in-love and *Abhisarika* denotes one of them.

*'Dasarupaka'*, another excellent work in the field defines her as one who being unable to bear the pangs of separation invites the lover to a tryst for the consummation of her passion. A critic states : She overcomes the coyness characteristic of a woman,

and this gives rise to the possibility of a conflict between bashfulness and earnest desire to meet her lover. Mostly, the circumstances are against her, so she secretly moves on a path, a sense of fear always clinging to her heart. Sometimes, Nature tries to obstruct her by means of rain or thunderstorm : or serpents, and even darkness on the way are not less frightening. Thus, for an *Abhisarika*, adventure involves great tension but, she is sure of his love for her.

**(see also 'Nayikas')**

**Abhivyakti**

Refers to expression, manifestation.

**Ābhoga**

A concluding section in chant or in a prabandha (an art song).

**Ābhoga see also Dhatus**

**Acharya**

It denotes a master, a teacher a preceptor or a director etc. (for example, Nātyacharya is used for a teacher of dramatics (*synonym-Guru*). Poets/drama composers, directors, stage managers, musicians, scene-designers, painters are some Acharyas in the domain of theatrical performances. The Natyashastra also refers to some Acharyas proficient in preparing material required for the stage and proficient in directing actors and actresses. We have many types of artisans like Mukutakara, Abharanakrit, Malyakrit, Vesakara, Chitrakara, Rajaka, Karuka and again Kushilava, Natyakara, Taurika etc.

This is also a mode of address in a Sanskrit play. The Natyashastra has prescribed a set of words for calling the different characters according to their position. A teacher is addressed as '*Acharya*'.

**Āḍambara**

This is a kind of drum; a drummer; Adambaraghāta is mentioned in a list of victims at the human sacrifice (Purush-amedha) in the Vajasaneyi Samhita.

This Āḍambara drum mentioned in the Mādhyamdina recenion (V 12-1) is referred to as Lambana in the Kaṇva recension (V. 10-1) of the Brihadāraṇyaka Upanishad.

**Adbhuta Rasa**

Adbhuta refer means 'Wonder, Marvellous, Prodigious' etc.

This is one of the nine rasas mentioned in the ancient treatises.

Adbhutarasa (Marvellous) the sentiment of wonder arises from the sthayibhava or permanent stage of 'Vismay' or Astonishment.

According to *Natyashastra*, the Vismay or Astonishment could be evoked by Vibhāvas such as sight of celestials, realisation of cherished objectives, approach of sylvan divinities and other unreal and, therefore, illusory spectacles as raised by magicians and jugglers, etc. The king and the other characters in Harsa's Ratnavali or Priyadarsika feel extremely distraught at the sight of the sudden outbreak of fire. But as soon as they realise that it was all a magician's trick, their afflicted senses give way to wonder and relief and joy.

Wonder is represented in acting by a gesture of surprise, joyful shaking of limbs, uttering amazing sounds, speaking words of appreciation, tremor, chocking of voice, perspiration and the like.

Varna: Pita (Yellow)

Mukharaga : Prasanna (Pleased)

Svara : Rishabha

Raga: As stated earlier, Amazement is the principal bhāva; wonder, astonishment, amazement, surprise, appreciation, admiration, adoration are all expressions in this rupture of wonder.

Joy, happiness and gaiety also tag along with this rasa. Thus aesthetic joy in music is also part of this rasa. Ragas employed to depict Adbhuta are :-

Bhauli, Devagāndhāri, Valaji, Shuddha Sāveri, Malayamārutha, Dhanyāsi, Bilahari, Mohana, Gaudamalhar, Kharaharapriya, Kedāragaula, Rāmapriya, Ārabhi, Schree,

Vasanthā, Ānanda bhairavi, etc.

Svara : Rishabha

Presiding deity : Brahma

**Adhama Nayaka**

Classical theorists classify male characters into three classes of Jyestha (Uttama), Madhyama (Madhya/A-mukhya) and Kanistha (Adhama, Hina, Nicha). This applies to the Nayaka, Neta or the leader of the principal dramatic action as well. *Bhavaprakashana* states that the Adhama is deficient in many. Pratinayaka or the counter-hero may be either a Madhyama or an Adhama type. Besides, the dramatic characters, that are supposed to be naturally low (Nicha) are Vidusaka, Shakara, Vita, eunuch and all servants

**(see also 'Nayaka's).**

**Adhama Nayika see Nayika**

**Adhama - Prakriti Pramada**

Bharata says this kind of female characters are like the low category of men and shares their traits.

**(see also 'Nayikas')**

**Adharabheda**

This means 'movements of the lip'. They are of six varieties as follows:-

(1) Vivartana (Twisting sideways)

To depict 'jealousy, pain, bashfullness'.

(2) Kampana ( Throbbing/quivering the lower lip)

To express 'laugh, smile, painting the lips.

(3) Visarga (Spreading)

To show 'painting the lips, feet, amorous mood.

(4) Viniğūhana (folding in of the lower lip)

Used for 'strenuous exertion'.

(5) Sandaṣṭaka (biting the lip)

To show 'anger, frustration, guilt, nervousness.

(6) Samudga (natural position of the lip)

To show 'sympathy, salutation and normal gesture.

**Adhikārī Netā**

The term is used for the hero who is entitled to the final fruit; also referred to as a Nāyaka in Sanskrit drama.

**Adhikarika Vritta**

The dramatic plot, according to Bharata's *Natyashastra* is of two types

(1) Adhikarika or Principal and

(2) Prāsangika or incidental, subsidiary.

Adhikarika Vritta or the Principal plot is that which has the inherent strength or potentiality to lead to the accomplishment of the desired fruit. It is also directed to lead to and connected with the final fruit 'phala' and its achievement.

*Dasarupaka* tries to define the term 'Adhikāra' and the cognate term 'Adhikārin' by stating that 'Adhikāra' (in the context of drama' means 'ownership of fruit', and Adhikārin' means the master (the leader of the actor or the hero of a drama) who owns that fruit. Therefore, the entire accomplishment leading to the final fruit which pervades the whole play is 'Adhikarika Vritta' or the Principal plot.

Some later thorists have used the term 'Mukhya' for this category.

**Adhira - Madhya Nayika see Madhya Nayika**

**Adhiṣthana**

*Natyashastra* while dealing with 'Theatre House' prescribes that the Natyamandapa should be provided with a plinth (Adhisthana) and Rangasirsa should be at the higher level than the plinth.

**(see also "Ranga")**

**Adityas**

Adityas are the sons of Aditi; solar divinities. Aditi is the mother of the gods, the mother of the world, the sovereign "mother". Adityas are among the presiding deities of the theatre, who should be worshipped with offerings and sacrifices, tells *Natyashastra*.

**(see also 'Devatas')**

**Āghāti**

In the Atharvaveda, this musical instrument is mentioned as Āgahāta. The Rigveda informs this as a musical instrument; the cymbal used to accompany dancing.

**Agni**

He is the 'Fire god', one of the presiding deities of the threatre to be worshipped with offerings and sacrifices.

It is said that Agni is the protector of the stage.

**(see also 'Devatas')**

**Ahārya Abhinaya**

Denotes external, effected by decoration or ornamentation, one of the four aspects of *Abhinaya* in Sanskrit theatrical tradition.

Refers to expression through costume and make-up or alankaras.

Chapter XXIII of *Natyashastra* explains this variety, ie, acting through costumes, and make-up. Here are given rules on the use of ornaments, costumes, their colours and the painting of various limbs.

This third genre of Abhinaya, as Bharata defines, is produced through Nepathya (*Natyashastra*; I, 2). Nepathya refers to painting and other make-up, costume, property, ornaments etc. required by the characters and are collectively called *Aharya-bhikaya*. Accordingly *Natyashastra* divides Nepathya into four divisions as *Pusta*, *Alankara, Angarachana and Sanjiva*.

This kind of Abhinaya, therefore, deals with the art of 'Get-up and Make-up'.

**Aharyabhinaya see also (Alankara, Angarachana, Nepathya, Pusta and Sanjiva)**

**Anata Nāda see Anāhata Nāda**

**Āhvāraka Svaras**

A collective term given to six techniques employed in singing the svaras of the Vedic Scales. These are Ayāmo, Dāruṇya, Aṇuta, Anavasarga, Mārdava and Nruta, of which the first three are used in the Utshepiṇi or upper tetrachord while the rest are employed in the Avashepiṇi or lower tetrachord.

**Ajjukā**

Bharata in his dramatic treatise '*Natyashastra*' has laiddown a set of words for calling the different characters according to their position. A courtesan is called 'Ajjukā', in a convention followed in Sanskrit plays.

**Ākashabhāṣita**

Refers to 'Speech in the air', an Indian stage technique when a characters on the stage enters into a dialogue with one who is not on the stage.

This is a *Natyokti* usually employed for economy of characterization. This kind of dramatic speech is open to all, but it has to use a particular convention and mode of Abhinaya is *Akashavhasita, Akashavachana or 'Aerial speech'.*

Natyashastra defines it as conversation carried on with someone situated far away; it is 'an unembodied communication; the (far-away) person is not visible to the eye of the spectators; he is concealed by the characters who is present on the stage before

t what he says or is supposed to say is reported

haracter present on the stage and that is how he

sation. Such a speech of the invisible character

chana'. The device of aerial speech comes handy

a character on the stage may be unnessary.

**Akashavachana see Akaskabharita**

**Akhyana**

It means 'Narration'; and also denotes story, tale; legend etc.

The early Indian dramatic representations were not merely Akhyana or story-telling by mimetic action (Anukriti) but it was a drama which Bharata testifies and Indian tradition upholds by showing that in it contained a spectacle of mythical, legendary or puranic happening, like the churing of the milk-ocean for nectar by gods and demons. Therefore Akhyana was retold by different actors by playing different roles incoporating movements and actions with appropriate make-up and the whole episode was 'acted' without the spoken dialogue. The speech was perhaps, added as an essential aspects of Natya in later period. Akhyana is the gist of the story, just one essential components of drama. The drama is, therefore, different from Akhyana in the form of public recitations of epic and puranic episodes by professional bards and story-tellers. But this factor must have helped in giving a formal shape to dramatic efforts.

**Aksara - samghāta (Compactness) see Vagyabhinaya**

**Aksaras (Tāla/Rhythm) see Laya**

**Aksepiki**

According to king Bhoja who wrote on poetry, drama and music, we learnt of a specific kind of music. In certain situations we require a certain melodic background and to impose this melody over the situation, a song was sung in which the *Rāga* also mattered, and not the words of the song. Bhoja refers to songs so used as Shravya or Aksepiki.

**Alambana see Vibhavas**

**Alankara**

It connotes 'Decoration'.

Bharata defines Aharyabhinaya as one which is produced through 'Nepathya'. The latter, he explains, is composed of Pusta, Alankara, Angarachana and Sanjiva.

In Alankara, he covers garlands, necklaces, ornaments worn on different parts of the body and dress. (XXI, 10)

There are three kinds of Alankara states Natyashastra. These are:

(1) **Ornaments** (made of coral, diamond, silver and gold).

(2) **Garlands** (made out of various types of flowers and wreathes.

(3) **Costumes**

Ornaments are of four types on the basis of way of wearing them. Bharata states them as Avedhya, Bandhaniya, Praksepya and Aropya.

Regarding ornaments, Bharata says "The variety in ornaments is greatly based on the difference between men and women, between region and region and between caste and case". (XXI, 15) The ornaments are worn not to make the characters look beautiful or attractive but look genuine int he context of the plot and the drama. *Natyashastra* stresses that ornaments for both men and women be chosen according to the region they belong, their caste with due consideration of place and time and it also discourages over-ornamentation.

Bharata prescribes the following ornaments for men: *cūdāmaṇi* [crest-jewel] and *mukuṭa* [crown] for the head; *Kuṇḍala* [ear-ring], *mocaka* [ear-pedant] and kīla [ear-top] for the ear; muktāvalī, [pearl necklace], *harsaka* [a snake shaped ornament] and *sūtra* [gold thread] for the neck; *vaṭikā* and *aṅgulimudrā* [finger-ring] for the fingers; *hastavī* and the *valaya* [bangle] for the fore-arm; *rucika* [bracelet] and *uccitika* for the wrist; *Keyūra* [armlet] and *aṅgada* [arm-band] for the upper arm; *trisara* [three-stringed necklace] and *hāra* [necklace] for the neck and chest; *tarala* and *sūtraka* [golden thread] for the waist; and suspended jewelled necklaces and flower-garlands for the entire body.

Ornaments for women are also given by Bharata. Women wear *pādapātra* on the *janghā* [shanks]; *aṅgulīyaka* [toe-rings] on the toes and *tilaka* on the big toes. *Nūpura, kiṅkiṇī, ratnajāla* [jewel-net] and ringing *kaṭaka* ornaments are worn round the ankle. An additional decoration of the feet will be the lac-dye applied on them in various patterns to impart to them the natural colours of Aśoka blossoms. Ornaments named *kañcī,* with a net of pearls, *mekhalā, raśanā* and *kalāpa* are worn round the waist. There is only one string in *kañcī,* eight strings in *mekhalā*, 16 in *raśanā* and 25 in *kalāpa*. *Hāras* were found to be of 8, 16, 32, 64, 100 strings. Women used to wear *hāraṣ* of different jewels on their bosom and round the neck. They are: *muktāvali* [pearl-necklace], *uyālapaṅkti* [snake-group], *ratnamālikā* [jewel-string], *ratnāvalī* [jewel-necklace] and *sūtraka* [neck-chain]. Different kinds of ornaments mixed with jewels were worn by ladies on the bosom or the back. On the fingers they used to wear rings. *Śaṅkakalāpī* [hastidanti cuḍiyān], *kaṭaka, patrapūraka, kharjura, aṅśopitika* ornaments were worn by women on the wrists. *Aṅgada* [arm-band] and *valaya* [bangle] were used on the upper arm. The *varjura* and the *svecchitika* are ornaments of the fore-arm. *Tilaka* and *patralekhā* adorned their temples. *Karṇikā, karṇavalaya, karṇamudrā* entwining the ear, *dantapatra* set with jewels, *karṇapūra* and *karṇotkīlaka* [ear-top] were prescribed for the ears. Bunches of flowers tied to the hair dangled above their eyebrows. They used *śikhāpāśa, śikhājāla, khaṇḍapātra, cūḍāmaṇi* [crest jewel], *makarikā, muktājāla* [pearl-net], *gavākṣa* and *śīrṣajāla* [hairnet] as ornaments for the head. Bharata has not mentioned any ornament for the nose which might have come into vogue in later times. Ornaments are to be worn according to emotions and sentiments and having a consideration of tradition measurements of the wearer and physical form.

Floral decorations is one of the essential components of Alamkara (embellishment). According to Bharata Garlands (Malya) can be categorised into five kinds as follows:-

(1) Veshtita (covered)

(2) Vitata (spread up loose)

(3) Sanghtya (with many strings)

(4) Granthima (tied up, knotted)

(5) Pralambita (hanging down)

So far as dress is concerned, the *Natyashastra* discusses in details proper dresses for male and female characters according to the part of the country and they belong, their age, their status or social standings and even different locales would mean a change in dress.

**Alankaras**

It denotes the 'Figures of Speech' and Bharata mentions four Alankaras available to a playwright. These are

(1) Upama (Simile)

(2) Rūpaka (Metaphor)

(3) Dipaka (Condensed Expression)

(4) Yamaka (Alliteration)

**Alankaras (Laksanas)**

It is accepted that the sentiments, plot character, acting etc together form a drama. But there are certain qualities which mark a good drama just like jewelleries, graceful behaviour etc adds to a person's deportment and over all impression. These marks are called Laksanas or Alankaras. There are thirty six marks of good dramatic composition as enlisted below:

(1) Bhusana (Ornateness)

(2) Aksharasamghāta (Compactness)

(3) Shobha (Brilliance)

(4) Udaharana (Parallelism)

(5) Hetu (Causation)

(6) Samasya (Hesitation)

(7) Dristanta (Favourable precedent)

(8) Prapti (Discovery)

A

(9) Abhiprāya (Fancy)

(10) Nidarshana (Unfavourable precedent)

(11) Nirukta (Convincing explanation)

(12) Siddhi (Persuasion)

(13) Vishesana (Distinction)

(14) Guṇātipāta (Accusation of virtues)

(15) Gunatishaya (Excellence)

(16) Tulya-tarka (Inference from Similitude)

(17) Padoccaya (Multiplex Predication)

(18) Dista (Description)

(19) Upadista (Pointed utterance)

(20) Viparyāya (Inversion)

(21) Bhramsha (Slip of Tongue)

(22) Anunaya (Demitation)

(23) Mālā (Series of offers)

(24) Dākshinya (Clever Manner)

(25) Garhana (Censure)

(26) Arthapatti (Presumption)

(27) Prasiddhi (Celebrity)

(28) Pricchā (Interrogation)

(29) Sārupya (Identity)

(30) Manoratha (Indirect expression of one's desire)

(31) Lesha (Wit)

(32) Samksepa (Brevity)

(33) Guna-kirtana (Enumeration of Merits)

(34) Anukta-siddhi (semi-uttered expression)

(35) Priyavacana (Compliment)

(36) Vichara (Deliberation)

**Alankaras (Pathyaguna / Sangita)**

Alankara denotes 'Ornament' (Melodic choices) Alankara is one of the attributes of musical rendering (Pathyaguna). There are six kinds of embellishments:-

(1) **Uccha (Highs):** Uccha is pitch produced from the *Shriasthana*. It is used while talking to some one at a distance, or express wonder, dismay, counter argument and in fright.

(2) **Dipta (Illuminated):** Dipta is louder than Uccha and produced from the *Shirasthana*. It is used in reproach, quarrel, dispute, annoyance, anger, arrogance, heroism, defence, wuttering sharp word, lamentation etc.

(3) **Mandra (Grave):** Mandra is lower than Uccha and produced from the Shirasthana. Used in desperation gloom, sportiveness, fainting, whisperng, secret conversation, when wounded etc.

(4) **Nīcha (Low Pitch):** Nīcha is lower than the Mandra and produced from the *Urasthana* (chest). It is used in normal conversation, ailment, weariness, tranquility, exhaustion, panic, while falling down etc.

(5) **Druta (Fast):** Druta is fast recitation and produced from Kanthasthana (throat) and is used in fear, cold, fever, panic, pain etc.

(6) **Vilambita (Slow):** This is a slow recitation and produced from Kanthasthana (throat) Used in Love and Pathetic ruptures (Shringara and Karuna Rasas) to indicate deliberation, discrimination, jealousy, anger, envy, inadequacy, expressive speech, bashfulness, anxiety, surprise, censure, chronic illness, while threatening, etc.

Sharangadeva stated that the aim of demonstrating the Alaṅkaras is to create delight, knowledge of the Svaras and the variety of melodic shapes.

Of Dattila's short list of Alankaras, some are shakes or quivers on a sustained tone, some are back-and - forth "swings" between two adjacent or non-adjacent tones, some are rapid touchings of a single higher or lower tone (to be struck "like lightning") and others are patterns with specific contours (with, for example, the lowest tone situated at the beginning middle, or end of the progression)".

According to Lewis Rowell, Professor of music theory at Indiana University "To put the three terms Varna, Alankara and Gamaka into their proper perspective, it is useful to imagine the decorative dimensions in Indian music as a hierarchy : If Varna represents the generalized shape of a given unit of melody, Alankara signifies the specific pattern of decoration within this general shape, and Gamaka refers to the transitive elements around and between the individual svaras - the microlevel of melodic structure progression from contour to patern to microstructure, we can also infer another progression : from ornaments as conceived to ornaments as performed; once again from the potential to the actual. The idea of Varna is readily grasped by the mind and described in words, but the microscopic subtleties of the Gamakas resist description and are best learned by demonstration and imitation.

In Music, the term Alankara refers to the pattern of surface decoration within an individual varṇa, and here the possibilities could in no way be restricted to any obvious set of exclusive choices. Alankara developed in an explosion of possibilities from Dattila's thirteen, to Bharata's thirty - three and subsequently to the sixty - three enumerated by Sharangardeva and the still larger numbers mentioned in later musical treatises.

**Alaṅkārasāśtra**

It means the science of rhetorics, poetics.

**Alapadma Hasta**

This is a single hand gesture in which all fingers stretched apart and the index finger stretched straight with the little finger bent inward. Alapadma is used to express "a full-blown lotus, wood apple, circular movement, a breast, separation from the beloved, face, the full moon, beauty, the hair-knot, a moon-tower (turret), a village, height, anger, cart a lake, a *chakrawaka* bird, murmuring sound and praise."

**Alapallava**

The gesture indicates full-blown lotus, anger, round face; ball, praise etc in Indian dance.

**Ālāpana**

A nonmetrical exposition of a Rāga at the beginning of a composition or performance is called 'Ālāpana'.

**Ālapti**

This is a version of Ālāpana that emphasizes the typical melodic contours of the chosen Rāga.

**[See Anibaddha Gāna]**

**Ālasya**

It denotes 'Indolence, Langour, Sloth, Laziness' etc.

Alasya or "Indolence" (is the seventh Mutable State/ Vyabhichari Bhava) which may be represented on the stage by avoiding activity, lying down, sitting listlessly, drowsiness, sleeping and dreaming.

**Āliḍha**

Refers to one of the standing positions denoting shooting, employed in performing arts.

**Amarsha**

It denotes, 'Indignation, Non-endurance' etc.

'Indignation' is the twenty-fifth Mutable State/Vyabhichari Bhava which should be represented in acting by shaking the head, perspiration, thinking, reflecting with downcast face, showing determination while working, looking for a wayout, for help and so on, mentions *Natyashastra*.

**Amatya**

This refers to 'Councillor'. The *Natyashastra* has prescribed a set of words for calling the different characters according to their position. A minister is addressed as 'Amatya' (councillor) or 'Saciva' (Minister) by a Brahmana and 'Arya' (Sir) by others.

**Ambhaṇā**

Resonator of the harp (Yāl) synonyms: Donior Doṇika (Pali).

**Aṁsha**

According to ancient musical theory there are three important notes in the Raga. Amsha is the predominant or main note, the soul of the Raga. Other being 'Graha', the starting note and Nyasa, the ending note. Sharangadeva in his treatise *'Sangita Ratnakara',* identifies the Amsha with the Vadi (Sonant). Because it is most used during a performance, the Vādī (Sonant) is called Amsha (main note). *Abhinavabharati* of Abhinavagupta states. "The Amsha svara is the same as the Vādī", therefore shares the same opinion.

Aṁsha is, therefore, the tonic or sonant note (the most prominent note in a jāti or grāmarāga).

**Amukha see Prastavana**

**A-mukhya Nāyaka see Madhayama Nāyaka**

**An-abhinaya see Itivritta**

**Anaddha**

*Amarakosha* enlists drum instruments 'Anaddha' as 'Ānaka, Pataha, Dhakkā, Bheri, Dundubhi, Damaru, Maddu, Dindima, and Zazzara (Rāigada is Marathi), Mardala, Mridanga, and Panava.

**Anāgata**

The previous note ending before the next note is sung. One of the defects to be avoided while performing the Karshana or Svarasandhi.

**Anāhata Nāda**

The primary preocenpathin of the musician is with sound, unmanifest and manifist. In musical ferms this becomes the concept of the instruck (Anāhata) and the struck (Āhata) sound. Practically all works of music begin their discussion on the nature of music with this conceptnal base. The Sangita Mākaraṇda defines the two as : 1 sound prudnced from either is known as 'Anāhata'. In theis unsthuck (Anāhata) *svara* the *devas* delight. The *yogis* and the great spirits projecting their minds by an effiort of the mind into this unstruck Sound depart, attaching liberation (mokṣa). The *Sangitaratna karn* devotes equal attcntion to Anāhata and speaks of Anāhata nāda as the means for inforse single minded (ekāgaṛactta) concentration.

**Anga**

Anga means 'the Limbs' six in number - head, hands, chest, armpits, waist and feet.

**(see 'Angika Abhinaya)**

**Anga see also Prasangika**

**Anga (Musical Rendering)**

This is one of the attributes of musical rendering. In all Shastras have provided six factors that govern the rendering of music Anga refers to speech delivery and there are six ways to render speech as follows:-

(1) **Viccheda (Separation):** This is a pause. It is indicates the ending of a sentence.

(2) **Arpana (Presentation):** This is a note during recitation that modulates a speech.

(3) **Visarga (Closure):** This is the completion of a sentence.

(4) **Aminamdha (Continuity):** This is a note or sign of separating two words by inhaling while reciting them.

(5) **Dipana (Brilliance):** This is a gradual augmentation of notes that proceed beautifully from the three voice sthanas, locations, Ura, Kantha and Shira.

(6) **Prashamana:** This is lowering the higher pitch smoothly.

**Anga (Prabandha)**

According to *Saṅgitaratnakara* of Sharangadeva, Prabandha consist of six angas : Svara, Biruda, Pada, Tena, Pāṭa and Tāla, like the limbs of the body, these are the integral parts of the configuration of a prabandha.

The Dhatus and Angas are the formal components of Prabandhas (art songs). In the earlier Brihaddeshi the formal structure of the various Prabandhas is described in terms of six Angas only, with their order left unspecified. The Angas are as follows:-

**Pada** (word), a passage of meaningful text (a word, phrase, line or stanza).

**Svara**, a passage of Sol-fa syllables.

**Biruda** (or Viruda), a passage of text extolling the subject of the song and including the singer's signature.

**Tena**, a vocalise on the word Tena with many repetitions.

**Pāṭa,** a passage of recited syllables onomatopoetic of drum strokes.

**Tāla,** a section regulated by one of the cyclical Deshi Tālas.

**Angahara**

According to *Amarakosha*, it is gesture, while Abhinaya is the expressive movement of hands.

*Nāṭyaśāstra* describes 32 aṅgahāra-s; a measured sequence of dance movements of the body arising out of a combination of two, three or four units (Karaṇa-s).

**Angarachana**

It connotes 'Painting of the Limbs'.

Aharyabhinaya is produced through Nepathya which is one of the four kinds of acting, comprises of painting, make-up, costume, ornaments, property required by the characters. Bharata divides Nepathya into four types, viz, Pusta, Alankara, Angarachana and Sanjiva.

Angarachana covers painting the face and body.

The characters in a play are usually painted not only to lose their previous individuality but also to look the character they are to portray. Angarachana should be governed by considerations of the art of painting, aesthetics and above all, of the drama. The make-up man should make character look not just beautiful and attractive, but real in the context, though the art of painting will have its say as far as the paint and its mixture is concerned. So Bharata stresses that one should know the process about (preparing and mixing) paints, about its lasting quality and fastness and also the region, the caste (family - heritage) and the age of the character (to be played). [XXI, 87]

Natyashastra instructs 'To make Pandu colour mix white and yellow; for *Padma* white and red; for *Kapota* white and blue; for *Harita* yellow and blue; for *Kasaya* blue and red; and for *Gour* mix red and yellow. After mixing the colours, the body of the actors should be painted according to the character, region, state and description.

Bharata adds A *Tilaka* applied with artistic design on forehead, a strand of hair in fine curls above the eyes are ornamental. Eyes and lips should be painted beautifully and in a pleasing manner. Teeth should be like pearls. *Alakta* (a red coloured liquid) has to be applied in various patterns on the feet and palms.

About facial make-up the Southerners should be made up as Asita (Non-white) the Easterners as Shāma (Darkish) and the Northerners as Gowra (White); followed by a detailed varities such as a forester be made-up black.

**Angika Abhinaya**

Denotes expression through gestures and movement of the limbs.

Angika denotes 'Bodily' and Angikabhinaya means acting expressed through physical action. In Agnikabhinaya, where the expressions are shown or conveyed through the physical movements of the body comprises of Shariraja, Mukhaja and Cheshtakrita. Shariraja denotes expressions through the limbs of the body and sub-divided as Anga, (major limbs), Pratyanga (minor limbs) and Shakha (branch limbs of the body). Mukhaja is expression through the facial features and cheshtakrita through the movements of the entire body.

**Angikabhinaya**

- Shariraja (The limbs of the body)
  - Anga (Major limbs)
  - Shakha (Branch limbs)
  - Pratyanga (Minor limbs)
- Mukhaja (Facial features)
  - Upanga
- Cheshtakrita (Movements of the entire body)

'Bodily acting' are therefore divided into three divisions:-

(I) Physical gestures (due to body or *Sharira*)

(II) Facial expressions (from different parts of face)

(III) Postures or movements (Ceṣṭā). (Deals with Cārī, Maṇdala, Gati-pracar, ie, gaits and movements) etc.

While referring to Angika Abhinaya, purely physical mode of expression, the *Natya Shastra* analyses the human form, dividing it into two principal sections as major and minor limbs. It deals at length with the nature and the meaning and the varieties of the acting of six Angas and six Upangas. Under 'Physical gestures' Bharata mentions six 'Angas' (Main limbs of the body, viz, hands, head, chest, sides (or hips), waist and feet. Each of these Angas have further sub-divisions. For example, in case of the 'Head' Bharata has prescribed thirteen kinds of movements, each conveying a meaning.

The Upanga or six minor limbs are eyes, eye brows, nose, lower lip and chin.

Facial expressions are conveyed by eyes, eyebrows, nose, lips, cheeks, and chin. These are Upangas (Subordinate or Secondary limbs).

Each of upangas have sub divisions. For example in case of 'Eyes', Bharata describes thirty six kinds of glances conveying thirty six different meaning.

Postures or the movements are further analysed in the following ways: The movement mainly with a single foot is called a '*Chari*'. The movement which combines both the feet and hands is called a *Karana*. The combination of three Karanas is called a Khanda.

Further, a *Mandala* is referred to as the combination of three or four Khandas. Sthanaka is a posture taken before the movement starts.

Chapters VIII to XIII of *Natyashastra* deals with the this Angikabhinaya, ie acting through limbs, ramified as gestures of minor limbs (Chapter VIII), gestures of hands (Chapter IX), gestures of other limbs (Chapter X), Chari, ie, movements employed in dance, fight, etc (Chapter XI), Mandal or circular movements arising out of the various Charis (Chapter XII), gaits suited to different characters (Chapter XIII).

Bodily gestures, etc, if unaccompanied by facial expressions do not convey any charm or attraction, physical gestures even if inadequate, will be twice effective if accompanied by facial expressions. Bharata's Natyashastra (VIII, 162 - 163) therefore says "like the moon during the night time" would be as dull as the moon during the day-time.

Angika (gesture) helps to a great extent in expressing one's mood or state in which one is involved be it grief, anger, pathos etc which are internal emotions, require the help of gestures to express them effectively.

**[see 'Chari' for pose; 'Gati - Prachar' for Gaits and movements; 'Mandala' for movement resulting from a number of Charis see also: Hasta Mudras and Karanas etc.]**

**Anibaddha Gāna**

Sharangadeva in his Sangitaratnakara has mentioned in the fourth canto that "The sages have declared Gāna to be two fold, namely Nibaddha (composed) and Anibaddha (Improvised). That which is composed of Dhatus (section) and Aṅgas (Limbs) is called Nibaddha. While 'Ālapti, which is free from such structural limitations, is known as Anibaddha.

**Anirukta**

Means Indefinite, unidentifiable.This is one of the tonal qualities mentioned in the Chandogya Upanishad. Anirukta denotes indefinite, unidentifiable voice (a tone quality).

**Anjali Hasta**

This is a double hand gesture in which both hands are joined in Pataka. This is used "to offer salutation to God, Guru and Brahmana holding the hands near the head, face and chest respectively." This gesture in Indian dance is therefore used to offer salutation. In case of God, it is held on the head, in case of elders near one's face and near the chest for friends and spectators.

**Anka**

According to Bharata, an Anka is rudhisabda, ie, he knows no etymology. The *Avaloka* on the *Dasarupa* states that the Anka signifies the mother's lap, because the Act helps the development of the theme.

This is also one of the ten recognised forms of drama, as mentioned in the traditional Sanskrit treatise; story is well known or not well known; Hero is an ordinary man; sentiment (rasa) is pathos; having just one act.

**[see 'Utsristkanka' & Javanikantara]**

**Ankamukha see Arthopakshepakas**

**Ankāsya**

In accordance with traditional Dramatic Theory, the character on the stage at the end of the preceding act introduces the beginning of the next act and the exits (the end of an act is usually indicated by the exit of all the characters on the stage.

This is, therefore, a linking devise - that part of an act wherein the subject of the act is intimated, also called Ankamukha.

**Ankavatara**

According to Sanskrit theatrical treatises, Ankavatara is a device in which the end of the preceding act telescopes into the beginning of the next act.

This is, therefore, a linking device and is that part of an act when the happenings in the next act are hinted at.

**Ankāvatāra see Arthopakshepakas (Indicatory scenes)**

**Anta**

It means the final component of a Gītaka. The latter denotes one of the compositions performed during the ritual prelude to a play.

**Antaḥpura**

It refers to the 'Harem of the King'. In the Royal Harem one can find innumerable characters of varied nature who serve the king. Such retinue comprises of both men and women such as Kañcuki, Pratihari, Shakāra, Varsavara (eunuchs) etc.

**Antara**

This denotes an interlude.

**Anubhava**

It means total impact of acting

**Anubhāvas see Vibhāvas**

**Anudarshana**

It means a perceptive aesthetic enjoyment.

**Anugata**

In the actual playing of the instruments, there are different methods. Three major styles are Tattva, Anugata and Ugha. Anugata is close accompaniment of the song.

**Anudātta**

This is a grave accent in Vedic recitation. Other than Rig and Sama Vedic verses, even the prose part of the Yajur - Veda are in Sanskrit with Vedic accents called as 'Udātta, Anudātta and Svarita. These acents were the musical notes, used in Vedic chants.

**Anudruta (Tala/Rhythm) see Laya**

**Anugānam**

A kind of Sāman, in which the sections are in different Gaṇa, each with different Rik, but treated as one complete Sāman; somewhat similar to Rāgamālika composition.

**Anukarana**

It is significant to mention here that Dhananjaya, used the term 'Rupaka' as a synonym for Drama. Drama is called 'Rupaka' as a synonym for Drama. Drama is called 'Rupaka' because it is a visual presentation; and there is also a metaphorical identification involved here, as when we call a face the moon, in order to imply its loveliness. In drama, there is a double identification or superimposition: A writer creates a character of Rama and we take it to be real Rama; this is one superimposition. When an actor play that part in a stage performance we accept that actor as the real Rama, atleast the time being, this is another supermposition. It is due to this supermposition that a drama is called 'Rupaka' and the principle behind this identification is Anukarana which leads to the belief of identity.

**(see also Bhavanukintana)**

**Anukirtana**

It denotes a specific cognitive process of aesthetic expression, artistic activity and aesthetic enjoyment, a creative exploratory interpretation.

**Anukta-siddhi (semi-uttered expression) see Vāgyabhinaya**

**Anukūla Nayaka**

The Anukula Nayaka is one who is sincerely and honestly devoted to the lady of his love. Bhavabhuti's Rama of Uttaramacharitam and Madhava of Malatimadhava fall into this category or Anukula or Eka-nirata lover.

*Bhavaprakashana* of Sharadatanaya classify the Nayaka (the Hero) in the context of love, implying the attitude and behaviour of the Hero in regards to the matters of love. His fourfold distinctions are:- Anukula, Daksina, Shatha and Dhrista type of Nayaka.

**(see also Nayaka)**

**Anukriti**

It denotes 'mimetic action'. It is believed in Indian tradition that early dramas presented by Bharata included Purvaranga, Nandi, an Anukriti and dance on the recommendation of Shiva. The story was presented by mimetic acting or Angika abhinaya, imitating the actions, movements and gestures, representing the action of the drama. Yet it was a drama and not mere Akhayana or story telling or ballad singing.

The early Indian dramatic performances may have been a simple Anukriti, without dialogue, but the story was told by actually portraying different characters by different actors with appropriate make-up, costumes, movements and actions and the whole show was 'acted'.

**Anunāshika**

Too much of nasal sound while singing is called 'Anunāshika'.

**Anurupa**

In Sanskrit drama, the roles were of three distinct qualities, namely, Anurupa, Virūpa and Rūpānusārinī. Anurupa refers to the similar to the nature of the person represented. Therefore, Anurupa is that which is represented by an actor of the same age and sex. *Natyashastra* admits of this mode of representation in which roles may be taken up by persons of appropriate sex and age.

**Aṇuta**

This is one of the six techniques employed in singing the svaras of the Vedic scales.

It refers to sharp intonation of the voice, while singing the higher notes from Dvitīya to Krushṭa, included in the Utshepiṇi.

**Anuvādi**

This is a neutral or subordinate note.

It means 'Assonant'. Bharata's *Natyashastra* divides Svaras (Notes) into four varities, namely, Vādī (Sonant), Samvādi (Consonant), Anuvādī (Assonant) and Vivādī (Dissonant), according to the number of Shrutis (Intervals) between them and ever since, this has remained the accepted categorization.

The notes of a Raga excluding the Vadi and the Samvadi are termed 'Anuvadi' and it enhances the beauty of the Raga. Vadi is the king of notes, while Samvadi is like a minister. But Anuvadi or Assonant notes are said to be the servants in relation to the king and the minister.

**Anvāvasaraga**

This is one of the six techniques employed in singing the svaras of the Vedic scales.

Contraction of the vocal chords while singing the lower notes from Chaturtha to Atisvaraya, included in the Avashepiṇi opposite of Ayāmo.

**Anya Nayika see Nayika, Parakiya Nayika**

**Apadhvānta**

This is one of the tonal qualities mentioned in the Chandogya Upanishad. Apadhvānta refers to tone resembling the sound emanating from a bronze vessel when broken (a tone quality).

**Apaghātila**

According to the *Lātyāyana Sharauta Sūtra,* the term 'Apaghātilā means a pair of musical instruments comprising of the instruments 'Pichchhola' or 'Pichchhora' and the Kāṇḍaviṇa, used in the recitation of Sāman in the Vedic period.

A pair of musical instruments played during the Mahā Vrata ceremony.

**Apasmāra**

It denotes 'Epilepsy, Falling, Sickness'.

Apasmāra or 'Epilepsy' is the twenty-second Mutable State/ Vyabhichari Bhava) which according to Bharata, should be represented on the stage by palpitation of heart, deep breathing, trembling, running, falling, perspiration, stillness, foaming, licking and so on.

**Apavaritaka**

This is a kind of Natyoktis, a special speech which contains a secret content, which is to be concealed from all characters concerned. This is employed mainly in Nataka and Prakarana in the context of doubt or hesitation. Denotes concealed speech related to some secret thought which the actor conveys to the audience by coming forward and then taking a turn; a Natyadharmi conventional speech.

**Apaviddha**

As mentioned in the *Natyasastra*, this is the fourth and one of the 108 Karanas or Cosmic Shiva Bharata Poses. Here the right hand in Sukathuda is placed on the right thigh. The left hand is held near the left breast in Katakamukhahasta.

**Apsaras**

Means essence (Rasa) of water (Ap), water nymphs, actress-dancers and courtesans of heaven.

Regarding Apsaras there is a myth that one day Indra, lord of the firmament, and some of the other gods grew bored with life, for they had everything at their command but nothing to look forward to. They implored Lord Brahma, the Creator, to find them a pastime that would please both the eye and the ear. Brahma with text taken from Rig Veda, song from Sama Veda, action from Yajur Veda and emotion from Atharva Veda created a new, fifth Veda called Natya Veda which he revealed to the sage Bharata. Bharata presented a threefold art, drama-music-and dance to Shiva who asked his celestial attendant Tandu to instruct Bharata in the art of tandava. Bharata compiled this knowledge in the Natya Shastra, a treatise on the art of dance. While rehearsing a dance-drama for presentation by his hundred sons in the court of Indra, he realised that the lasya could only be performed by women. He informed Brahma about the problem whereupon the all-powerful lord created Apsaras, celestial nymphs, to entertain the gods. According to another legend, the Apsaras (essence of waters) sprang up from the ocean during the Amrit Manthan (churning of the ocean) by the gods and the Asuras (demons) in search of the elixir of immortality. As neither the gods nor the Asuras would accept Apsaras as wives, they became common property known as *sumad-atmajas* (daughters of pleasure), to be enjoyed in heaven as well as upon earth. They delighted the gods by dancing merrily to the accompaniment of music by Gandharvas, the celestial singers.

In a dignified Sanskrit dramatic composition, a celestial woman is not usually appear as heroine which depicts a celestial or royal character as a hero. An exception to this rule is 'Urvashi', a celestial courtesan. In Kalidasa's drama 'Vikramorvasia' she is represented as a heroine by the side of 'Pururavas', a royal hero.

**Anunaya (Mediation) see Vagyabhinaya**

**Arabhati Vritti see Vrittis**

**Arala Hasta**

A single hand gesture, adopt the *pataka* and bend the index finger such that the tip of the thumb touches the middle phalange of the index finger. Arala is used to denote : poison, nectar, violent wind and such other things. This gesture in dance is also used to express courage, beauty drinking poison, dressing the hair and decorating the face, etc.

**Ārambha**

This is the third constituent parts of the Purvaranga [Preliminaries of a play], performed behind the curtain. It means the beginning of the rehearsal song of the chorus.

**Arambha see also Mukha-Samadhi**

A young tree, the thinness and fatness of the waist.

**Archika**

In the beginning, the Rigvedic chants were simple in form and were sung on one note. This earliest chants of the Rigvedic hymns were of a recitative nature than musical which lacked pitch and rhythm, monotonous without any melodic life and character. This hymnal period has been called 'Archika' pivoting on the raised note called 'Udātta'.

**Aradhachandra Hasta**

A simple hand gesture, first to adopt the *pataka* and stretch the thumb outward and four fingers pointing sidewards, palm facing the body and the thumb up.

This is used to denote phase of the moon on the eighth day of the dark fortnight, a hand seizing the throat, a spear, consecrating or doing *abhishekam* on deity, a dining plate, origin, thinking about oneself, meditation, prayer, touching the limbs, obeisance, a young tree, the thinness and fatness of the waist etc.

**Ardhamagadhi**

This is one of the seven principal Prakrita dialects used in the Sanskrit plays.

Ardhanmagadhi is spoken by Chetas [slaves], Rajaputras [sons of kings] and Shresthins [masters of guilds].

**Ardhanikuttaka**

*Natyasastra* of Bharata prescribes this tenth and one of the 108 Karanas or cosmic Shiva Bharata poses. It is just the half of Nikuttaka. One hand touches the shoulder while one heel stamps the ground. The hands should face each others.

**Ardhapataka Hasta**

A single hand gesture which requires to adopt *tripataka hasta* and bent the little finger Ardhapataka is used to denote.

Leaves, a board for writing or painting, the bank of river, saying 'both', a cutting saw, knife, flag, tower and horns of animals.

**Ardharechitha**

*Natyasastra* of Bharata mentions this twelfth and one of the 108 Karanas or Cosmic Shiva Bharata Poses. According to it, the hands should be in Suchimukha mudra with the feet stamping the floor. One side reposes in Sannata (one side bent).

**Ardhasuchi Hasta**

This is a single hand gesture. In the *kapittha,* the index finger is stretched upwards. Used to express "a sprout, young ones (of a bird) and big worms."

**Ārohī**

It means 'Ascent', one of the four kinds of Varna (melodic movement). Others are Sthayi (level), repetition of the same sound; Avarohī (descent) and Sañcāri (wandering or ascent and descent combined).

**Aropa**

It denotes 'Superimposition' It is Dhananjaya who used the term 'Rupaka' of Bharata as a synonym for Natya. It states that Drama is Rupaka because it is a visual presentation; and there is also a metaphorical identification involved here, as when we call a face the moon, in order to imply its loveliness. In drama, there is a double identification or superimposition: A writer creates a character of Rama and we take it to be real Rama; this is one superimposition. When an actor plays that part in a stage performance we accept that actor as the real Rama, atleast for the time being; this is another superimposition.

It is due to this superimposition that a drama is called 'Rupaka' and the principle behind this identification is Anukarana which leads to the belief of identify.

**Aropya**

This is one of the four kind of ornaments according to the method of wearing them, states *Natyashastra*. Aropya covers Hemasutra [gold chains] and necklaces that are to be worn round the neck.

**Artha**

Artha means 'prosperity'; one of the four aims of life, the others being Dharma, righteousness, that is fulfillment of one's duties according to one's station; Kāma, fulfillment of the needs of love and sexual desire; and fourth and ultimate, Mokṣa, release from all the other aims - total liberation.

In a Sanskrit dramatic composition the Hero (The principal character) directly by his own efforts or through the endeavours of his ministers and helpmates, stands as the leader of an action and obtain its fruit (Phala). The Phala, as *Nataka-Laksana-Ratnakosa* points, out in the traditional manner is the *Purusartha* (Dharma, Artha or Kama).

Artha is accomplished when the Hero obtains something he did not have before like a new or lost kingdom.

**Artha (Natyartha)**

Denotes 'Inner meaning of a dramatic composition (or a poetry) - its rasa content - Natyartha.

**Arthahīna see Dosas**

**Arthāntara see Dosas**

**Arthāpatti (Presumption) see Vagyabhinaya**

**Artha - prakriti**

Sanskrit dramatic treatises hold that the plot of a dramatic composition comprises of five parts which it calls Samdhis or Junctures and each such Samdhi is itself constituted by an amalgam of an Arthaprakriti and an Avastha. The former refers to the different essential elements of the theme or the plot. There are five Artha - prakritis as mentioned below:-

(1) Bija (The germ)

(2) Bindu (The sign of continuity)

(3) Patākā (The episode)

(4) Prakari (The incident)

(5) Karya (The purpose to be achieved)

**[see also Samdhis]**

**Artha - Sachiva**

The dramatic character or Pātrāni of Sanskrit drama may be categorized in three context of Dharma, Artha and Kāma, in which matters they counsel and assist a Royal Hero, states *Bhavaprakashana*. Artha in connection with a Royal Hero means polity and economy of the state, and prosperity which results from the practice of a correct and wise administrative policy. In this domain, the King's ministers (Mantri) can be placed int he fronk rank. Others to be included are the political friends of the king, prince, vassals, officers, commanders of army and soldiers, foresters, king's brother-in-law of a lower caste etc, who all have their own uses, and who may come under the three divisions of high, middling and low, according to their individual qualities and socio-cultural status.

*Natyashastra* mentions that the minister shculd be endowed with superior intellect and a light sense of religious morality, expert in political science, never lazy or indolent, a pleasant talker, highly skilful in detecting the weak points of others and of the opponents and fully equipped to take advantage of them, possessing an excellent knowledge about organising military compaigns at correct times and seasons, clever and skilful in interpreting the precepts of political and administrative theory, having a noble lineage and very much devoted to his master, a man who has an expert knowledge of the proper time and place for commencing and executing a significant mission.

From *Daśarupaka*, we learn that a Dhiralalita Hero leaves his state affairs to be attended to by his minister (the principal associate of king in the field of Artha-Sachiva). Other types of Heroes rely on themselves, or on their minister, or both act together, a required by the particular political and administrative situation.

**Artha-vyakti see Ganas**

**Arthopakshepakas**

These are indicatory scenes, some minor technical devices employed to bridge the gaps in the development of the plot and helping situations on the way to further advance in the direction of the final goal of the drama. Subsequently Arthopakshepakas make a drama compact and pleasing by avoiding unnecessary and unwanted details through such devices. These are of five varities:-

(1) Viskambhaka (Explanatory scene)

(2) Chulika (Behind the scene revelation)

(3) Praveshaka (Introductory scene)

(4) Ankāvatāra (Transition to the next Act) and

(5) Ankamukha (Preface to an Act)

Out of these five, Chulika, Ankavatara and Ankamukha are mere technicalities and have no distinct existence of their own. But Viskambhaka and Praveshaka are very significant. Both consists of a brief scene with two or more characters in it. Apparently both seem alike, but a technical difference exists between them.

In Viskambhaka, according to Bharata's *Natyashastra* and later theories, one can find dramatis personae of middling status and also those of low status. Therefore the speechis either in Sanskrit if it has only middling characters or an admixture of Sanskrit and Prakrit, if its characters hail from low class speaking Prakrit alone. But in Praveshaka, only 'low' characters can participate, the speech is only in Prakrit language. Another difference is that the Viskambhaka occur in the beginning of a drama, while Praveshaka can occur only in between two Acts. However *Natya-darpana* rejects this theory. But most striking aspect is however in their affinities with regard to ultimate purpose. Such indicatory scenes contain dialogues mainly narrative in nature, giving information about certain happenings, which cannot be shown on the stage by reason of their impropriety on impossibility. However, such happening have a significant role on the future course of the plot. Therefore, the help of Viskambhaka or Praveshaka is undertaken to bridge the gulf.

**Arya**

It denote 'noble one'. A Brahmana is addressed by 'Arya', according to *Natyashastra* which has prescribed a set of such words for calling the different characters according to their position.

A minister is called 'Amatya' [councillor] or 'Saciva' [Minister] by a Brahmana and 'Arya' by others Arya or Aryaputra is a mode of address in a Sanskrit drama in which women in their youth should also address their husbands as 'noble one' (Arya), says Bharata in Natyashastra.

**Aryabhasa see also Bhasavidhanam**

**Asamyuta Hastas**

It refers to single hand gestures which are the real essence of dance language. They are used to symbolise animals, gods, emotions etc. The same gestures when used in different directions conveys altogether different meanings.

**Asamyutahasta : (*Pataka*)**

Asamyutahasta : (*Tripataka*)

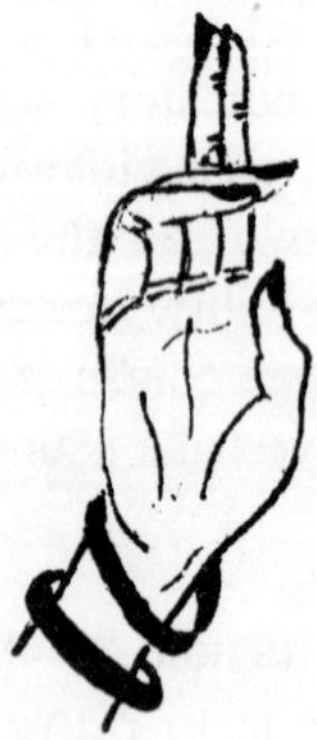

Asamyutahasta : (*Ardhapataka*)

According to *Abhinaya darpana,* they are:-

1. Pataka 2. Tripataka 3. Ardhapataka 4. Kartareemukha 5. Mayura 6. Ardhachandra 7. Arala 8. Shukatunda 9. Mushti 10. Shikhara 11. Kapittha 12. Katakamukha 13. Suchi 14. Chandrakala 15. Padmakosha 16. Sarpasheersha 17. Mrigasheersha 18. Simhamukha 19. Kangula 20. Alapadma 21. Chatura 22. Bhramara 23. Hamsasya 24. Hamsapaksha 25. Sandamsha 26. Mukula 27. Tamrachooda 28. Trishoola.

Certain other *Asamyuta Hastas* like *Vyaghra* and *Ardhasuchi* have also come into common usage. *Natyashastra* has given another variety called "*Urnanabha*' which is not mentioned in *Abhinaya Darpana*.

**[see also Hasta Mudras]**

**Asarita**

This is the ninth and the last constituent parts of the Purvaranga (the preliminaries of a play) which is performed behind the curtain. In all there are twenty different items (inclusive of both off and on stage rituals) of Purvaranga.

Asarita means 'entrance and practice of the dancing girls' After Asarita, the rest are presented on the stage.

**Ashirvachana**

In means 'Blessings'. The Bharata's *Natyashastra* mentions that the Nandi or benediction part of Purvaranga [Preliminaries] should have words invoking Ashirvachana [Blessings]. Sutradhara recites the Nāndi in a middle tone, while his Pariparsvikas says evamastu [so be it] at the end of every foot [Pada].

**Āshravana**

This is the fourth constituent parts of the Purvaranga [Preliminaries of a play] taken up behind the curtain. It means 'tuning of instruments which are played upon by striking [Atodya].

**Ashru**

This means "Tears, weaping etc" (Seventh Sattvika Bhava/ Emotional State) which Bharata states, should be represented on the stage by wet eyes, rubbing of the eyes, and shedding tears, now and then.

**Asragīta**

Denotes 'Background music' *Sahityadarpana* while mentioning Ullāpya as a minor type of drama states that it has asragīta which is played in it from behind the stage with reference to the plot.

**Astitānta**

This is the undue elongation of the final or the next note. A defect to be avoided in singing the Karshana.

**Asura(s)**

It denotes :-

(1) The God head

(2) The great pristine gods; Varuna, Agni and Soma in particular.

(3) A demon.

Asuras are often represented on the stage as demons.

**[see also Daitya, Danava & Rakshasa]**

**Asūyā**

It means 'Envy, Jealousy, Intolerance' etc.

Asūya is the fourth Mutable State/Viyabhichari Bhava which should be conveyed by accusations, ignoring virtues of others, jealosy, looking down, twisting of eyebrows, avoiding and ignoring others, etc.

**Atibhasa see also Bhasavidhanam**

**Atihasya (Excellence) see Vagyabhinaya**

**Atmagata speech see Svagata**

**Atikrama**

This means 'leaving one note in between two notes in the descending order. This is similar to Datu Svara of Karnatic Music. Opposite of Pratyutkrama. It is one of the Gīti-upāyās or aids to the recitation of the Sāma-Veda.

**Atikranta**

The singing of the second note after the first note completely ends. One of the defects to the avoided while singing the Karshana.

**Atodya**

It refers to 'Musical' instruments.

Regarding the origin of musical instruments there are certain legends. Anil Baran Ganguly informs: Once the ten-headed Rāvaṇa was caught under mount Kailāsa and it became impossible for him to get himself free, then he tried to sing some beautiful notes to be able to come out. He needed some instrument to give him support for the recital of his music. (For such purposes, a musical instrument like an Ektārā of today was generally used even in those days). So Rāvaṇa chopped off one of his ten heads, cut cut a nerve from his huge body and tuned it to the pitch of his voice by tying the end to the head thus cut by him and held the other end tightly with his left hand. He then sang sonorously and soulfully till he pleased Lord Śiva, who at once released him.

Thus, probably, this single-string Ektārā was the earliest instrument used in Indian music. There is another legend regarding the origin of musical instruments.

Mahādeva (Śiva), the creator of music, once saw Pārvatī, his consort, reposing most gracefully, breathing like soft music and her exquisite bosom rising and falling rhythmically and the bangles on her hands producing a tinkled melody by their movement.

Lord Śiva watched absorbingly for some time in silence. Intoxicated by the captivating spectacle, he thought of a way of permanently recording her beauty. He invented the Rudra Vīṇā representing the long neck and the straight slender figure of Pārvatī, the two supporting gourds, being her breasts, the metal frets her bracelets and, most expressive of all, the sound, her rhythmic breathing.

Another legend goes like this that one day during the rainy season, the great sage Swati went to a lake to fetch water. As he entered the lake, the clouds started gathering and the raindrops started falling one after another. Soon it started raining heavily. Instead of taking shelter from the heavy downpour the sage was attracted by the mysterious and fascinating sounds of the water dropping on the lotus leaves. He stood there spellbound and thrilled by the sounds created by nature. He realised that the sounds produced by the raindrops falling on the various shapes of the leaves created a variety of sounds ranging from high pitch to medium to low pitch. These sounds, he felt, were majestically deep, melodius, and delightful. This variation in sound inspired him to develop the various percussion instruments. The sage Swati sought the help of Vishvakarma to create instruments like *mridanga, pushkar, panava, and dardura*. When he made instruments like *muraja, alingya, urdhavaka and angika* he was inspired by the *dundubhi of devas*. He covered *avanaddha* instruments (*mridanga and dardura*) with leather and *panava* with strings. He made some more drums like *jhallaru, pataha* etc. The great sage Swati and Narada discussed about the Gandharvas playing on the stringed instruments accompanied by various other instruments and devised the method of playing musical instruments with extended amplitude and other similar features.

*Natyashastra* divides the Music into two categories, namely Gāna (Vocal) and Atodya (Instrumental). Regular musical instruments are of four types, viz Tata (Stringed), Avanaddha (Covered), Ghana (Solid) and Suṣira (Hollow). Ghara and Aranaddham are rhythmic instruments that use a pair of sticks or Lands to prodnce the beat, while the Tatam and Suṣira aṛe melodic instruments.

The stringed are those with strings, the 'covered' means the drums, the 'solid' are the cymbals, and the 'hollow', the flutes. Bharata has dealt, in detail on every aspects of this instrumental music in his dramaturgy.

Amarakosa also classify musical instruments into following categorizes :-

(1) String (Tata) like the Vina with seven strings;

(2) Stretched leather (Anaddha) like the drum.

(3) Reedy (Susira) or wind, like the flute, trumpet and

(4) Percussion (Ghana) like a bell.

In one of the verses in Chapter VI of Natyashastra, Bharata has furnished eleven elements of Drama which can be collectively called the '*Digest* of *Natyashastra*. These significant dramatic components are :-

Rasa (Sentiment)

Bhava (Emotion)

Abhinaya (Acting)

Dharmi (Modes of representation)

Vritti (Styles of expression)

Pravritti (Local usages)

Siddhi (Success of production)

Svara (Note)

Atodya (Musical instruments)

Gana (Song)

Ranga (Theatre)

**'Dhatu', [see also 'Dhatu', 'Vadya', 'Deva Vadya' etc.]**

**Attā**

Bharata has prescribed a set of words for calling the different characters according to their position. An old woman was addressed as 'Attā' in Sanskrit plays.

**Attikā**

This is also a dramatic appalation and refers to the elder sister, say Amarakosha.

**Auḍava Raga**

The Ragas of Indian classical music are conventionally divided into three classes (jatis). These are Saṁpūrna (of seven shrutis), Ṣādava (of six Shrutis) and Auḍava (of five Shrutis). An Auḍava Rāga is obtained by deducting two of the seven Shrutis. A discarded Shruti (or the removal of a Shruti in the process of composing a new Rāga) is called Varja.

**Autsukya**

It denotes 'Eagerness, Impatience, Anxious' etc.

Autsukya or 'Eagerness' is the twentieth Mutable State/ Vyabhichari Bhava which Bharata states should be represented in acting by deep sighs, worrying, downcast looks and face, sleep, drowsiness and desire for lying down.

**Avahittha**

It denotes 'Dissimulation, Concealment' etc.

Avahitha or 'Dissimulation' is the twenty-sixth Mutable State/ Vyabhichari Bhava which according to Bharata should be represented on the stage by irrelevant talk, looking down, broken speech and pretended patience.

**Avahittha Hasta**

This is a double hand gesture. Bent fingers of two *shukatunda* are interlocked near the chest are bent forward and lowered slowly and the gesture is calleld 'Avahittha'.

This Indian dance gesture indicates weakness, amorous actions, eagerness, interest and keeness, displaying a slim body.

**Avakāshika**

A speech uttered in the space without the appearance of a character is called 'Avakāshika', according to '*Natya-Laksana-Ratnakosha* of Sāgaranandin.

**[see also Akashabhasita]**

**Avamarsha - Samdhi**

According to Sanskrit dramatic theory, the plot of a dramatic composition comprises of five divisions which it call 'samdhis' or junctures, a blending of Arthaprakriti (essential element of the theme) and Avastha (stage of development of the plot). Avamarsa - Samdhi is the fourth juncture having *Prakari* as the 'Arthaprakriti' and *'Niyatapti'* as Avastha. This juncture 'Avamarsha or Vimarsha is the juncture of taking thought or pondering or assessing the gains and losses after the head-on-clash represented by the Garbha-Samdhi. This is a stage of relief and relaxation during which future course of action is deliberated upon and fresh attempts to put in once again (Vimarsha - Avamarsha) *Natyadarpana* observes Vimarsha as deliberation, hesitation or doubt where the hero, though he visualises his goal as very near, cannot help being filled with doubt because of the circumstances which are beset with difficulties.

Avastha '*Niyatāpti*' is apt because at this stage, difficulties do exist obstructing the smooth progress of the situation, yet remedies are easily at hand to counter them. The Arthaprakriti is '*Prakari*', a short episode bearing no specific or individual fruit to offer, nor does it have any great impact, but adorns the drama as a flower-bouquet would beautify a place.

**Avanaddha**

Regular musical instruments, according to Bharata, are of four varities, viz, Tata (stringed), Avanaddha (covered), Ghana (Solid) and Suṣira (Hollow). The Avanaddha ie, the covered denotes the drums.

Presently we have Membranophones or generally Percussion instruments like Mridangam, Dholak, Tabla, Pakhawaj, Morching, Main Kanjira etc as 'Avanaddha'.

**Āvāntara Svaras**

This is a name given to a set of eight methods or aids (Gīti-upāyam) adopted in the singing of the Sāma-Veda. They are, Pratyutkrama, Atikrama, Karsana, Svara, Vinata Praḥata, Utsvarita, Abhīgita.

**Avanti**

It denotes the province or region lying around Avanti (modern Ujjain) such as Vidisha, Saurastra, Malava etc Bharata in his *Natyashastra* prescribes four Pravrittis or Local Usages to the producers of plays to create ambiance or to give realistic touch to the production one should reflect in their performances the locale of the various regions of this vast land. Avanti is one such pravrittis which takes into consideration the peculiarities and practices, costumes, languages and manners of this region.

**[see also Pravrittis]**

**Avantija (Avanti)**

This is one of the seven principal Prakrita dialects used in the Sanskrit plays and is spoken by Rogues.

Avantija or Avanti was employed by Śudraka in his magnum opus 'Mrcchakatika'.

**Āvāpa**

It refers to one of the four silent Tāla gestures (right palm up wit fingers folded)

**Avara Natyamandapa see Ranga**

**Avarohi**

It means 'Descent' and refers to one of the four kinds of Varṇa (melodic movement). Others being Sthāyī (level), repetition of the same sound, Arohī, ascent and Sañcārī (wandering or a scent and descent combined).

**Āvarta**

This denotes a rhythmic cycle.

The circle of Tala in Indian musical system. In it, a set of rhythmic units [Mātras] are juxtaposed in a cycle and repeat themselves.

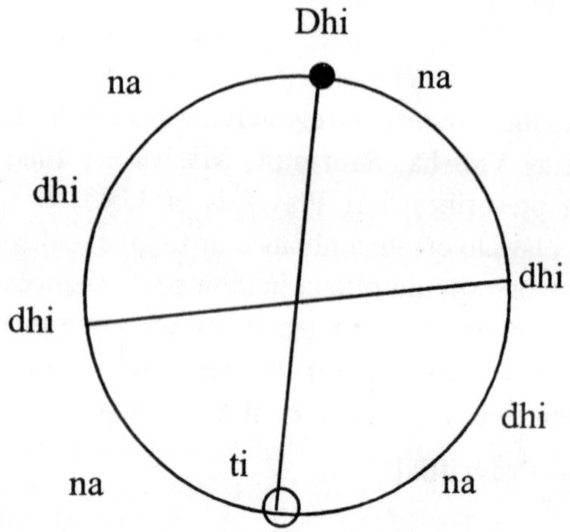


The above figure show one such cycle or Avarta in which ten units or matras are divide. This is a circle of ten beats, but this really is a 2+3+2+3 rhythm and all the beat not of the same quality. Emphatic beat on 1; 3, 8 less so (mild beat); 6 is vacant (a wave of hand on 6). The other beats are identical. Beat 1 is called 'Sam' and 6 is 'Khali'. If we actually beat the rhythm in the following manner, a fairly good idea of what this Tala would sound like can be drawn. First to give a strong beat on 1, faint claps on 3, 8 wave the hand on 6, and count mentally the rest (2, 4, 5, 7, 9, 10) naturally spacing the beats uniformly. What we have counted is one cycle of the Tala and such circle is an avarta, a cycle or 'repetition'.

**Avashepiṇi**

This refers to technique employed in the singing of the lower notes from Chaturtha to Atishvāraya, corresponding to the lower tetrachord or Purvānga of a scale.

**Avastha**

It means 'condition', *Dasarupaka* of Dhananjaya defines Natya as 'an imitation of the (physical and phychological) conditions (avastha) of life. It comprises of pathya, gita, abhinaya and rasa. Natya is both Anukarana and Bhavanukirtana. The creative artist produces characters, situations and incidents and the sometime, he also creates their actions, speeches, passions and emotions. In all this he imitates life either at first hand or from his observations of human behaviour and in one word, eventually the emotional experience of the entire world of beings.

**Avastha (Samdhis)**

Sanskrit dramatic theory states that the plot of as dramatic composition comprises of five parts which it calls Samdhis or Junctures and each such Samdhi itself constituted by an amalgam of an Arthaprakriti and an Avastha. The latter refers to the stage of development of the plot, ie, the different stages in the progress of the themes towards it fulfilment. In all there are five Avasthas, viz.

(1) Arambha (The beginning)

(2) Yatna (The effort)

(3) Prāptyasa (The prospect of success)

(4) Niyatāpti (Certainty of success)

(5) Phalāgama (Attainment of the result)

**[see also 'Samdhis']**

**Avatarana**

This is the second constituent parts of a **Purvaranga**

(Preliminaries of a play) performed behind the curtain. It means the placing of singers (gayaka).

**Avedya**

This is one of the four kinds of ornaments according to the method of wearing them stated in the *Natyashastra*. Avedhya covers the Kundala (ear-rings) and other ornaments for the ear which are fixed in holes pierced in the skin. Other kinds are Bandhaniya, Praksepya and Aropya.

**Āvega**

Refers to 'Agitation, Flurry' etc.

Avega or 'Agitation' is the sixteenth Mutable State/ Vyabhichari Bhava which according to *Natyashastra* should be represented in acting by loose limbs of the body, disturbed mind, change in colour of the face, sadness and surprise.

**Aviddha Prayoga**

Denotes a play production in vigorous style.

In Nātya, there are two kinds of performances, namely, Sukumara and Aviddha that are followed to present emotions and sentiments, the soul of Sanskrit drama.

Aviddha is full of war, motions and agitation. Unlike Sukumara which is delicate, it involves too much of violence, cutting, tearing and fighting with enormous indecent languages. Hence women should not take part in it. Aviddha performances were to be carried out by devas, danavas and raksasas who were violent by nature and full of vigour, states *Natyashastra*.

*Natyashastra* recognises this two kinds of production keeping in mind plot and the characters of a play. A director has to consider whether the play revolves around ordinary people or divine characters, demons with their super-human qualities and actions; whether to delineate everyday life of pain and pleasure of wickedness, cruelty, deceit, etc. So we have Aviddha style as one which according to traditional norms.

Bharata says that in presenting Samavakara, Dima, Vyayoga and Ihamriga, one has to employ Aviddha style. Hence the methods (vritti) should be Sattvati and Arabhati, ie plenty of movements, actions, fights, magics etc.

**Avyaktam**

In music, it refers to the lack of clarity in pronouncing the Sāhitya according to its grammatical construction.

**Ayamo**

This is one of the six techniques employed in singing the svaras of the Vedic scales. Ayamo is adopted in the Utshepini or upper tetrachord.

**Ayoga Sringara see Sringara Rasa**

**Ayusman**

It denotes 'Long-lived one' Bharata has prescribed a set of words for calling the different characters according to their position. For e.g. the lord of a chariot was addressed by the charioteer as 'Ayusman'.

# B

**Bahlika**

This is one of the seven principal Prakrit dialects used in the Sanskrit plays. Bharata states that this is the native speech of the Khasas who belong to the north.

**Bahubheda**

This refers to the movements of the arms and are of ten kinds:-

(1) *Tiryaka* (stretched sideways)

(2) *Urdhwastha* (stretched above the head)

(3) *Adhomukha* (moving towards the ground)

(4) *Anchita* (a circularl movement from the chest, to upwards)

(5) *Apaviddha* (moving in a circular way)

(6) *Mandalagati* (moving around like brandishing a sword)

(7) *Swastika* (crossing and touching each other at the wrists)

(8) *Prishthanusari* (moving towards the back)

(9) *Udhveshtita* (moving out from the wrist and brought back to position)

(10) *Prasarita* (stretched in any direction).

**Bakura (Bākura)**

This musical instrument is described in the Rigveda where in the Asvine are said to have blown their Bakura against the Dāsyus. According to Roth, the object that was blown was a musical instrument.

**Balavat Slakshaṇa**

This is one of the tonal qualities mentioned in the Chandogya Upanishad. Balavat slakshana refers to voluminous, yet brilliant voice.

**Bandhaniya**

This is one of the four kinds of ornaments according to the method of wearing them, stated in the *Natyashastra*. It covers Angada [arm-band] and girdles. Other kinds are Avedhya, Praksepya and Aropya.

**Bandhavahasta**

It refers to Hastas for relatives. They are:

(1) *Matru*-mother: *Ardhachandra* in the left hand is placed near the navel with *sandamsha* in right and then the left hand rotated around the belly in *mrigasheersha*. This can be used for indicating daughter also.

(2) *Pitru* -- father: It is the same as *matru,* except *shikara* in right hand. This can be used for son also.

(3) *Dampati*--wife and husband: Left hand in *shikhara* and the right hand in *mrigasheersha.*

(4) *Shvashru*--mother-in-law: *Hamsasya* in right hand near the throat and *sandamsha* in left hand circled around the navel and held in *mrigasheersha.*

(5) *Shvashura* -- father-in-law: Same as *shvashru* except that instead of *hamsasya, shikara* sould be held.

(6) *Putra* -- son: Hold left hand in *shikhara* with the right hand in *sandamsna* circling round the navel.

(7) *Putri*--daughter: Same as *hasta* for the son except that instead of *shikhara*, *katkamukha* should be held.

(8) *Jyeshtha kanishthabhartru*--elder and younger brother: *Mayura* is shown by both hands in the front on the two sides.

(9) *Bhartrurbhratru* -- husband's brother: Left hand in *shikhara* and the right hand in *kartareemukha* placed on the sides.

(10) *Nanandru*--husband's sister: Right hand in *shikhara* and right hand in *mrigasheersha*.

(11) *Snusha* - daughter-in-law: The son's hand first and then *mrigasheersha* with right hand.

(12) *Sapatni*-co-wife: After showing *pasha,* show *mrigasheersha* in both the hands.

**Bhagavan**

This denotes 'a Holy one' Bharata prescribes a set of words for calling the different characters according to their position. Gods, great sages, learned persons well versed in different Vedas and priests were called by men and women alike as 'Bhagavan'.

**Bhāṇa**

One of the ten major recognised forms of drama, mentioned in the traditional Sanskrit Treatise. The story conceived by the playwright; a Rouge (only one character in this play) is the Hero; the sentiment is love (Sringara) or heroic (Vira).

This variety of Sanskrit drama, presented in the form of a monologue portray the Viṭa or rake, a thoroughly disreputable character walks through the less respectable parts of the town holding imaginary coversations with the people he meets.

Bhana is a one-act play, a short piece presented by a single actor, as said before, who appears as a man of the world and indeed as the principal Viṭa. For this purpose, he describes his own adventures and partly those of others. He uses the monologue and [Ākāśabhaṣita] and pretends to see and hear others. He acts, speaks, asks questions and answers on behalf of the imaginary person and make appropriate gestures.

It is believed that Bhana emerged out of the Pantomine or the musical dance and this explains why Lāsya is employed in it.

Bhanas are preserved in the collection known as '*Chaturbhani*'.

**Bhānda**

It refers to 'Drum', a musical instrument which is very spirit of the ancient dramas. There is a Sanskrit proverb 'Amridangam natakam', ie, any thing strange is like "a drama without a drum".

**Bhanga**

This means 'the bending postures of the entire body' and falls under the head 'Cheshtakrita' (comprises the movement of the entire body) which comes under Angikabhinaya.

Bhanga or the bending postures of the entire body are of four varities as follows:-

(1) *Abhanga (Slightly bent)*

Sculpturistic poses like Rama's.

(2) *Atibhanga (Fully bent)*

Tandava aspect like Shiva's.

(3) *Samabhanga (Straight)*

Performing penance like saints and Rishi's.

(4) *Tribhanga (Three fold bent of the body near the head, waist and knees)*

Lasya dance, portraying female deities like 'Parvati'.

**Bhanika**

This is a minor type of drama (Uparupaka), an one-act piece. According to Avaloka on the Daśarupa, Bhani is a kind of musical dance.

**Bharata Putraka**

It means 'An actor'

**Bharata vakya**

An actor's benediction is called Bharatavakya. It, denotes the last verse or verses in a drama, a sort of benediction.

**Bharativritti see Prastavana and Vrittis**

**Bhartri-dārika**

This is a mode of address in a Sanskrit drama (as stated in *Natyashastra*), unmarried princesses are to be addressed by their handmaids as 'young mistress' (Bhartri-darika).

**Bhasavidhanam**

Bharata in his *Natyashastra* has prescribed some rules on the 'Use of Languages' under this head. In this he has stated his preferance for chaste and polished Sanskrit as the language of a play, but as all the dramatis personae cannot be expected to do so, he advocates Prakrit for them Sanskrit when changed and devoid of the quality of polish' is Prakrit which is of three types.

1. **Samana - Shabda:** (When the original words of Sanskrit are followed without any modification, it is termed as 'Samāna-shabda' such as the terms Amala, Renu, Taranga, Lola etc.
2. **Vibhrasta (Corrupt)** Sounds which change their combined form or vowels or sustain loss, and that often in the middle of a word are corrupt such as 'Acchariya' from '*Acharya*' and '*Khu*' from '*Khalu*'.
3. **Deshi** (Indigenous) Indigenous words that are derieved from the regional languages are termed as 'Deshi'.

Further, *Natyashastra* categorize such regional languages into Super human language (Atibhasa), Noble Language (Aryabhasa).

The common language (Jati-bhasa) and the Animal language (Yonyantri-bhasa). The first is the language of the gods, the second for the kings, the third has various forms and comprises many terms of barbarian origin and the last one has its origin in animals and birds of different species.

Bharata also recommends the use of dialects for different characters in a play and provides seven major dialects. These are Magadhi, Avanti, Prachya, Shauraseni, Ardhamagadhi, Bahlika and Dakshinatya.

He further mentions some sub-dialects [Vībhāsas] such as Shakari, Abhiri, Chandali, Shabari, Dravidi, Audri and Vanaukasi. Neither Bharata nor Sagaranandin speak of 'Maharastri'. However, *Sahitya darpana* of Vishvanatha, a later work (About 1380 A.D.) informs about Maharastri which has, nevertheless, no place in Sanskrit dramas.

Thus language or dialect to be used by an actor would depend on the social standing and background.

**Bhāshika Svaras see Gātika and Anudātta**

**Bhatta see Rajan**

**Bhattini**

This is an appalation used in drama alone and Bhattini refers to a king's wife who is not the consort, crowned with him, states *Amarakosha*.

**Bhāva**

Means 'Being, existing, existence. Refers to inner states of being as represented in a work of art for evocation of nava nātya-rasas.

It is rightly been stated that the concept of the Rasa and Bhava is so prodigious that it can't be explained in general terms.

Some scholars use the term 'Emotion' for Bhava. Of late, even 'Sentiment' is being in usage. Other in vogue are 'Feeling' "State" etc.

Mostly drama theorists use 'States' for Bhava. According to *Natyasastra*, Bhava is that, which by the '*abhinaya*' of word, gesture and physical modifications expresses the mood of the poet.

In *Daśarupaka* it is described as a State which is brought about by emotional mood, such as pleasure or pain. The Bhavas invoke a response in the spectator's heart. They, then, give rise to Rasa.

Bhāvas are (1) *Sthāyi Bhāvas* (Permanent States). These States are powerful ones and pervade all the sentiments. Therefore, Rasas have corresponding Permanent States, very alike in their nature to Rasa (Principle Emotion/Sentiment).

(2) *Vyabhichari Bhavas* present 'passing emotions' which later get developed into Sentiment. According to *Natyasastra* it is that which by words, acting and emotions *leads* to one to realise a Sentiment. *Dasarupaka* describes it as those which especially accompany the Permanent State in cooperation, emerging from it, and being submerged in it, like the waves in the ocean.

(3) *Sāttvika Bhāvas:* The Vyabhicari and Sāttvika Bhavas help in the invocation of the Sthayi-Bhāvas. It is only Dhanika in his commentary on *Dasarupaka* deals at length with Sattvika Bhavas. He defines Sattva as a mental condition which is highly sympathetic to the joys and sorrows of the others. Sattva is a mental state (born of the mind) and it arises when the mind is in a state of composure. Therefore, tears, horripilation etc which a person experiences in a state of joy or sorrow are merely produced from this Sattva and so are called 'Sattvika Bhavas' or 'Sattva-produced'

In one of the verses in Chapter VI of *Natyashastra*, Bharata has furnished eleven elements of Drama which can be collectively called the '*Digest of Natyashastra.* These significant dramatic components are:-

Rasa (Sentiment)

Bhava (Emotion)

Abhinaya (Acting)

Dharmi (Modes of representation)

Vritti (Styles of expression)

Pravritti (Local usages)

Siddhi (Success of production)

Svara (Note)

Atodya (Musical instruments)

Gana (Song)

Ranga (Theatre)

Bhava is, therefore, an essential component in drama that denotes an emotion and its external expression. If the spectator absorbs the Bhava it produces Rasa or an enjoyment of the Bhava. Rasa and Bhava are represented through the skilful and sensitive handling of facial expressions supplemented by the body movement of a dancer. A rasa is a result of Sthayi Bhava (Permanent State) producing a pleasurable sensation through the operation of transitory (Vyabhichari) State. The Rasa is a response to bhava. Static emotions are love, mirth, grief, anger, enthusiasm, fear, disgust, surprise placidity that gives rise to Rasas Sringara, Hasya, Karuna, Rudra, Vira, Bhayanaka, Bibhatsa, Adbhuta and Shanta respectively.

**[see also 'Rasas']**

**Bhāva**

It also denotes a venerable man, a term of address in Sanskrit drama.

**Bhavaka**

One having a taste for the beautiful.

**Bhavanukirtana**

To Bharata, Natya is Anukarana and Bhavanukirtana. Its essential components are Pathya, Gita, Abhinaya and Rasa. Bhavanukirtana is the sole aim of traditional Indian drama. Drama presents an emotional experience of the entire world of beings. A playwright produces characters, situations and incidents and further he goes on to create their actions, speeches, passions and emotions. In this he imitates life and this is the Anukara part.

In the same way an actor also act to portray a character on the stage. This is Abhinaya with the help of make-up, costume, movements etc. the actor's histrionics is based on the anukarana of things in real life. Thus when some emotional experience is properly created by a playwright and presented by an actor appropriately, it becomes enjoyable to the reader as well as the spectator. This is rasa the emotional content of drama and the relish or enjoyment it affords.

Natya is, thus, an admixture of experience of sorrows and happiness of all humanity rendered by Abhinaya. The Rasa element may be, as said before, may be referred to the pleasure the spectators derieve from the performance and the whole process is called the 'Bhavanukirtana'.

**Bhavavastha**

Means the inner states of being (of a character) in a specific situation in a play.

**Bhaya**

It refers to 'Awe, Fear' etc.

Bhaya, the Permanent State (Sthayi Bhava) is usually experienced by women and lower classes of people. It is produced by displeasing the master and the king, roaming in a lonely forest, house, deep hills, seeing an elephant or a serpent, rebuke, a frightful garden, misfortune, darkness of night, sound of owls, fearful animals and the like.

This sixth Sthayi Bhava is projected by tremor of limbs, state of panic, terror, dried up mouth and lips, wide eyes and the like.

**Bhayanaka Rasa**

It connotes 'Fear, Terrible, Terror, Horrific' etc.

According to Bharata's *Natyashastra*, when a fight becomes fierce with terrifying noises, or killing and capturing, etc take place, or when a jackal cries or an owl hoots, such events fill an anxious heart with fear. Or, when any great calamity befalls a near and dear one, a sense of terrible loss seizes one such are the Vibhavas which help the proper portrayal of this Rasa. Vibhavas like entering an uninhabited house or a dense forest unaccompanied, or the sight of ghost may also induce a sense of fear.

The Vyabhichari states constituting this Rasa are depression, agitation, distraction, fatigue etc.

The sense of fear is predominant in this Rasa 'Fear' the Sthayi Bhava or the Permanent feeling which with proper treatment gives rise to Bhayanaka Sentiment.

Fear is represented in acting by tremor of hands and feet, steadiness, trembling of body, palpitation of heart, dryness of lips, the mouth, the palate and the throat.

*Varna* : Krishna (Black)

*Mukharaga* : Shyama (Dark)

*Hasta* : Hamsasya

*Svara* : Dhaivata

*Raga* : Ragas that depict this rasa are Pharaju, Revathi, Thodi, Sahāna, Shubhapanthuvarāli, Bhavapriya, Gaulipanthu, Sahāna, Mukhāri, Shanmukhapriya, Vachaspathi, Dvijāvanthi and Sarasāngi

*Presiding deity* : Kala.

**Bherunda Hasta**

This is a double hand gesture in which the two hands in the *Kapittha* are joined at wrist.

In Indian dance, the gesture indicates a couple of Bherunda birds.

**Bhesaghara**

It means the 'Green Room', where the theatrical characters get their make-ups, costumes etc.

**Bhinnārtha see Dosas**

**Bhītam**

Denotes the fear while singing. One of the fourteen Gāyaka doshas.

**Bhitti**

It denotes the wall of the theatre-house.

**[see "Ranga"]**

**Bhogini**

In Sanskrit drama, the Bhogini is that type of woman who belongs to high lineage and blameless character, she receives worship and honour by her own qualities, such woman is soft, never rash, a little detatched, forbearing, and worthy of confidence.

**Bhrama**

This is the synonym of 'Shanka' (Third Vyabhichari Bhava/ Mutable State)

**[see 'Shanka']**

**Bhramara Hasta**

This is a single hand gesture in which the middle finger and the thumb should touch each other with the index finger curved and the last two fingers stretched outside. It denotes "bee, parrot, wing, crane, cuckoo, etc."

This Indian dance gesture also represents the plucking of flowers with long stemps.

**Bhramari Bheda**

This denotes 'Whirling movements'. Bhramari Bheda is one of the major divisions of Cheshtakrita (movements of the body). The latter comes under the Angikabhinaya. According to *Abhinaya darpanam,* there are seven types of whirling movements as follows:-

(1) **Utpluta (Jump):** The whole body whirls around with a jump, in the *Samapada* position.

(2) **Chakra (Wheel):** The hands in *Tripataka* and the body whirls around like wheel, keeping both the feet on the ground.

(3) **Garuda (Bird):** Knee of one leg is rested on the ground while other leg is stretched and body whirls around with stretched arms.

(4) **Ekapada (One leg):** The body is rested on one foot while whirling around.

(5) **Kunchita (Small):** Body whirls around with bent knees.

(6) **Ākāsha (Aerial):** Jump and place both the legs wide apart before whirling.

(7) **Anga (Body):** Jump and place the legs half a cubits apart after whirling.

**Bhramsha (Slip of Tongue)** **see Vagyabhinaya**

**Bhrubheda**

This means 'movement of the eyebrow' and are of seven types as follows:-

(1) *Utkshepa* (raised up separately)

(2) *Patana* (lowered seperately)

(3) *Bhrukuti* (bringing together)

(4) *Chatura* (extended in pleasing manner)

(5) *Kunchita* (little bent together or separately)

(6) *Rechita* (Raised in a graceful manner)

(7) *Sahaja* (natural position)

**Bhrukuṁsa**

This refers to a dancer in women's garb (with expressive movements of the eyebrows).

In Mahabhasya, we can trace the word 'Bhrukumsa' which referred to a male who was inpersonating as female. The assumption of women's roles by men has, therefore, very early evidence. The *Natyashastra* has expressly admits of this mode of representation in drama called '*Rupanusarini*' where a man portrays the part of a woman. Though this was not an usual practice, the job was entrusted to the '*Nati*' who normally played an importnat female role as in the *Karpuramanjari*

**[see also Rupanusarini]**

**Bhumika**

It denotes 'Theatrical dress, the costume of any character, represented on the stage; and also roles of characters of the play.

**Bhumika (Roles of characters)**

[*see under Anurupa, Virupa, Rupasarini, Sukumara, Aviddha, Sutradhara, Natyacharya, Acharyas, Nati etc.*]

**Bhusana (Ornateness) see Vagyabhinaya**

**Bibhatsa Rasa**

It denotes Abhorrence, Disgust, Odious, Detest, Loathing etc.

In Bibhats rasa or the Sentiment of Disgust, Jugupsā or the state of repulsion is the basic permanent state with the help of which this develops.

The Vibhavas in this, according to *Natyashastra* are bad omens, or hearing of something repulsive. This feelings of repulsion can occur due to many reasons. When something horrible as a murder is witnessed, or some nauseating smell or the icy hand of a ghost is felt, if some revolting action like the drinking of human blood takes place, or eerie sights like headless torsos dancing on the battle field or the gruesome details of human sacrifices etc are described, there is awakened the feeling of repulsion, disgust, and even contempt.

The Vyabhicharibhava (The Transient states) in Bibhatsarasa are epilepsy, delusion, pongs of death, illness, agitation, etc.

The horrible acts and terrifying scenes required for the depiction of this sentiment cannot be presented actually on the stage, so the necessary effect has to be created with the help of narratives or description of events such as sacrifices and slaying etc.

Abhorrence is represented in acting by contorting the mouth and eyes, covering the nose, tilting the head and walking unsteadily.

*Varna :* Nīla (Blue)

*Mukharaga :* Shyama (Dark)

*Haśta :* Kartarīmukha

*Svara :* Dhaivata

*Raga:* Ragas employed in this rasa are serious and sad in nature namely Purvikalyāni, Gamanaschrama, Varāli, Mukhāri, Mandāri, Vasantha Bhairavi, Āhiri, Ghantā, Bhairavi, Mānji, Punnāgavarāli, Nādanāmakriya, Bhavapriya, Kanakāngi, Rishabhapriya, Schubhapanthuvarāli, Sāveri, Sindhurāmakriya, Māyāmālavagaula etc.

*Presiding deity :* Mahākāla

**Bija see Mukha-Samdhi**

**Bindu**

It means point, seed, a drop.

This is a part of the five Arthaprakritis of the plot progression of a Sanskrit drama.

**[see Pratimukha-samdhi]**

It means 'drop', also in the sense of (1) a single ornamental tone, or (2) a metaphorical reference to the spreading properties of a drop of liquid.

**Biruda**

A panegyric, often the final component of a *prabandha* (an art song).

**Brahma**

The creator, the first deity of the sacred Hindu Trinity

One of the presiding deities of he theatre, stated Bharata who is said to have received a revelation of the dramatic art from Brahma, the creator, who entered into meditation and from the depths of the divine thought brought forth the arts of drama, music and dance for the joy of the universe.

This presiding deity of theatre, according to *Natyashastra*, must be worshipped with offerings and sacrifices.

According to this treatise of Bharata (6, 45), Brahma is the God of Wonder (Adbhuta Rasa).

**Brahmana Svaras see Gātika and Udātta**

**Brinda see Kutapa**

# C

**Cācapuṭaḥ**

One of the five Mārga Tāla patterns, with a proportional structure of 2:1:1:2.

**Caccatpuṭah**

One of the five Mārga Tāla patterns, with a proportional structure of 2:2:1:3.

**Cari see Chari**

**Ceta see Cheta**

**Chadma Griha**

Sanskrit term meaning 'Green Room' which is usually located near the main auditorium from here the dramatic personae appear and make their entry and also retire in the Chandma- Griha.

**Chakra Hasta**

This is a double hand gesture in which the hand in *ardhachandra* are brought together with the palms facing each other at right angle.

This gesture in Indian dance is used to show the chakra of Mahavishnu.

**Chamatkara**

Amazing delight which constitutes the essence of an art experience.

**Chandali**

This is one of the Vibhasas or sub-dialects of Prakrita used in the Sanskrit plays and is assigned to the Pulkasas and the like. This sub-dialect was used by Sudraka in his '*Mṛcchakatika*'.

**Chandra**

It denotes '*the moon god*'. Bharata states that he is one of the most prominent deities of the theatre to be worshipped with offerings and sacrifices.

Chandra protects the main building of the playhouse and keep it cool and peaceful.

**Chandrakala Hasta**

This is a single hand gesture in which the thumb should be stretched outward in suchi.

The gesture is used to denote moon, the face, a measuring index, objects of that shape, the crown of *Shiva,* river *Ganga* (Ganges) and a baton.

**Chapalatā**

It denotes 'Agitily, Restlessness, Inconsistency'.

Chapalata is the fourteenth Mutable State/Vyabhichari Bhava and according to *Natyashastra*, Agility should be represented in acting by using harsh words, rebuke, hitting, killing, capturing and irritating.

**Charaṇa**

An wondering actor or singer or a dancer or a mimic bard was called Charaṇa in ancient times. There was a tradition of employing musical band, in the royal procession as one see in the first act of the play 'Ratnavali' of Harshadeva.

**Chari**

Part of the Bodily acting 'Angika Abhinaya' Chari means 'pose which brings in a line waist, hips, thighs and feet. Bharata's famous dramaturgy *'Natyashastra'* furnishes a number of poses which represent actions of different kinds. It is neither a movement nor a gesture but comes naturally like nodding the head. It is a deliberate stance. Bharata says "except by a chari there shall be no movement in a play".

Shooting an arrow, riding a chariot or holding the reins of the horses are some examples of 'Chari'. Bharata in *Natyashastra* (X, 45-56) states that in all such poses the hands, feet, hips and waist must be in line with the action suggested. To quote Adya Rangacharya What the author [Bharata] wants to convey is that on the stage one's movements should be not only deliberate but artistic. As everyone from the auditorium is watching the actor, he has to stand, turn, move about, etc, in a manner in which the spectator feels pleased and interested. Therefore, Cārī or poses-stylised movements - are prescribed both *Bhaumya* ie, belonging to or treading on the earth or *Ākāśikī* in the air, ie, to convey running, jumping, etc.

Chari is a stage walk that depends on the simultaneous action of feet, shaks and hip where the movement of one foot is suggestive of different actions. The *Natya Shastra* analyses the various body movements : the movement mainly with a single foot is called 'Chari'.

*Natyashastra*, therefore, recognises only two kinds of Chari, *Bhumi* and Akshiki (the earthly and aerial respectively).

The Bhumi or earthly has following kinds:-

Samapada

Sthitavarta

Shakatasya

Adhyardhika

Chasagati

Vichyava

Edakakridita

Baddha

Urudvritta

Addita

Utsyandita

Janita

Syandita

Apasyandita

Samotsarita

Mattali

Akashiki or the aerial has following forms:-

Atikranta

Apakranta

Parshvakranta

Urdhvajanu

Sūchi

Nupurapadika

Dolapada

Akshipta

Aviddha

Udvritta

Vidyudbhranta

Alata

Bhujangatrasita

Harinapluta

Danda

'Chari' denotes the 'movement of the feet' and falls under the main head '*Cheshtakrita*' (comprises the movements of the entire body). The latter comes under '*Angikabhinaya*'.

*Abhinaya darpana* recognises eight kinds of '*Chari*' movement of the feet as follows:-

(1) **Chalana (Motion):** One foot is moved forward from its original position.

(2) **Chankramaṇa (Walking):** The feet are turned out slowly lifted and placed sideways alternately.

(3) **Sarana (Quick motion):** The feet are moved such that the toes of one foot touch the heel of the other alternately, crawling movements of a leech and the hands are in *Pataka*.

(4) **Vegini (Swift):** One hand in *Alapadama* and other in *Tripataka*, moving forward either on the heels or entire sole.

(5) **Kuttana (Pounding):** Striking or stamping the floor with the heel or with the forepart or with the entire sole.

(6) **Luthita (Rolling):** In position of *Swastika* (crossed feet), execution of Kuttana with the toe or forepart of the foot.

(7) **Lolita (Agitated):** From the position of Kuttana, foot move slowly without touching the floor.

(8) **Vishamasanchara (Uneven):** Here the feel is placed alternately from left to right and from right to left side.

**Chari (Purvaranga)**

In the context of drama, this is one of the twenty constituent parts of Purvaranga (preliminaries of a play), performed on the stage. This item is preceded by Rangadvara, when the play (abhinaya) begins, the Sutradhara recites a new verse and bows before Indra's banner 'Jarjara'. After Rangadvara, Chari features different paces and gestures with an erotic sense, followed by Mahachari, similar paces, but more impetuous in degree.

**Chārin**

It means "steps," poses.

**Charita see Itivritta**

**Chatura Hasta**

This is a single hand gesture in which the little finger is straight down, the other three fingers bent upwards with the thumb curved to touch the three middle fingers. This is used to express "musk, a little bit, gold, copper, iron, wet, sorrow, aesthetic pleasure, the eyes, the difference of castes, proof, sweatness, slow gait, breaking to pieces, face, oil and ghee."

This hand gesture is also used to represent policy, discipline, afflicted person etc in Indian dance idiom.

**Chaturasra Tāla**

Denotes a musical rhythm pattern with eight time beat. A Tala with eight matras-s. It is a '*Jati*' of *Chanchutputah Tala,* the ancient basic Tāla, prototype mentioned in the *Natyashastra*.

**Chaturatodya**

This denotes the four types of musical instruments:

(1) Stringed (Tata; such as Veena)

(2) Covered (Avanaddha; like drum, tabor)

(3) Solid (Ghana; like cymbal, gong)

(4) Perforated (Susira; like flute)

**Chatuṣshruti Raga**

Ragas of Indian classical music are conventionally divided into three classes (Jatis) : Saṁpurna (of seven shrutis), Ṣāḍava (of six shrutis), and Auḍava (of five shrutis).

Chatuṣshruti Raga means a Raga having four Shrutis. However such a Raga is an oddity from the point of view of treatises on Indian classical music, and is generally unknown to musicians. None of the musical treatises mention such a jāti. But many a scholars feel that in the past, there was such a jati, but baffles many as how could a Raga of a more four svaras be expanded for the purpose of building a melody. H.V. Sharma writes "Dhruvagana, according to *Nātyashastra* did not always use all the seven svaras.

Dhruvas may have been song even in a smaller number of Svaras in Sanskrit plays, though in the context of Pūrvaraṅga, they would have been sung using all the seven svaras selectively, or even over stepped a Saptaka marginally. The contexts here suggest these probabilities. Chatuṣshruti, Auḍava, Ṣāḍava and Saṁpūrṅa may all have coexisted, in relation with or independent of each other, supporting nāṭya performances:

Isolated from nāṭya catuṣśruti rāgas may have had an independent existence as a jāti with no relationship with rāgas of other jatis employing a larger number of Śrutis. Combination of jātis seems to have been a later development.

**Cheshtakrita**

This refers to expressions through the movements of the entire body, which comes under Angikabhinaya. They are Mandala (static posture), Bhaṅga (bending postures of the entire body), Sthanakas (positions of the feet in standing posture), Utplavana (Leap), Bhramari (whirling movements), Chari (the movements of the feet) and Gati (way of walking) *Natyashastra* gives two divisions for both Mandala and Chari. They are Bhumi (earthly) and Akashiki (Aerial).

**Chestima see Pusta**

**Cheṭa**

It denotes the servant of the hero in a Sanskrit drama.

*Rasarnavasudhakara* points out that "a ceta like Kalahamsa in the Malatimadhava can play a very significant role in establishing a link between the hero and the heroine. Though a servant, a carrier of messages, this dramatic character of low class can rise to the nobel level of humanity by his utterly honest and selfless deed, as proved by Śakara's Ceta when he jumps down from the terrance, in his shackles, in order to save the life of Carudatta, the hero of Mrcchakatika.

**Cheti**

It refers to a female servant in a Sanskrit drama.

**Chibukabheda see Dashana-Chibuka - Hanubheda.**

**Chiddrāni**

In Pali it is 'Chiddāni', refers to the holes in the sounding board through the strings of the harp (Yāl) pass.

**Chinta**

It denotes 'Anxiety, worry' etc.This 'Anxiety' is the ninth Mutable State/Vyabhichari Bhava which should be conveyed on the stage by deep breath or sighing, lamentation, deep thinking, keeping the face down, disturbed thinking and weakness of body, etc.

**Chitra-Abhinaya**

This is a part of the Abhinaya (Acting), but falls outside the four components of Abhinaya, ie, Angika, Vachika, Aharya and Sattvika. In *Natyashastra*, Chapter XXV Bbharata furnishes some miscellaneous rules and directions regarding. Abhinaya which are placed under the head 'Chitra'. In XXVI he defines 'Chitra - Abhinaya' as that which expresses, by means of gestures and looks etc, that which is 'not mentioned'. Modern critic Adya Rangacharya culls some modes of Chitra-Abhinaya from *Natyashastra* as follows:-

(1) Expressing thrill (i.e., hair standing on end) one should act the touch to the body or to the mind of things soft or sweet-natured (XXV,9).

(2) By acting avoiding touch or repulsion one should express the presence of harsh or undesirable things (XXV, 10)

(3) With body trembling with fear and eyes closd, one should convey the sense of lightening striking or of a deafening sound or of a fire emitting sparks (XXV, 15).

Chapter XXVI of *Natyashastra* therefore deals with Chitrabhinaya, ie, varied representation. It provides detailed instructions regarding the gestures to be made in response to environmental changes, e.g. to indicate moonlight, sun, smoke, dust, the appearance of repugnant objects, etc.

It is varied representation of different activities, moods, animate and inanimate objects through hand gestures, facial expressions and the body movements.

**Chitra Purvaranga**

According to Bharata, there are twenty different constituent parts of a Purvaranga. The first nine are presented off stage (behind the curtain) and the rest on the stage. They are the part of a regular Purvaranga or a chaturasra Purvaranga. In the Chitra [variegated] Purvaranga strewing of flowers and dance of the gods etc are added.

**Chitrakara**

According to *Natyashastra*, poets (drama composers), directors, stage managers, musicians, scene-designers fall under the category of Natyacharyas. There are other Acharyas and artisans seem to have been necessary in the presentation of Sanskrit drama. The Chitrakara is one who paints pictures.

**Chittavritti**

It refers to changes in the state of mind, wavering in the inward working of mind.

**Chulika**

According to traditional Dramatic Theory, Chulika is the device in which a character, off the stage, introduces the scene, and then enters on the stage and narrates what has passed in the meanwhile and what is to follow. It is, therefore, a linking scene - an intimating speech in an act from behind the curtain suggesting an explanation of the matter on the stage.

**[see also Arthopakshepakas]**

**Costumes see Aharyabhinaya, Alankara etc.**

# D

**Dainya**

It means 'Depression, Despondence, Miserable.

"Depression" is Eighth Mutable State/Vyabhichari Bhava which should be represented in acting by lack of self-control, headache, dullness of body, absent-mindedness, uncleanliness, etc.

**Daitya/Daiteya**

It means 'A demon, (descended from Diti) an Asur, the titan or giant of Hindu mythology.

In the context of drama, it denotes such characters represented in a dramatic composition. *Natyashastra* states that those who are fat and tall, whose voice was deep like thunder and who had terrifying eyes, eyebrows and faces, were selected for the roles of Daityas, Danavas and Rakshas. The Aviddha type of performances which is full of war were to be done by them, as they were violent in nature and full of vigour. Such characters are seen in Dima, Samavakara, Vyayoga and Ihamriga etc.

**Daiva Viṇa see Viṇa**

**Ḍakkinī**

The *Natyashastra* helds music, an indispensable adjunct of Sanskrit drama. It informs about some musical instruments like Mridanga, Paṇava, Dardura, Dundubhi, Muraja, Jhallari, Pataha, Vaṁsha, Shaṅkha and Ḍakkinī.

**Daksina Nayaka**

*Bhavaprakashana* of Sharadatanaya classify the Nayaka (the Hero) in the context of love, implying the attitude and behavioour of the Hero in regards to the matters of love. His four fold distinctions are Anukula, Daksina, Shatha and Dhrista type of Nayaka.

According to *Sahityadarpana*, the Daksina kind is represented by a Hero who shows the same courteous and just attitude to all the women for whom he has love;they are the Heroine and the previous wives or queens of the Hero. The Royal Heroes of Sanskrit drama generally appear to be of this variety.

**[see also 'Nayaka']**

**Daksinatya**

This is one of the seven principal Prakrit dialects used in the Sanskrit plays. Bharata opines that it should be used by warriors, police officers and gamesters.

**Daksinatya (Pravritti)**

It refers to southern provinces/regions Bharata's *Natyashastra* explains four Pravrittis or Local Usages to the producers of plays to give authenticity to the production by reflecting in their performances the locate of the various regions of this vast land. Daksinatya is one such Pravritti which takes into consideration the perculiarities and practices, costumes, languages and manners of this region.

**Daksinya (Clever Manners) see Vagyabhinaya**

**Danavas**

It refers to 'demons' (descended from Dānu), titan or giant etc.

In the context of drama, it denotes such characters represented in a dramatic composition. *Natyashastra* states that those who are fat and tall, whose voice was deep like thunder and who had terrifying eyes, eyebrows and faces, were selected for the roles of Daityas, Danavas and Rakshas. The Aviddha type of performances which is full of war were to be done by them, as they were violent in nature and full of vigour. Such characters are seen in Dima, Samavakara, Vyayoga and Ihamriga etc.

**Daṇḍa (Dandaka)**

This refers to the arm of the harp, together with the doni or ambhaṇa (resonator), forming the whole frame.

**Dandas**

From *Natyashastra*, we find that measurement for the building of theatres was dependent upon the conception of Hasta and Danda. 24 Angulas mean one Hasta, four Hastas one Danda. This measurement matches with the one given in the Arthashastra of Kautilya.

**[see 'Ranga']**

**Dardura**

The *Natyashastra* describes music as an indispensable adjunct of Sanskrit drama. It mentions about musical instruments such as Mridanga, Paṇava, Dardura, Dundubhi, Muraja, Jhallari, Paṭaha, Vaṁsha, Shaṅkha and Ḍakkinī.

**Dāruṇya**

Singing of the higher notes from Dvitiya to Krushṭa, with a stress; included in the Utshepini. One of the six techniques employed in singing the svaras of the Vedic Scales.

**Dashana - Chibuka - Hanu bheda**

This means 'the movements of the teeth, chin and jaw and are of seven kinds as follows:-

(1) *Kuttana* (gnashing of the teeth)

Used to express fear, cold, anger, depiction of a sick man.

(2) *Khandana* (separating and joining the jaws repeatedly)
To express 'praying (chanting silently), studying, speaking, eating.

(3) *Chhinna* (setting the teeth and lips together tightly)
To show 'sickness, fear, cold, anger, while doing exercise, and for offended look.

(4) *Chukkita* (lips and jaws are held wide apart)
To depict 'yawning'.

(5) *Lehan* (biting the tongue)
To show 'greediness'.

(6) *Sama* (natural position slightly apart)

(7) *Dashta* (lower lip is bitten by the teeth)
To express 'anger'.

**Dasharupa**

Bharata in his *Natyashastra* (Chapter XVIII) has stated ten varieties or genres of drama which can be collectively termed 'Dasharupaka'. He tells about the ten Rupakas, their names, their content (krama) and their performance. The forms are

(1) Nataka
(2) Prakarana
(3) Aṅka
(4) Vyāyoga
(5) Bhaṇa
(6) Samavakara
(7) Vithi
(8) Prahasana
(9) Dima
(10) Ihamriga.

The third chapter of Dhananjaya's '*Daśarūpaka*' thus describes the ten forms (daśarūpa) of drama which as said earlier are Nāṭaka, Prakaraṇa, Bhāṇa, Vyāyoga, Samavakāra, Īhāmṛga, Aṅka (or Utsṛṣṭkāṅka), Dima, Vīthī and Prahasana.

| Ramification of Drama | Act | Rasa | Saṃdhī |
|---|---|---|---|
| *Aṅka* | 1 | *Karuṇa* | 2 |
| *Bhāṇa* | 1 | *Vīra or Śṛṅgāra* | 2 |
| *Dima* | 4 | *Dīpta Raudra* | 4 |
| *Ihāmṛga* | 4 | *Śṛṅgāra* | 3 |
| *Nāṭaka* | 5 - 10 | *Vīra or Śṛṅgāra* | 5 |
| *Nāṭikā* | 4 | *Śṛṅgāra* | 5 |
| *Prahasana* | 1 | *Hāsya* | 2 |
| *Prakaraṇa* | 5 - 10 | *Vīra or Śṛṇgāra* | 5 |
| *Samavakāra* | 3 | *Vīra* | 4 |
| *Vīthī* | 1 | *Śṛṅgāra* | 2 |
| *Vyāyoga* | 1 | *Dīpta Raudra* | 3 |

**Dasi**

This refers to 'Maids', also called Ceṭi, an associate of the Heroine, (as stated by Dhananjaya in his *Daśarupaka*).

**Dashavatara Hastas**

It means Hastas of ten incarnations of Vishnu. They are:-

(1) *Matsyavatar* - incarnation as fish - *matsya hasta.*

(2) *Kurmavatar* - incarnation as a tortoise - *kurma hasta*

(3) *Varahavatar* - incarnation as a boar - *varaha hasta*

(4) *Narasimhavatar* - incarnation as half lion and half man- *Simhamukha* in left and *tripataka* in right hand indicating half lion and half man.

(5) *Vamanavatar* - incarnation as a dwarf -*Mushti* in left hand pointing upwards and *mushti or mrigasheersha* in

right hand pointing downwards holding the umbrella and the *kamandal* (small pot with water)

(6) *Parashuramavatar* - incarnation as an axe wielder-Left hand in *ardhachandra* is placed on the waist and the right hand in *ardhapataka* suggesting *parasu* (axe).

(7) *Ramachandravatar* - incarnation as a noble king - *Shikhara* in left and *katakamukha* in right hand held straight down holding bow and arrow.

(8) *Balaramavatar*- incarnation as a plough wielder -*Pataka* in right and *mushti* in left hand to indicate wielding the plough as a weapon.

(9) *Krishnavatar* - incarnation as a preacher of Bhagavat Gita - *Mrigasheersha* in both hands near the right side of the face horizontally, suggesting flute.

(10) *Kalkiavtar* - *Pataka* in right and *tripataka or kapittha* in left hand indicating horse and the rider.

**Deshi**

Belonging to a region, a country, a province, popular - contrasted with *'Margi'*.

**Desi Sangita**

Brihaddeshi of Matangamuni states that the word 'Deshi (popular) applie;s to all earthly music. Dvani (sound) goes everywhere in every place and comes to the lips in the form of a 'melodious movement' (varna), giving rise to Desi Sangita. Hence it is called 'Deshi'.

According to authorities on the art of music, there are two main distinctions in the theory and practice of Sangita. We have Marga Sangita (the High style) and Desi Sangita.

Deshi Sangita is opposed to Marga Sangita and refers to those current in different places. This terrestrial music varies from country to country according to the tastes of the people of a particular region and is a source of pleasure.

Deshi Sangita is, therefore, regional, provincial; the assimilation of regional musical traditions ca. A.D. 500 - 1000.

**Deva see Rajan**

**Deva Vadya**

This denotes the divine instruments. Seven deities of the Hindu pantheon are believed to have played music on different instrument Vina, Venu and Mridanga are called 'Deva Vadya'. Goddess Sarasvati is depicted as playing the Vina, Lord Krishna (Vishnu) playing the Venu (Flute) and Nandi playing the Mridangam.

For Lord Shiva's cosmic dance, the music ensemble included, apart from the above three instruments, Lord Brahma wielding the cymbals and sage Narada providing vocal support.

**Devata (Dramatis Personae)**

It means 'god, a deity or divine being. In the context of drama, it refers to divine characters in a dramatic composition. Such divine personages were represented by persons whose physiques were well built and who spoke delightfully, mentions Sanskrit dramaturgic treatise.

**Devatas (Theatre deities)**

Bharata gives greater emphasis on the forms and ceremonies for worshiping some 'Devatas' called the presiding deities of the theatre. They are Chandra [moon god], Lokapālas [guardians of the world], Mārutas, Mitra, Agni [fire god], Varuna, Adityas, Rudras, Bhutas, Apsarasa, Yaksinya, the Ocean god, Kritānta, Nāgaraja, the Rod of Yama, Niyati, Mrityu, Indra, Vidyut [Lightning], Yaksas, Pishachas, Guhyakas, Vajra, powerful Jarjara, Brahma, Vishnu, Shiva, Kārtikeya, Sarasvati and Onkara. They should be worshipped with offering [Bali] and sacrifices.

**[see also Nandi]**

**Devatahasta**

It refers to the Hastas (Hand gestures) for deities. They are:-

(1) *Agni : Tripataka* in the right and *kangula* in the left hand.

(2) *Brahma : Chatura* in left and *hamsasya* in the right hand.

(3) *Indra : Tripataka* in both hands in *swastika* posture.

(4) *Kubera : Alapadma* (lotus) in left hand and *mushti* (mace) in the right.

(5) *Lakshmi : Kapittha* in both the hands held near the respective shoulders to suggest holding of lotuses.

(6) *Manmatha : Shikhara* in the left and *katakamukha* in the right hand near the chest suggesting arrow and flower.

(7) *Nirriti : Khatva* first and then *shakata* on both the sides of the face.

(8) *Parvati : Ardhachandra* in left is held down in *varada* (boon) pose and the right hand in *ardhachandra* is held up in *abhaya* (protection and blessing) pose.

(9) *Saraswati : Suchi* in right hand and *kapittha* in the left hand raised to the shoulder level.

(10) *Shanmukha : Trishula* in the left and *shikhara* in the right hand.

(11) *Shiva : Mrigasheersha* in the left and *tripataka* in the right hand.

(12) *Varuna :* The right hand in *pataka* and left in *shikhara,* both held near the respective shoulders.

(13) *Vayu : Arala* in the right and *ardhapataka* in the left hand.

(14) *Vinayaka : Kapittha* hands on the thighs or near the chest facing each other.

(15) *Vishnu :* Both the hands holding *tripataka*

(16) *Yama : Pasha* in the left and suchi in the right hand.

**Devi**

This is a mode of address in a Sanskrit drama in which the king's wives are to be addressed by their attendants as 'Devi' (Lady), other modes are 'Bhattini' (Mistress) and Svamini (Madam).

In Sanskrit plays, other queens, not crowned, having high virtues but lacking the superior polish, are Devi. They are proud, jealous of the love of their royal husband and therefore entering into rivalry with their competitors in love.

**Dha (Dhaivata)**

This is the sixth scale degree.

**[see Dhaivata]**

**Dhaivata**

This is one of the seven svaras (Notes) and according to *Ragavibodha, Sangitaparijata, Sangitamakarandah* etc, the sounds of music are first perceived as relative pitches or intervals and then from the twenty two Shrutis (Main Intervals) come the seven Svaras, namely Ṣaḍja, Ṛṣabha, Gāndhāra, Madhyama, Pañcama, Dhaivata and Niṣāda. It is interesting to mention here that the traditional authorities on music refer each Svara or Note to the sound of some animal.

Dhaivata is the croaking of the frog in the rainy season.

**Dhakki**

This is a sub-dialect of Prakrita used in the Sanskrit plays. Dhakki was used by Śudraka in his master piece 'Mṛchhakatika'; alongwith others dialects and sub dialects.

**Dharma**

Dharma denotes cosmic order, rightenousness, that is, discharge of one's duties according to one's station.

*Natyashastra* tells us that the drama emerged out of the need for entertainment. But he did not design it for that purpose only. Bharata used the terms Vilasa, Sukha and Vinoda to suggest instruction. But also used such terms as Dharma, Dhriti and Nigraha to underscore instruction and believed that the Drama will be instructive through the sentiments arising out of it, the true function of it is the blending of instruction with entertainment. The playwright has a moral obligation too and admitted the seductive power of dramatic art and, therefore, laid equal stress on both entertainment and instruction.

**Dharmaphala**

In a Sanskrit dramatic composition, the Hero (The principal character) directly by his own efforts or through the endeavours of his ministers and helpmates, stands as the leader of an action and obtains its fruit (phala). The Hero, as *Nataka - Laksana - Ratnakosha* points out in the traditional manner, is the Purusartha. (Dharma, Artha or Kāma) The Nayaka (Neta) or the Hero who accomplishes something for others or in spiritual interest, this is 'Dharmaphala'.

**Dharma-sachiva**

*Bhavaprakashana* describes dramatic characters in the context of Dharma, Artha and Kama, in which matters they counsel and assist a royal hero. Dharma - sachiva usually refers to king's religions counsellor. There may be Ritvik (a priest) or Purohita (a king's official or family priest). According to *Natyashastra*; they come from high and noble families, endowed with splendid intellect, wise in the knowledge of many sciences, affectionate, incapable of being enticed by the king's opponents, ever alert and never blundering, native and patriotic, free from greed, properly trained and modest, pure in thought and conduct and, above all, deeply religious.

*Bhavaprakashana* calls them 'Narma-sachiva', because they are expected to give pleasant company to the royal hero and, besides advising him on the matters concerned, should also be capable of pleasing him by their pleasant talk and gentle wit.

Others associates of this nature, according to *Bhava-prakashana* is Hermits, according to *Dasarupaka*, a philosopher who advice on propound metaphysical matters. A Brahmin who is well-versed in the Vedas or man who practise religious vows also belong to this category.

**Dharmi**

Bharata emphasized dramatic realism and idealism under the heading 'Dharmi'. The former is called Lokadharmi and the latter he termed 'Natyadharmi'.

Dharmi refers to the 'modes of representation'. Chapter XIV of *Natyashastra* contains an explanation of this two types of Dharmi. In one of the verses in Chapter VI of *Natyashastra*, Bharata has furnished eleven elements of Drama which can be collectively called the *Digest of Natyashastra*. These significant dramatic components are:-

Rasa (Sentiment)

Bhava (Emotion)

Abhinaya (Acting)

Dharmi (Modes of representation)

Vritti (Styles of expression)

Pravritti (Local usages)

Siddhi (Success of production)

Svara (Note)

Atodya (Musical instruments)

Gana (Song)

Ranga (Theatre)

Dharmi is, therefore, an essential component of Drama.

**[see : Natyadharmi and Lokadharmi]**

**Dhātreyi**

Dhananjaya in his dramatic treatise mentions about this kind of female characters in a drama and she is the daughter of the nurse, foster - sister.

**Dhatu**

A primary or elementary substance, a verbal root, a note made on a '*Vina*' with a special stroke of plektrum.

In Bharata's *Natyashastra,* the technique of playing upon the Vina is referred to collectively as 'Dhātu' (XXIX - 81) and is of four kinds, of which Vyañjana is one, which is again of ten varities (V. 89-95). They are Kāla, Tāḷam, Nishkotiteṁ, Utkrishtam Repam, Avamrishṭam, Pusham, Anusvana, Bindu, Adhara Kāla is the plucking the strings with two thumbs; Tāḷam is striking hard with the left finger; Nishkotitem is striking the string with two thumbs; Utkrishtam is the striking the string with left palm Repam is "All the fingers striking the strings simultaneously; Avamrishtam denotes playing one the string in three different ways; Pusham is playing with the small finger; Anusvara is 'playing on the strings with the middle of the palm; Bindu refers to 'plucking the string to produce a strong note; Adhara denotes 'playing with the two small fingers.

According to Sharangadeva 'Dhātu' is the structural element of Prabandha and is shown to be fourfold : the first is Ugrāha, then Melāpaka, Dhruva and Ābhoga.

The formal components of the Prabandhas or art songs are Dhātus and Aṅgas. The archetyped are:-

(i) Introduction

(ii) An Interlude

(iii) Main section

(iv) Prefinal Interlude; and

(v) Conclusion.

The second, fourth, and fifth components were optional. The fourth of these, Antara (Intemediate) seems never to have been much more than an occasional option, and later theories generally agree on a set of four.

According to Sameshvara's *Mānasollāsa* :-

*Udgraha* should be first division, then Melāpaka, And next Dhruvaka should occur, and then Ābhoga is desired.

The song is (first) grasped (*udgrāhyate),* hence the name *udgrāha.*

*Melāpaka* (uniting) is link binding together *udgrāha and dhruvaka.*

*Dhruvaka* is so-called because it is rendered again and again, and because it is obligatory *(dhruvatvāt).*

*Ābhoga* receives its name because it completes (*ābhoga*) the *dhruvaka.*

The following is considered to be a general rule pertaining to all the songs.

Namely, that *melāpaka* and *ābhoga* may or may not be included.

*Udgrāha* is said to consist of a pair of rhymed lines, followed by an ornamental passage,

And then a passage of text describing the subject of the song.

Thus there should be a pair of lines in *udgrāha,* and also in the third section.

Then *melāpaka* should be rendered, adorned with ornaments.

And next *dhruvaka* is to be performed, free from the regulation of metric *gaṇas,*

And finally *ābhoga* is sung, incorporating the name of the singer.

Once *ābhoga* has been sung, the *dhruvaka* should be repeated by the performers.

Thus the *dhātus* have been declared to be the body of all the componenets of *tāla.*

Dhatu is therefore, "Element", in the sense of a formal component of a prabandha (art song) (2) an instrumental finger stroke.

**Dhiradhira Madhaya Nayika see Madhya Nayika**

**Dhiralalita Nayaka see Nayaka**

**Dhira - Madhya Nayika see Madhya Nayika**

**Dhirashanta Nayaka see Nayaka**

**Dhirodatta Nayaka see Nayaka**

**Dhiroddhata Nayaka see Nayaka**

**Dhrista Nayaka**

*Bhavaprakashana* of Sharadatanaya classify the Nayaka (the Hero) in the context of love, implying the attitude and behaviour of the Hero in regards to the matters of love. His fourfold distinctions are - Anukula, Daksina, Shatha and Dhrista type of Nayaka. According to *Sahityadarpana*, the Dhrista (Bold) Nayaka is fearless although he has given cause to his wife for feeling offended; he is above any feeling of shame even though he may be threatened; he does ot mind lying or bluffing when caught red-handed in a guilty behaviour. Kalidasa's Heroes like Agnimitra and Pururavas to some extent are made to behave like Dhrista Nayaka.

**[see also : Nayaka]**

**Dhriti**

It denotes 'Contentment, Satisfaction, Holding etc.

Dhriti or 'Contentment', is the (Twelfth Mutable State/ Vyabhichari Bhava) and according to Bharata's theory, contentment should be represented by enjoying the attainments, forgetting te losses and not worrying about things gained or lost, etc.

**[see also Dharma]**

**Dhruvaka**

This is the main section of a prabandha (art song).

**[see 'Dhatus']**

**Dhruvas**

These were the most important and charming songs associated with the Sanskrit drama. *Natyashastra* states that they were to be sung during Pravesha (At the time of entrance), Āksepa (Diversion), Niṣkrāma (Departure), Praśādana (Calming) and Antara (Transition) and are, therefore, named accordingly. In his dramatic treatise, Bharata gives a detail description of their metres, aspects, contents, language, and the time and occasion beffiting their performance. He also discusses them in the light of various sentiments (rasas). The song (Dhruva) based on rasa and context, make the drama dazzle as the heaven with the stars. As without colour, a drawing is not beautiful, so is drama not attractive without music.

In the English translation of *Natyashastra*, Manmohan Ghosh states in the introduction to volume II that "The Dhruvas from their detailed description seem to have been a sort of "background" music suggesting acts and moods of different characters in a play.

In the words of V. Ranghavan "These *dhruvās* are remarkable for certain features; They are always in Prākrit language, which on one hand lights up their popular origin and on the other emphasizes their adaptability for musical treatment. Secondly, they are always symbolical, e.g., the effulgent and pure sage Viśvāmitra is described in terms of the sun; Candragupta in terms of the moon and his inimical surrounding and the dark hint of bloodshed in terms of the red evening sky; mad Purūravas as a king of elephants restlessly roaming in the forest; the two lady friends of Ūrvaśī as two female swans on the lake. Bharata sets forth a brief list of images suitable to different categories of characters for employment in *dhruvā*-compositions.

The evidence available is in favour of taking these *dhruvās* as being sung by the musicians from behind the curtain; the practice in the surviving traditions in the country also points to this view; but the concerned actor himself, who had to identify himself with the theme of the song, was in the habit of joining in a snatch or two of it."

**[see also: Gana, Sangita etc.]**

**Dhvani**

Resonance or reverberation of sound, one of the main feature of poetry where implied or suggested meaning is more striking than the expressed idea.

**Dikpalastuti**

In the Purvaranga (preliminaries in a drama), there is an item called Parivartana is performed on the stage which involves stalking round the stage with praise of the guardians of the world ie, Dikpalastuti and adoration of Indra's banner.

**Dima**

This is one of the main genres of drama [Rupaka] and according to the commentary on the *Dasarupa*, the name Dima is equivalent to Samghāta Injuring, in as much as the Heroes always come to blows among themselves. It is also to incorporate events such as earthquake, fall of meteors, an eclipse of the sun or the moon, battle, personal combat, challenge and angry conflict. The subject-matter of Dima must be a familiar one and all the styles are allowed except the gay style and also to omit Hasya and Sringara rasas. The Rasa is probably Adbhuta or Bibhatsa or Vira because of magic, witch craft, fighting, etc; having four acts. Heroes of Dima should be gods gandharvas and demons all of them vehement. They should be sixteen in number. The drama '*Tripuradāha*' is a dima.

**Dipaka (Condensed Expression)**

This is one of the four Alankaras (Figures of speech) available to a dramatist Dipaka literally means 'Illuminator. This third variety is the condensed Expression, and that it is combining of words in different topics in a single sentence for their mutual illumination. *Natyashastra* gives an example (XVII, 59). "In that region (lit., there) fullness (lit., want of emptiness) was always effected by swans in the lakes, by flowers in the trees, intoxicated bees in the lotuses, and by friendly groups of men and women in the gardens and the parks.

**Dīṣṭa (Apt Description) see Vagyabhinaya**

**Divya Nayika**

Bharata's fourfold division of Nayikas (Heroines) are Kulaja, Divya, Ksatriya and Panyakamini. Unlike later theorists, only *Natyadarpana* reverts to this categorization and divides each into further categories according as they possess the qualities of fortitude (Dhairya), grace (Lalitya) or nobility (Udāttatva).

According to it, Divya Nayika should show all the three different qualities separately.

**Dola Hasta**

This is a double hand gesture in which the hands in *Pataka* are stretched down on the sides.

This is used "at the commencement of '*Natya*' (dance)."

**Dombi**

This type of drama is mentioned by *Bhavaprakashana* alone. It is a one-act play. The heroine is noble lady, an artisan or a maid. A woman being in the lead, the impulse to heroic activity is slight, which is carried out by speeches, as the love - element is presented in graceful mode and fine and colourful costume.

**Doṣa (Nātya)**

Means 'Demerits or short comings in a work of art'.

The composer of a play should avoid ten faults or dosas, recommends *Natyashastra*. These are:-

(1) **Gūdhārtha (Circumlocution):** Mentioning anything by means of a synonym which is more difficult than the original or the common expression is circumlocation.

(2) **Arthantara (Superfluous Expression):** Mentioning anything that is superfluous or unnecessary, is Superfluous Expression.

(3) **Arthahina (Want of Significance):** An expression which is irrelevant or which remains incomplete, is an instance of 'Want of significance'.

(4) **Bhinnārtha (Defective significance):** An expression which is not refined or is worthy of a rustic is an instance of 'Defective Significance'.

(5) **Ekartha (Tautology):** Saying of the same thing in many words is called 'Tautology'.

(6) **Abhiluptārtha (Want of Synthesis):** When a sentence is complete within each foot of a verse (and all the sentences are not connected with one another by sense) it is an instance of 'Want of Synthesis'.

(7) **Nyāyād-apeta (Logical Defect):** Anything devoid of reasoning is an example of Logical Defect.

(8) **Viṣama (Metrical Defect):** It is a lopse in the metrical structure.

(9) **Visandhi (Hiatus):** It is keeping words separate whereas they should have been combined in Sandhi.

(10) **Shabda-cyuta (Slang):** Literally shabda-cyuta means 'Lapse in a word'. Use of vulgar words in slang and be avoided.

**Doṣa (Sangita)**

A defect or blemish is called 'Doṣa'. And in Music,. the *Naradi Siksha* that deals with different aspects of music in connection with the Sāma Veda, has explained fourteen Gāyaka doshas they are Sankita, Bhītam, Ughrishta, Avyakta, Anunāsika, Kākasvara, Sirasigata, Sthānavivarjitam, Visvaram, Virasam, Vislishta, Vishmāha-tam, Vyākula and Tālahīnam. Sankita means shyness in singing. Bhitam denotes fear while singing. Ughrishta means restricted pronounciation, Avyakta refers to 'oppose of vyakta' ie, impurity in pronouncing the sāhitya, therefore, not according to its grammatical construction. Anunāsika indicates too much of nasal sound. Kākasvara means singing like the crow. Sirasīgata refers to excessive shrilliness in the voice. Sthānavivarjitam is singing in all the three sthanas that which is to be sung in one particular svarasthāna. Visvaram means not conforming to the rules of singing to svaras in correct places.

Virasam denotes lack of concentration. Vislishta is separating the words in irregular places. Vishmāhatam refers to confused utterance of mātras hrashva, dīrgha etc. Vyakulata is the opposite of Saṃa (Samam is the uniformity in singing adding or deleting svaras according to some rules).

Tāḷahīnamdenotes lack of sense of rhythm and layas.

**Dosha (Svarasandhi)**

The *Naradi Shiksha* deals at length with different aspects of music in connection with Sāmagāna. Regarding the Svarasandhi, ie, passing from one note to another, the Shiksha stresses that the change over should not be artificial nor cutting, but must be natural and soft. The Svaras must be close to each other like the shadow closely following the light. While performing the Karshana, that is, singing the Svarasandhi, Narada states that six defects (doshas) may likely to appear and must be avoided. They are :- Anāgata, Atikranta, Vichchhinna, Vishamāhata, Tanvantara and Astitānta.

Besides slipping off from the original note and not singing in the correct Svara (Sthāna) is to be avoided. This is called 'Visvaram' by the Sāmagas and as 'Viraktam' by the Vīṇāvādi or the Viṇa player.

**Dravidi**

This is one of the sub-dialects of Prakrita used in the Sanskrit plays. However Dravidi dialect is not available in any extant dramas. This Vibhasa was prescribed for forest-dwellers and the like.

**Dristanta (Favourable Precedent) see Vagyabhinaya**

**Drishtibheda**

The expressive eye movements of 'Angika Abhinaya' is called 'Dristi'. Drishtibheda denotes the movements of the glance and according to *Abhinaya darpanam*, there are eight types of glances as follows:-

(1) **Sama** (Keep the eyes open normally without blinking) Used to show 'balance, to form a decision or another

thought, surprise, the image of god and in the beginning of 'natya' in dance.

(2) **Alokita** (open the eyes wide and roll them in a circle) Used in depicting 'glancing or rotating potter's wheel, looking at on showing different sorts of objects.

**Drishtibheda:** ***Sachi***

(3) **Sachi (Side glance) :** Used in secret hinting, touching of beard, aiming an arrow, parrot, remembering, information, tasks etc.

(4) **Pralokita** (Look both sides, one after another) To denote watching things on both sides, excessive affection, moving.

**Drishtibheda:** ***Milita***

(5) **Milita** (Keep the eyes half open) To denote 'snake, being under another's power, uttering (prayers etc); meditation, salutation, lunacy and keen observation.

**Drishtibheda: Ullokita**

(6) **Ullokita** (Raise the eyes and look upwards) To denote 'top of a flag, a tower of the temple (gopura), the heaven; of previous birth; height and moon light.

(7) **Anuvritta** (Look up and down) To denote 'angry looks, and invitation to beloved.

(8) **Avalokita** (Look down wards) To show looking at the shadow, recollection, discussion, study, looking at one's own limbs.

**Drisyakavya**

Connotes a visual poetry, a drama.

**Druta (Tala/Rhythm) see Laya**

**Drutam**

According to *Amarakosha* it denotes rapid dance. It is also called 'Ogha'.

**Dukhātmaka dramas see Rasa**

**Dundubhi**

The drum 'Dundubhi' is often mentioned from the Rigveda onwards. It was used in both war and peace. In the Tandya Maha Brahmana it is mentioned that the instrument was used on the occasion of Mahavrata ceremony, a rite performed at the winter solstice, for the purpose of driving away influences hostile to the return of the sun.

The Saman singers were accompanied on this musical instruments and in order to bring out the sounds (dhvani) hidden in the trees, the drum Dundubhi was sounded in the four corners of the of the Mahāvedi, herein the inference is that the Dundubhi was made of wood which represented the trees in which the sound is hidden.

The *Natyashastra* helds music, an indispensable adjunct of Sanskrit drama. It mentions some musical instrumentals such as Mridanga, Paṇava, Dardura, Dundubhi, Muraja, Jhallari, Paṭaha, Vaṁsha, Shaṅkha and Ḍakkini.

**[see also 'Dundubhyāgāta']**

**Dundubhyāgāta**

This refers to the player on the Dundubhi. According to Bhatta Bhaskara, player on the paṭaha. In the Purushamedha Prakayana of the Taittiriya Brahmaṇa (3rd Ashtaka and 4th Prashana), names of professional artists and musicians are given whose services were required in the sacrificial hall. Dundubhyāgāta was one of such musician.

**Durmalli**

This is a minor type of drama (Uparupaka) and according to *Sahityadarpana* it has four acts. The first act lasts for three Nāḍikās and the Viṭa appears in it. The second in which the Vidusaka emerges, lasts for five Nāḍikās, and the third, with the Pithamarda lasts for six Nāḍikas. The fourth is that in which citizens emerge for ten Nāḍikās.

**Duta**

Messengers, male or female may be of three types, states traditional doctrines. They are :- Nisristārtha, Mitārtha and Karyapresya.

**Duti**

It refers to a female messanger, a confidante, a go-between for the lovers.

Analogous to male messengers, a Duti (female envoy) may also be a three kinds Nisristartha, Mitartha and Kāryapresya.

In Sanskrit drama, female messengers are usually deputed to contact the men in the first affairs of love, and to reconcile the lovers separated from each other due to pride, quarrel or estrangement. A duti may contact a man during a festival, a night stroll, in a garden, in the house of an acquaintance, or that of a female friend (of the Heroine) or in the house of the nurse, or in a deserted house, under the pretext of inviting him or visiting him during a supposed illness, and so on.

**Dvār**

It refers to the 'doors' of the theatre-house.

**[see 'Ranga']**

**Dvibhumi**

It means 'Two level of a building'. Dvibhumi is a theatre having the height equal to a mandapa of two storeys, described in *Natyashastra* (2-80).

**[see under 'Ranga']**

**Dvija (Vidusaka) see Vidusaka**

# E

**Ekaharya Abhinaya**

It denotes Abhinaya or acting of a solo actor who portrays a variety of roles without the change of getup; also called '*Ekapatraharya*'.

**Ekartha see Dosas**

**Ekartha Abhinaya**

It refers to that kind of Abhinaya (Acting) where an actor portrays diverse incidents and situations under one theme.

**Ekatala**

It is beat-an inadequate mention of a whole system of beats (Amarokosha).

**Ekavidya**

In the context of drama, it refers to character in a Sanskrit drama who is proficient in one of the fine arts, music, dance, or poetry. The character 'Viṭa' is technically described in the dramatic treatise as Ekavidya. But a Vita is equally gifted in the arts of love, an associate of the hero in love matters (Kama-sachiva).

**[see Kama-Sachiva and Vita]**

# G

**Ga (Gāndhāra)**

This is the third scale degree.

**[see Gāndhara]**

**Gajadanta Hasta**

This is a double hand gesture in which both the hands in *sarpasheersha* touch the arms of opposite sides on shoulders or elbows to represent carrying the bride and bridegroom, lifting a heavy weight, holding a pillar and uprooting a boulder. This is given by *Natyashastra*, but not mentioned in *Abhinaya Darpana*.

**Gamaka**

In music it denotes 'Transition', a melodic choices or melodic transition or vocal ornament.

Gamaka is 'Grace'. The ornaments of the svaras (notes) consist in Gamakas or Graces. According to *Sangitasamayasara*, "When in singing, a note rises from its own pitch and moves towards another so that the second sound passes like a shadow over it, it is called a 'Gamaka'.

According to lewis Rowell, Professor of music theory at Indiana University. "To put the three terms Varna, Alankara and

Gamaka into their proper perspective, it is usefil to imagine the decorative dimension in Indian music as hierarchy : If Varṇa represents the generalized shape of a given unit of melody, Alankara signifies the specific pattern of decoration within this general shape, and Gamaka refers to the transitive elements around and between the individual svaras - the microlevel of melodic structure progression from contour to pattern to microstructure, we can also inter another progression : from ornaments as conceived to ornaments as performed; once again from the potential to the actual. The idea of Varna is readily grasped by the mind and described in words, but the microscopic subtleties of the Gamakas resist description and are best learned by demonstration and imitation.

The first description of the Gamakas appeared in Parshvadeva's '*Saṅgītasamayasāra*'. Parshvadeva's list contain seven that includes such familiar ornaments as a tremor on a single tone, one tone sliding gradually into another, a second tone begun without a new stroke or articulation, two degrees of oscillation between two tones (one rapid and one slow), and other staples of the Indian melodic tradition. Pārshvadeva's list has been expanded to fifteen in *Sangitaratnakara* of Sharangadeva and the number has grown in subsequent treatises on music.

**Gāna**

It means 'a song'. Natyashastra has given Gana of five variations.

Also denotes a *Deshi* music constituting songs where more importance is given to the words than the note or the time measure.

The genre of incidental music for the ancient theatre in known as 'Gāna'.

In one of the verses in Chapter VI of *Natyashastra*, Bharata has furnished eleven elements of Drama which can be collectively called the 'Digest of Naṭyashastra. These significant dramatic components are:-

Rasa (Sentiment)

Bhava (Emotion)

Abhinaya (Acting)

Dharmi (Modes of representation)

Vritti (Styles of expression)

Pravritti (Local usages)

Siddhi (Success of production)

Svara (Note)

Atodya (Musical instruments)

Gana (Song)

Ranga (Theatre)

Bharata has thus assigns due place to music in drama and has devoted six chapters of his Natyashastra to an exposition of the Theory and Practice of Music. Of all the songs associated with the performance of dramas, *Dhruvas* appear to be most charming, says *Natyashastra*. They are to sung on five occasions at the time of entrance, diversion, departure, calming, and transition. They also comprised back-ground music suggesting acts and moods of diverse characters. As the production of Rasa being the main purpose of ancient dramas, music was given full importance in it.

**[see also 'Dhruvas' and 'Sangita']**

**Gaṇaka**

This refers to one who is well versed in the jatis or classifictions of Shrutis, the Svaramandala, ie, Saptasvaras. In short, Gaṇaka is well versed in the science and the art of music. In the Purushamedha Prakayana of the Taittiriya Brahmaṇa (3rd Ashtaka and 4th Prashna), names of professional artists and musicians are mentioned whose service were required in the sacrificial hall and it includes the name of Ganaka.

**Ganam**

Under the heading 'Gānam', the 'Chāndogya Upanishad (II Adhyaya, 22 Khanda) furnishes different tonal qualities. They are:-

1. *Vinadri* : Voice resembling that of Rṣhabha.
2. *Anirukta* : Indefinite, unidentifiable.
3. *Nirukta* : Definite, identifiable.
4. *Mridu slakshaṇa* : Soft, sweat and brilliant.
5. *Balavat Slakshana* : Voluminous yet brilliant.
6. *Krouncha* : Voice that has an effect of creating pathos or karuna, like the bird 'Krouncha'.
7. *Apadhvānta* : Tone resembling the sound emenating from a bronze vessel when broken.

**Ganapati**

Ganesha, leader of Gaṇas (ie, spirit attendants of Shiva). He is the elephant headed son of Parvati and Shiva. Also known as Omkara. According to *Abhinaya-darpana*, in 'Nandi' (Benedictory verse), many kinds of charming tones are performed in honour of Ganapati, the god of the Muraja drum and other gods.

In *Natyashastr*a we find that there are various Indian deities deputed to protect different dramatis personae where they are performing on the stage. A verse says : Let Indra protect the actor playing the role of hero, Saraswati assume the role of heroine, Onkara (Ganesa/Ganapati), the Vidusaka and Siva the rest of the characters.

**Gāndhara**

This is the third scale degree (Ga/Gāndhara), one of the seven Svaras (Notes) and according to *Ragavibodha*, *Sangitaparijata*, *Sangitamakarandah* etc, the sounds of music are first perceived as relative pitches or intervals and then from the twenty two shrutis (Main Intervals) come the seven svaras, namely Ṣaḍja, Ṛṣabha, Gāndhāra, Madhyama, Pañcama, Dhaivata and Niṣāda. It is interesting to mention here that the traditional authorities on music refer each Svara or Note to the sound of some animal.

Gandhāra is said to represent the bleat of the goat.

**Gandharva**

It refers to celestial musician inhabiting Indra's heaven. Gandharvas are the celestial guardian of Soma, of the flowing supernal light. These celestial beings are proficient in song and dance and wear fragrant garments.

This also refers to sacrosanct exclusive margi music used in the preliminaries of dramas where nuances of notes and time measure were more important than the words. The Sanskrit drama had a religious origin. Bharata himself recommends. Natya and Gandharva, ie, Drama and music, as a supreme way of pleasing gods. Music (Gandharva) dance and drama were the ways and modes of propitiating the divinities and obtaining their pleasure and blessings. It is rightly stated by a critic that the recitation or spoken dialogue and acting modes are the characteristic aspects of drama; emotional representation and emotional response are its objectives, and Gandharva and dance are its pleasurable accompaniment. (Sources of enjoyment).

This is therefore the genre of ritual music performed during the prelude to a play.

According to Abhinava gupta Gāndharva is the genre of ritual music, unlike the incidental music, was fixed in all aspects of its structure - melodic, rhythmic, and formal. The musical elements dominated the text, and the aim of thẹ genre was adrista phala ("unseen benefit"), not the immediate pleasure of the spectators: The most of the available information on the structure and style of the early theater music pertains to the ceremonial music of the Pūrvaranga which is a sacrifice, a religious ritual designed to propitiate the presiding deities, to purify both the performers and the stage, and to lead the audience step by step from the sacred plane of the opening ceremonies into the mundane world depicted in the play.

**Gaṅgāvataraṃakarasạ**

A cadence of movement literally meaning the discant of the rivers Gāngā (Gangas).

**Ganika**

This refers to courtezans.

When represented on the stage, she is one of three major kind of heroines in a Sanskrit play. She is under the category 'Sādhārani or Samanya'.

*Dasarupaka* and *Rasarnavasudhakara* describe her as endowed with cunning, boldness and maturity, and skill in various arts. The Ganika as a heroine may be shown to be actually in love or merely playing the game of love.

*Dasarupaka* and *Natyadarpana* categorically state that in a drama other than Prahasana type, a Ganika should always be portrayed as a woman who is really in love and is sincere, attached and devoted to the Nayaka (the hero), like Vasantasena to Charudatta in the famous classic 'Mrcchakatika'. However in a Prahasana, a courtesan may asume the role of a non-loving and insincere, as a play of this nature aims at evoking only laughter and merriment.

Another important points is that when the hero of a dignified dramatic composition is a celestial or Royal one, Ganika should not be firgure as a heroine. An exception to this rule is a celestial courtesan. In Kalidasa's Vikramorvasiya, one can find 'Urvasi' as a heroine by the side of the Royal hero 'Purūravas'.

Bharata has also suggested that the names of courtezans should end in datta, mitra and sena, while laying down rules for assigning names to characters.

**Garbha**

It denotes 'Arrogance, Pride, Haughty'.

Garbha or "Pride" is the Eighteenth Mutable State/ Vyabhichari Bhava which according to Bharata should be represented by an actor on the stage by intolerance, arrogance, contempt, insult, refused, looking over the shoulder, mockery, harsh words, disregarding elders, rebuking etc.

**Garbha - Samdhi**

Dramatic theory holds the view that the plot of a drama is

divided into five divisions which it terms 'Samdhis'. 'Garbha - Samdhi' is the third in the series and comprise of '*Pataka*' (essential element of the plot) as Artha - prakriti and 'Praptya's as Avastha (stage of development of the plot. *Natyashastra* defines Garbha - Samdhi as that stage of play where the seed sprouts up, and there is satisfaction as well as frustration followed by renewed struggle. Garbha show the 'Bija' develping towards the 'Phala'. When sufficient efforts have been put in and the drama attains a stage where the possibility of attaining the end seems to be in view - such a stage in called 'Garbha - Samdhi. Hence Praptisambhava is a constituent of this juncture (through a blending of favourable and adverse situations) alongwith Pataka ie, an extra help is provided to the hero/heroine for attaining that great fruit and this is done by incorporating a subsidiary plot, Pataka solely employed to help the theme of the main plot.

In Mudraraksasam, the second act begins with Garbha - Samdhi. Chanakya's plans gradually succeed, as expected by him. This brings Praptyasa. The episode of 'Kusuma Pura' is the Patākā.

**Garhaṇa (Censure) see Vagyabhinaya**

**Garuda Hasta**

This gesture in Indian dance is used to represent Garuda, the vehicle of Vishnu.

This is a double hand gesture in which the palms of the hands in *ardhachandra* are kept one above the other with the palms facing the body and the thumbs kept together.

It denotes "*Garuda*, the king of eagles."

**Gātha see Gātika**

**Gati - Prachar**

It refers to the gaits and movements, the last of the four kinds of 'Bodily Acting' or Angika Abhinaya. This is an altogether different kind of actions and movements, discussed by Bharata in his *Natyashastra*. Chapter XII deals with Gati - Prachar where the actors are told how to walk when someone feels cold, how to glance when one fleeing from some terror, to walk as a merchant or as king would walk, quick steps to show the moving of a chariot, with bow and arrow the warriors in the chariot, to keep face up, if one is flying into the skies, with face down if the character is descending to the earth and so on.

'Gati' is the way of walking and Gatibheda is one of the major divisions of 'Cheshtakrita' (ie, the movements of the entire body) the latter comes under 'Angikabhinaya'.

The *Natyashastra* has given about sixty types of *Gatis*, based on different age, conditions, situations, castes, professions, character, moods and sentiments of human beings and the types of their rides either on vehicles or on animals.

*Abhinaya darpanam,* however, given ten types of Gatibheda (way of walking/stepping) as follows:-

(1) **Hamsi (Goose):** One foot is placed slowly after the other at a distance of half a cubit and bent on each side alternately with hands in Kapittha.

(2) **Mayuri (Peacock):** Holding Kapittha in both hands, stand on the toes and move (bend) the knees alternately.

(3) **Mrigi (Deer):** Holding Tripataka hands and hoping forward or sideway like a deer.

(4) **Gajalīlā (Elephant):** Holding *Pataka* hands on both sides and moving slowly in Samapada (natural) lifting the left like an elephant.

(5) **Turangini (Horse)**

Right hand in *Pataka* and left in *Shikhara* lift the right foot and jump alternately in quick succession.

(6) **Simhi (Lion)**: Standing on the toes, jump forward quickly holding both the hands in Shikhara.

(7) **Bhujangi (Snake):** Walking with the feet moving like a snake with Tripataka hands.

(8) **Mandūki (Frog):** Standing on the toes and jumping forward quickly, with both the hands in Shikhara like Simhi.

(9) **Vīra (Heroic):** Moving forward with force as though coming from a distance holding Pataka in right and Shikhara in left hand.

(10) **Manavi (Human):** Moving about or around with right hand in Katamukha and left hand on the waist.

**Gātika**

The earliest Rigvedic hymns were based on one (raised) note called Udātta lacking pitch and rhythm. Taking the hint from the rise and fall in the voice of everyday speech, the early Aryan must at one stage had begun to chant the words of the text to fluid rise and fall of the voice. This stage referred to is singing to the two primary notes, ie Udātta (raised) and Anudātta (not raised).

This represented the two main pitches of the speaking voice. In the *Nāradi Shiksha* which provides a link between Vedic and Post-Vedic music calls there two notes Udātta and Anudātta as Brahmana Svaras and Bhāshika Svaras respectively. This period has been style as 'Gātha' or 'Gātika' period of vedic singing when only these two notes were in vogue.

**Gāthika see Svaras (Vedic)**

**Gatraviksepa**

It means 'Bodily movement'.

**Gayika**

It means a female singer.

**Ghana**

Regular musical instruments, according to Bharata, are of four varities, viz. Stringed (Tata), covered (Avanaddha), Solid (Ghana), and Hollow (Susira). The Ghana or the 'Solid' are the cymbals. This is the 'solid' category of instruments, ie, idiophones.

The idiophones or anything solid-like sticks and stones, pots and pan might have been the oldest musical instruments used by mankind. However as they are not capable of producing definite pitches that are required for creating a melody, they donot find a place in classical music with two exceptions - Ghatam and Jalatarang.

**Ghana**

Presently we have idophones and autophones like Jalra, Jhallari, Thalam (cymbals) Jalatharang, Ghatam etc.

**Ghana see also Madhyama**

**Ghātas**

It means 'obstacles' during a dramatic performance and therefore points to the 'defects of a Natakamandali (Theatre Troupe) Bharata has mentioned obstacles (Ghatas) arises from four sources : from the fault of actors, from an enemy, from gods and finally from portentous calamity.

**[see also "Siddhis"]**

**Gita**

In the description of the genesis of Natyaveda, it is stated that *Natyashastra* as fifth Veda was a creation from the four Vedas. The components of Natya suggested are Pāṭhya, Gita, Abhinaya and Rasa. The Sanskrit dramatic theory leans heavily on Anukriti (mimetic representation), carried out by appropriate Abhinaya. Natya is an admixture of experience of sorrow and happiness of all humanity rendered by Abhinaya. The Rasa element (emotional experience) may be referred to the pleasure the spectators derive from the performance; and the Gita, if it comes as an accomapniment, may be yet another source of enjoyment.

Gita means 'song'. In Bharata's time which covered a period from 100 BC to 400 AD even the Prabandha Gāna was not there. Varities of Dhruva Gana which were in vogue them were classified according to Tālas or Rhythm and not according to Rāgas or melody.

**Gita (Purvaranga)**

This is the first constituent parts of Purvaranga (Preliminaries of a play) taken up on the stage. This is preceded by nine items performed behind the curtain. First comes Gita, meaning song in praise of gods and followed by Utthapana, Gita (song) on the setting up of the banner of Indra (Jarjara).

**Gītaka**

This is one of the compositions performed during the ritual prelude to a play.

**Gīti**

In Rhythmic system, this is "text setting" also style in general.

**Glani**

It means 'Remorse, Aversion, Weakness' etc. Glani is the second Vyabhichari Bhava or the Mutable State which should be conveyed by a weak voice, eyesight and cheeks, depressed stomach, slow gait, trembling, disappointment, slackness of limbs, change of colour, change of voice, etc.

**Gobrāhmananripādi**

In *Agnipurana* it is to be found that Nandi is regarded as one of the twenty two divisions of the Purvaranga. It adds to Bharatas Ashirvachana, prayers to the elders and benedictions of cow, Brahmana and King etc (Gobrahmananripadi) in the Nāndi ritual.

**Gosthi**

This is a minor type of drama (Uparupaka) and according to *Sahityadarpana*, an one-act play in which nine or ten ordinary men and five or six women appear.

### Graha

According to ancient musical theory, there are three important notes in the Raga, namely Graha, Amsha and Nyāsa. The Graha is the starting note, Amsha the main or predominant note and Nyāsa, the ending one.

### Grama

It means 'Scale'.

A combination of Svaras in called 'Grama'. Indian music is traditionally based on the three Gramas named Sadja, Madhyama and Gandhara. Sadja and Madhyama Gramas are found on earth while Gandhara is reserved for heaven. Three svaras (notes) namely Udātta (raised), Anudātta (not raised) and Svarita (Circumflex) of the Veda are not included in the Grāma. Sadya Grama is the best of all the Gramas.

Raga is the basis of melody in our music. Ragas (modes) necessarily depend upon two Gramas and are mainly produced from Sadja Grama.

### Grāmārāga

This is a scalar mode.

### Grivabheda

Refers to the movements of the neck.

According to Abhinaya darpana this is of four types :-

(1) **Sundari** (Moving the neck to the sides): Used in attention, striving, full expanse, acceptance with pleasure and beginning every item (attami).

(2) **Tiraschina** (Moving the neck from one side to the other like the movement of a snake): Used in 'exercise with a sword and the movement of a snake'.

(3) **Parivartita** (Moving the neck sideways in the form of half moon): Used in Lasya (amorous dance), kissing, admiration.

(4) **Prakampita** (Moving the neck forward and backward like a pigeon): Used to denote 'You and I, us, you and me, you and mine etc.

Apart from Abhinayadarpanam, we have *Natyashastra* that furnishes few more varities of neck movements. They are :-

(i) **Sama** (Natural position): Used in 'meditation, uttering prayers and natural position'.

(ii) **Nata** (lowering down the neck): Used in 'putting on an ornament or putting arm around someone's neck.

(iii) **Unnata** (Raising up the neck): Used in 'looking up and reaching a high place'.

(iv) **Tryasra** (Tilting the neck to a side): Used in 'weight lifting and sorrow'.

(v) **Rechita** (Shaking or moving the neck both sides): Used in suggesting charn, coquetry, and churning.

(vi) **Kunchita** (Bending down or contracting the neck): Used in 'pressure of load and protecting the neck from injury.

(vii) **Anchita** (Tilting the neck backwards): Used in 'combing hair, looking upwards.

(viii) **Valita** (Turning the neck sideways): Used in 'looking behind or turning the face back.

(ix) **Nivritta** (Brining back the neck from *Valita* the original position): Used in 'going back to one's own place.

**Gūḍhārtha see Dosas**

**Guhyakas**

It refers to "the Hidden Ones", gnomes or spirits forming the retinue of Kubera; guardians of hidden treasure. They are a kind of demigods, generally distinguished from the Yakshas. One of the presiding deities of theatre, states *Natyashastra*, they should be worshipped with offerings and sacrificies.

**Gulma**

Denotes a collective dance, ie, a group of dancers who follow after the main dancer.

**Gulphabheda**

This denotes the movements of the ankles and are of five kinds:-

(1) Angushthasamshlishta (Ankle touches the big toe of the other foot)

(2) Antargata (turned inside)

(3) Bahirgata (turned outwards)

(4) Mithoyukta (joined together)

(5) Viyukta (separated)

**Guna - kirtana (Enumeration of Merits) see Vagyabhinaya**

**Gunas**

Merits in a work of art; Attributes, characteristic of all substance or property belongong to all created things (Sattva, Rajas, Tamas). It denotes three constituents of Prakriti: *Sattva*, illuminating, cohesive tendency; *Tamas*, 'darkness' disruptive tendency; *Rajas*, revolving, activating tendency.

In the context of dramatic composition, while dealing with Diction (Vagabhinaya) Alankaras (Figures of speech) etc in *Natyashastra*, Bharata prescribes ten Gunas (Merit) to the playwright. There are :-

(1) **Shlesa (Synthesis):** It refers to the union of words linked through intended meaning.

(2) **Prasada (Perspiquity):** It is easy comprehension through the use of simple words and expressions.

(3) **Samatā (Smoothness):** When Alankaras and Gunas match and illuminate one another, it is an instance of Smoothness.

(4) **Samādhi (Concentration):** It is condensation of meaning with the help of figures of speech.

(5) **Mādhurya (Sweetness):** When a sentence, heard or uttered many times, does not tire, it is sweetness.

(6) **Ojas (Grandeur):** When a composition, censured and deficient in quality, reflects an exalted sense through its wealth of words and meanings, it is an instance of Grandeur.

(7) **Saukumārya (Softness):** When a composition consists of words easy to pronounce, euphonically combined, and giving agreeable meaning, it is an instance of softness.

(8) **Artha - vyakti (Clarity of Expression):** When the meaning becomes clear to the penetrating mind just after recital, it is an instance of 'Clarity of Expression'.

(9) **Udātta (Exaltedness):** When a composition includes witty and graceful words having many special senses which are marvellous, it is an instance of Exaltedness.

(10) **Kānti (Loveliness):** When a composition gives delight to the ears as well as to the mind on account of its well-put together words, it is an instance of loveliness.

**Gunapata (Accusation of Virtues) see Vagyabhinaya**

**Gunas (Gāna)**

'The *Naradi Siksha*' which deals with different aspects of 'music in connection with the Sāma Veda has provided ten excellences or guṇas of lay and sacred music. These guṇas are:- Raktam, Purnam, Alankrita, Praṣanna, Vyakta, Vikrushṭa, Slakshanam, Saman, Sukumāram, Madhuram.

It is added that one must possess all these qualities because the audience will be invariably comprising of people of different tastes and liking. For example the Sāma will be appreciated by the Acharyas or Preceptors. Vyakta is preferred by pundits, scholars and musicians. Madhuram will be relished by women and Vikrishta to be liked by others.

Raktam is the harmonious blending of the notes of the Vīṇa and the Veṇu (flute). It also indicate the sweetness got by the agreement of the two instruments and the singer.

Purnam in this context (in music) means fullness of Svara and Shruti. In Sahitya it means the fullness of metre, pāda and akshara.

Third excellence is Alankrita, ie, adorns by the change of register from throat to chest and to head.

Prasanna indicates the clearness of music. Vyakta denotes purity in pronouncing the sãhitya according to its grammatical construction. Vikrushṭa means purity of words and increase in the volumes of tone. Slakshanam refers to the observance of the rules Vilambita, pluta, high, low etc. Saman indicates uniformity in singing adding or deleting svaras according to some rules Sukumaran means soft pronounciation of words by modulating the voice. Madhuram is natural sweetness of the words/voice.

**Gunotkirtana**

It means 'praises of merit'. *Natyadarpana* tells us that the Benedictory part (Nandi verse) should have six or eight pādas and adds the terms Saraswati (goddess of learning), Kavi and Gunotkirtana.

**Guru**

It means 'teacher' but in music and poetry, it denotes long duration.

# H

**Hala**

It is dramatic appalation used for a female friend.

**Hallisha**

This is a minor type of drama, an one act, with the Kaishikivritti, a predominant feature in it with plenty of music and dance, states *Sahityadarpana.*

**Hamsapaksha Hasta**

This is a single hand gesture in which one has to keep the little finger straight in *Sarpashirsha.* This is used to denote "number six, construction of a bridge, putting nail marks and a covering."

It also represents offering water and gifts, decoration of cheek, etc in Indian dance.

**Hamsasya Hasta**

This is a single hand gesture in which the first finger is bent to touch the thumb while the other three fingers are stretched straight. This is used to express "Blessing, auspiciousness, tying with thead, ascertaining, instruction, thrill (sensation), pearls, putting the wick of lamp, touchstone, jasmine flower, painting, snakebite, dam."

It also represents the swan beak, certainty, a drop of water etc.

**Hanjā**

This is a dramatic appalation and according to *Amarakosha* it is used for a female servant.

**Hañje**

It means 'Hey child'. Bharata in his treatise has laid down set of words for calling the different characters according to their position. A slave girl was addressed as 'Hañje'.

**Hand Gestures see Hastamudras**

**Hanubheda see Dashana - Chibuka - Hanubheda**

**Harinapluta**

"Jump of a dear;" the name of a cadence of movement.

**Harsha**

It denotes 'Joy, Bristling, Happiness'. This 'Joy' is the fifteenth Mutable State/Vyabhichari Bhava which according to Bharata should be represented by a happy face and eyes, sweet words, embracing, horripilation, tears, perspiration and the like.

**Hāsa**

It means 'Laughter, Amusement, Cheerful' etc.

Hāsa or "Laughter", is the second Permanent state (sthayibhava) which is produced by means of caricaturing the actions of others, loose and irrelevant talk, stupidity and absurdity, by smile, laughter, excessive laughter and the like.

**Hasta Mudras**

According to *Natyashastra* tradition, there are 24 single hand gestures (Asamyuta Hasta) and 13 double-hand gestures (Samyuta Hasta) and 30 Nritta hastas.

The hastas or hand gestures facilitate the expression of the chosen composition or sahitya. Each hasta carries a different shade of meaning. *Abhinaya Darpana* of Nandikeshwara which is dated around A.D. 1000 gives 28 single-hand gestures and 24 double-hand gestures.

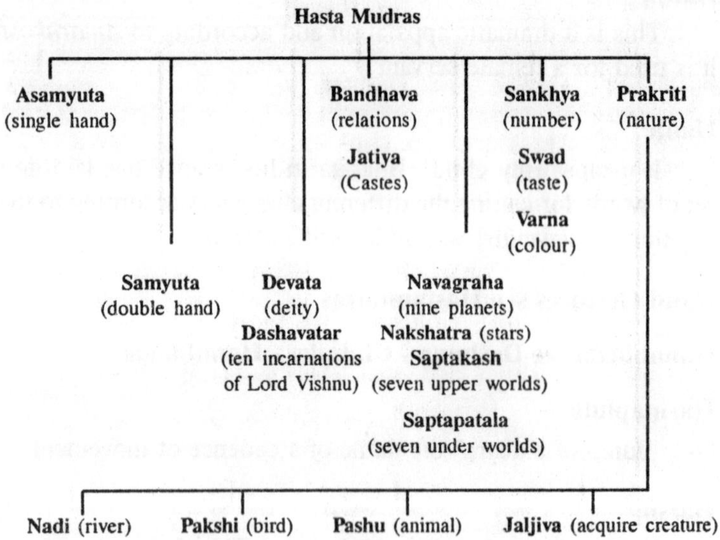


**[see also 'Asamyuta Hasta, Samyuta Hasta, Devata Hasta, Rakshasa Hasta Dashavatar Hasta, Jatiya Hasta, Bandhava Hasta, Navagraha Hasta, Nakshatra Hasta, Saptakash/Saptatala Hasta, Sankhya Hasta, Varna Hasta, Prakriti Hasta, Pashu - Pakshi Hasta]**

## Hastas

From *Natyashastra,* we find that measurement for the building of theatres was dependent upon the conception of Hasta and Danda. According to it, 21 Angulas means one hasta, four hastas one Danda. This measurement matches with the one given in the *Arthashastra* of Kautilya.

**[see 'Ranga']**

## Hasya Rasa

Hasya refers to 'Humour', Comic, Rejoice, Mirth. This is

one of the Navarasas and second most important sentiment in a drama, placed after Śringara rasa. Without humour or Hasya, a play is likely to becomes monotonous, serious and heavy, *Natyashastra* defines Hasyarasa as having Hāsa as its Permanent state, the Sthayibhāvas.

The Vibhāvas are funny dress, ornaments, shamelessness, vulgarity etc. The Vyabhicharibhavas for this sentiment are dissimulation, indolence, sleep, jealousy etc. Thus humour is created by funny dress as well as humorous acting and speech. The characters figuring in Hasyarasa are usually of low type.

*Natyashastra* classifies Humour further into six varities such as Upahasita (a scornful laugh, employed to ridicate) while Apahasita is mockery. They represent satire.

Humour is conveyed in acting by uncouth behaviour, old speech, wearing unusual ornaments and dresses, etc.

*Varna* : Shveta (white)

*Mukharaga* : Prasanna (Pleased)

*Hasta* : Sandamsha

*Svaras* : Madhyama, Panchama

*Raga* : In this Rasa, Ghana and joyous Ragas generally employed to radiate this rupture 'Hasya Rasa' or Humour.

Presiding deity : Pramatha

**Hāva**

This denotes the erotic expression and according to *Amarakosha*, there are six expressions of erotic sentiments of woman. The commentary mentions ten varieties, quoting *'Nataka Ratnakosha'*. These are Lila Vilasa, Vichitti, Vibhrama, Kilakinchit, Mottayita, Kuttamita, Vivvoka, Lalita, Vihrita.

Vichitti is disdain of ornaments due to consciousness of beauty. Kilakinchit is humming out of joy. Mottayita is yawning et cet. expressive of yearning for the loved one. Kuttamita is apearance of pain in excessive pleasure. Notable among these being Vivvoka, ie indifference (I don't care attitude).

**Hetu (Causation) see Vagyabhinaya**

**Hina see Adhama**

# I

**Ihamriga**

This is one of the major genres of drama (Rupaka), and according to the commentary on the *Dasarupa*, This form derieves its name from the fact that in it a maiden, who is as difficult to be obtained as a gazelle, is demanded.Ihamriga is of four acts having three junctures.

The plot of the Ihamriga is of mixed nature, partly legendary and partly invented. It contains mixed story of gods and men; any Rasa except Hasya and Sringara (like Vyayoga type).

The Nayaka (Hero) and the Pratinayaka (The opponent of the hero) may be either human or divine, wellknown, self controlled and vehement, the latter committing improper acts by mistake. It contains scenes of wrath but the characters are not shown to be dashing into battle by some artifice. The play 'Rukminiharana' is a Ihamriga variety.

**Indra**

He is the creator God of the aeon prior to that of Rudra Pashupati.

He is the chief of the Vedic gods, the god of rain and one of the presiding deities of theatre, according to ancient dramatic doctrine.

In *Natyashastra* we find that there are various Indian deities deputed to protect different dramatis personae where they are performing on the stage. A verse says :

Let Indra protect the actor playing the role of hero, Saraswati assume the role of heroine, Onkara the Vidusaka and Siva the rest of the characters.

*Natyashastra* (6, 45) mentions Mahendra is the God of Chivalry (Vira rasa). Mahendra or Indra is regarded as the leader of gods.

**[see 'Jarjara puja' 'Ranga devatas' 'Devatas']**

**Istartha**

This apparently means one to whom wealth is desirable and in the context of Prashnika (judges of a dramatic performance) he is a bard and is included to judge the praises and songs addressed to the Royal Hero.

**Itivritta**

To denote the plot of a play, Bharata in his *Natyashastra* uses the term 'Itivritta' and calls it 'Sharira' the body of it. Even *Bhavaprakashanam* also states that the plot of drama is designated as 'Itivritta because it has to be so conceived, designed and presented as to seem that it has really happened. The dramatic plot has synonyms like Vastu (Plot), Katha (Story), Vrittanta or Charita (happening, life and activities).

Abhinavagupta in his commentary has described that an epic or a narrative poem and a drama both must have a plot or a story to tell. But a poem uses only Vritta, incidents or happenings it is to be read or listened to and enjoyed (anabhinaya) while, Natya must use Itivritta, ie, incidents or happenings which have been built and polished or perfected in a particular manner, so that the Natya can be presented through histrionic devices on a theatre stage, it is to be seen and heard, acted on a stage, thus enjoyed (Abhinaya).

**[see "Adhikarika Vritta" "Prasangika" and "Vastu".]**

# J

## Jaḍata

It denotes 'Stupor, Stiffness, Senselessness'.

Jaḍata or 'Stupor' is the seventeenth Mutable State/ Vyabhichari Bhava which according to Bharata's *Natyashastra* should be represented by an actor by keeping silent, uttering inaudible words, remaining absolutely quiet, unblinking eyes and needing support from others.

## Janantika

This is a conversation with a person, in the presence of many, who are within hearing distance; the speech is supposed to be guarded from one particular person only; the others present may hear it; the person who is not to hear it is excluded by the *Tripatāka-hasta* gesture, three fingers raised, the second near the small finger and thumb bent, and the hand raised as a sereen (antara) before the person to be excluded; this is called 'Janāntika'. A stage convention where one's private feelings are conveyed to another character in the presence of other character characters who are not supposed to hear.

**Jangha bheda**

This refers to the movements of the shanks and are of five kinds:-

(1) Avartita (crossed)

(2) Nata (bent)

(3) Kshipta (stretched out)

(4) Udvahita (raised up)

(5) Parivritta (turned back)

**Janubheda**

This means 'movements of the knees' and are of seven types:-

(1) **Samhata** (one knee touches the other): Shown in shyness, anger and jealousy.

(2) **Kunchita** (folded so that thigh and shank touch each other)

(3) **Ardhakunchita** (waist and knees are lowered down wards): Shown in 'bending'.

(4) **Nata** (touching the ground): Used in 'falling and protesting'.

(5) **Unnata** (lifted upwards almost to the height of the chest): Used to show climbing

(6) **Vivritta** (turned outwards): Depicts sitting on animals like horse, camel etc.

(7) **Sama** (normal position): Used in 'standing straight'.

**Jarjara**

This is Indra's [the lord of the gods, Vedic God of rains] banner staff, presented to Bharata and his drama troupe.

Brahma, Shiva, Vishnu, Kartikeya and the three great serpents Shesa, Vasuka and Taksaka are supposed to preside in the five knots of the flag-staff. The first part of the staff is wrapped in white linen, the second in blue. the third in yellow, the fourth in red and the fifth in multicoloured cloth.

The Jarjara is regarded as very powerful and prominent presiding deity of theatre, states Bharata and should be worshiped with offerings and sacrifices.It is essential for Sanskrit drama performance where it is installed during the preliminaries. Infact the setting up of the flag-staff of Indra is the most significant and auspicious rites on the stage. The day preceding the festivity, the Jarjara is erected in the stage in the evening after the Mantras have been chanted.

On the day of performance, the Jarjara is worshipped alongwith all prominent gods.

**Jarjara puja**

In the Purvaranga (preliminaries of a play), there is an item called Parivartana which involve stalking round the stage with praise of the guardians of the world 'Dikpalastuti' and adoration of Indra's banner called 'Jarjara puja'.

**Jarjara shlokas**

This is one of the twenty constituent parts of Purvaranga [preliminaries of a play], performed on the stage. The item is preceded by 'Shuskavakrista'. Once the latter is over, Jarjarashlokas takes place in praise of the god whose worship is being celebrated, or in praise of a king or of Brahmā.

**Jati**

It denotes the parent modes or scales from which the Rāga later developed, provided the melodic settings for both songs and instrumental music. Intervals (Shruti), Notes (Svara), and Modes (Jāti) suited to different rasa and situations are mentioned by Bharata.

As music compositions, the Dhruva songs have their two essential aspects of melody and rhythm. All the illustrative songs in ancient music treatises from Bharata down to Sharangadeva in the earlier section of his chapters, are connected with dance and drama. In Bharata they were *Jatis*, in late writers, the *Ragas*. These melodic modes were analysed with reference to their emotional suitability. The intervals, notes and modes were all studied from the emotional view point and schemes of harnessing different moulds for different dramatic situations were formulated. Bharata has shown the emotional values of Svaras and Jatis. To quote V. Raghavan from his essay on *'Music in ancient Indian* drama'. "Of the *jātīs*, Saḍijodīcyavatī and Ṣaḍjamadhyama are to be employed for love and fun, Ārṣabhī and Ṣāḍjī for the heroic, the wonderful and the terrible and so on. A larger analysis of music is also given with reference to the five junctures through which the plot of the play progresses from inception to *denouement:* In the opening Madhyama-grāma; the Ṣaḍja-grāma in the progression; the Sādhārita in the development; Kaiśikamadhyama in the pause; and Kaisika in the conclusion. The relation between *rāga* and *rasa* is further worked out by Mataṅga and Kaśyapa. To illustrate with some stray applications - Mataṅga says: Of the Bhinna class of *Rāgas*, Bhinna Ṣaḍja is usefulfor the entry of a hero proceeding on hunt; of the Gauḍa group, Gauḍa-pañcama in separation of lovers; of the Vesāras, Śauvīraka is good for quietude and scenes of recluses and sages; of the Sādhāraṇa *rāgas*, Bhammana-pancama for fatigue *en route* or in forests. The lost treatise of Kaśyapa is replete with further intricate schemes on this subject; a few random examples from the extensive citation made by Abhinavagupta will suffice to show the extent of Kaśyapa's analysis. When tranquility follows anxious thought, Mālavi followed by Gurjari is helpful; Āndhālī may be employed when intoxication waxes; when a low character is indulging in the comic, Gāndhāra-pañcama; a lady's cogitation, as distinct from a gentleman's may be properly backed up by Mālava-pañcama. Nānyadeva, in his *Bharatabhāṣya*[7] of which only a single corrupt ms. is known, gives the *rāga, tāla* and *rasa* for every *dhruvā* metre in Bharata. When the undeniable relation of melody and emotional effect is granted, the artistes may deduce their schemes. The very name *rāga* has an emotional significance. Mataṅga suggests that *jātīs* are so called because etymologically they are productive of moods. It is well known that a class of *rāgas,* in the classical period, was known as *kriyāṅga;* and the name is explained in the music treatises as referring to the dramatic use of these modes for emotional situations, exhilaration, sorrow and so on. The practice of making such studied use of *rāgas* in dramas was so well settled that Kālidāsa refers to it in his *Kumārasambhava* when he makes the divine couple grace with their presence a dramatic performance done by the celestial damsels in honour of their marriage; and Ānandavardhana, the critic, presses the emotional suggestiveness of *rāga* more than once in support of his argument for the acceptance of the comprehensive principle of suggestion.

Bharata has mentioned earlier of *Melodic Jatis* and then of *Rhythmic Jatis*. The latter are the eighteen in number some are Shuddha, Ekarūpa, Deshanurupa, Deshad-apeta-rupa, Viskambha, Paryasta, Parsnisamasta, Duskarakarana, Urdhvagostika, Ucchitika etc. The memonics of rhythm-syllables composing or indicating each and the characters and the situations, he gives more elaborately the rhythm - syllables for the instrumental music.

Early compilation of Ragas were then known as Jatis. Matanga muni regards Raga as one of the seven clases of Jatis current in his time. He believes Jati generates the Grama raga withthe usel of predominating note (Amsha Svara). In Brihaddesa (4-9th c.A.D.), he mention of Grama raga.

**Jatibhasa see also Bhasavidhanam**

**Jatiya Hasta**

It refers to the Hastas (Hand gestures) for castes. They are :-

(1) **Brahmana:** Left hand in *shikhara* held above the left shoulder and right hand is held horizontally below the waist on the right side of the thigh to indicate the sacred thread.

(2) **Kshatriya:** Left hand held horizontally in *Shikhara* and the right hand in *pataka*.

(3) **Vaishya:** *Hamsasya* in left and *Katakamukha* in right hand.

(4) **Shudra:** Left hand in *Shikhara* and the right hand in Mrigashirsha.

**Javanika**

Javanika is a handheld mobile curtain used in Sanskrit Theatre.

Javanika, Yavanika and Yamanika are three recognised form of the word for 'Curtain'. Javanika is the Prakrit form of Yavanika.

The word 'Javana' means going fast and is derieved from the root 'Ju'. The feminine form of 'Javana' is Javanī or Javanika. It may refer to a curtain which was to be drawn with force.

The word 'Yavanika' is derieved from root 'Yuñ bandhane', yuñ, yunāti, badhnāi avrinoti va anaya iti ie, anything by which something is covered from the sight of the spectators, ie, Curtain.

The word 'Yamanika' comes from the root 'Yaṁ' 'to stop or restrain', denoting a covering or curtain and the word Yamani, from which Yamanika is directly derieved can be traced in the Vajasneyi - Samhita.

Neither in the *Natyashastra* nor in the *Abhinavabharati*, there is any reference to the drop curtain. The ending of acts in Sanskrit dramas does not require any drop scene and it never ended abruptly like modern plays. So there was no drop - curtain in ancient India Theatre. It had only one curtain and that it was placed between the Rangashirsa and the Rangapitha.

**Javanikantara**

Dramas are usually divided into acts. The common word for an act is 'Anka'; only in the sub-class, Saṭṭaka, the act is called 'Javanikantara'.

**[see Saṭṭaka]**

**Jhallari**

The *Natyashastra* helds music, an indispensable adjunct of Sanskrit drama. It informs about some musical instrments like Mridanga, Paṇava, Dardura, Dundubhi, Muraja, Jhallari, Paṭaha, Vaṁsha, Shaṅkha and Dakkinī.

**Jihvabheda**

This denotes 'the movements of the tongue'. They are of six varities as follows:-

(1) **Rijvi** (tongue stretched out from the open mouth):Used to show 'feeling of extreme thirst, exhausion'.

(2) **Unnatā** (tongue is raised up in the open mouth):To show 'yawning and looking into the mouth'.

(3) **Lolā** (tongue moving and waving in the open mouth): To portray 'removal of obstacles'.

(4) **Lehinī** (lips and teeth are licked by the tongue):To show 'tasting'.

(5) **Vakra** (tip of the tongue is curved or twisted):Depicts Narasimha (the man - lion)

(6) **Srikkānugā** (lips are licked by wet tongue): To denote 'seeing delicious food'.

**Jugupsā**

It means 'Disgust, Revulsion, Scornful, etc.

Jugupsā is a Permanent State, Sthayi Bhava, relates to women and lower class of people. It is produced by the sights and sounds of dirty and distasteful objects. It is shown by an actor by covering the nose, contracting the physical limbs, uneasiness and holding the heart and the like.

**Jyestha Natyamandapa see Ranga**

**Jyestha Nayaka**

Classical theorists classify male characters into three classes of Jyestha (Uttama) Madhyama (Madhya/A-mukhya) and Kaniṣ tha (Adhama, Hina, Nicha). This applies to the Nayaka Neta or the leader of the principal dramatic action as well.

*Bhavaprakashana* gives the Jyestha Nayaka as one who has all the commended qualities and is therefore, Uttama Nayāka.

**[see also 'Nayaka']**

# K

**Kahali**

Brass made funnel like trumpet is called 'Kahali'.

**Kaishiki Vritti see Vritti**

**Kakali**

This is an overlapping note between the two voice registers.

This is the musical sound which Amarakosa defines as a low sweet sound; and if it is indistinct it is Kala; if deep, as from the throat, Mandra; if high pitched, Tāra.

**Kaksya Vibhāga**

This refers to Natyadharmi zonal division. Kaksyas denotes the divisions of the stage to represent change in scenes and other objects.

*Natyashastra* prescribes that Kaksyavibhaga or divisions into parts should be made in a regular order. Probably on both sides of the pillars in the Rangashirsa, there were Kaksyas. These were three in number close to the Nepathyagriha there were Abyantara Kaksya [Internal] closely attached to the Rangapitha was the Bāhyakaksya [External] and in between these Kaksyas there was the Madhya Kaksya [Middle].

In Kaksyavibhaga of the stage, we see that there could be as many divisions as the plot required to represent houses, cities, countryside with gardens, villages, forests, ocean, islands, mountains, three worlds with animate and inanimate objects, world of gods, demons and nether regions etc.

Kaksyas were required when a change of scene was to be effected; inside and outside intermediate positions, distance and near, places etc.

**[see also 'Parikramana']**

**Kaku**

This denote 'change of the voice under different emotions, such as fear, grief, anger etc.

This is therefore, 'Modulation of Voice' to express different emotions.

Kaku is one of the attributes of musical rendering (Pathyaguna) there are two ways of intonation or effective modulation of voice. They are:-

(1) Sākanksha (Expectant)

(2) Nirakanksha (Devoid of Expectation)

**Kakusvara (Kākusvram)**

This denotes a defect in singing, means, singing like the crow.

**Kalā**

Musical time measure; a division of time variously computed (one minute fortyeight seconds or eight seconds).

In Rhythmic system, Kalā is a division of time, also a silent gesture demarcating such a duration.

**Kāla**

According to *Natyashastra* (6, 45), Kāla is the God of fear (Bhayanaka rasa).

This deity is regarded as a regent of the death.

**Kalahantarita Nayika**

*Natyashastra* has give eight varieties of Heroine - in - love and Kalahantarita is one of them. *Dasarupaka* describes her as "one who has quarrelled with her lover". The cause for the quarrel could be some misunderstanding or due to jealousy. The Heroine in such a state is torn by mental conflict, as a result of doubt and jealousy that some other woman may be in her way. Eventually she is not ready to approach her lover or speak with him.

**Kalpita (Smile of Conceit) see Alankaras & Upama**

**Kalpita Sangita**

It denotes 'previously composed music. It is sung as it was originally composed by composer.

**Kāma**

In a Sanskrit dramatic composition, the Hero (The principal character) directly by his own efforts or through the endeavours of his ministers and helpmates, stands as the leader of an action and obtains its fruit (Phala). The Hero, as *Nataka - Laksana - Ratnakosha* points out in the traditional manner, is the 'Purusartha' (Dharma, Artha or Kāma).

Obtaining the woman of one's love is an achievement by the Nayaka (The Neta) in the sphere of Kāma.

**Kāmadasha**

Convention of the ten stages of love to be portrayed in works of art.

**Kama - Sachiva**

Apart from the Hero and Heroine, the dramatic characters (Pātrāṇi) of Sanskrit drama are considered in the context of Dharma, Artha and Kāma, in which matters they counsel and asist Royal Hero. Associates can be male or female may appear in secondary, minor or negligiable roles *Bhavaprakashana* place them under the three heads of Dharma - Sachiva, Artha - Sachiva and Kama - Sachiva. Kāma - Sachiva are those associates of the Hero who help him in the context of love matters.

They are:

(1) Pithamarda (a Patākānayaka, the Hero of the sub - plot) or Upanayaka, a secondary hero.

(2) Viṭa

(3) Vidūṣaka

(4) Ceṭa

The Hero's helpmates in love belong to different strata of the society In general, the Pithamarda hails from the Uthama class, Ceta to the Adhama class. *Sahitya dapana* regards Vidusaka and Vita as characters of the middling rank. But in Bhāna, the Vidusaka and Viṭa are treated as *Nicha patras.*

**Kañchuki**

Kañchuki, the Royal Chamberlain is also known as Kañcukīya or Kāñcukiya and so called because he wears a long robe as a uniform in his office. This is a typical character of a Sanskrit play. He and the Varṣavara (eunuchs) are stated by *Natyashastra* to be employed in the Royal Harem and the given the charge of looking after the young maidens and princesses. They exercise authority and attend on the king and Queen in their daily routine.

They are carriers of news concerning everything that takes place in Harem. They enjoy so much confidence of their masters that even a Queen may give them duty in the apartment of her royal husband. Bharata mentions that the Kancuki is usually a Brahmin, very old, and possess high skill required for the execution of his ttrusted and confidential duties. Their other salient features are that they are either impotent or effiminate or atleast not sex-minded at all. They are well trained and modest and never give themselves high airs. G.K. Bhat, renowned Sanskritist points out that the Sanskrit drama often shows that Kañcuki grieving over his old age and complaining that the big cane staff that he first took in his hand as a mark of his authority when he joined the *Antaḥpura* as a young person has now become, with advancing years, his chief means of physical support in his movements in the Royal Harem. Kañcuki is, recognised as a typical type of dramatic character, moulded by convention.

Kañchuki is, therefore, the Chamberlain of a royal palace, a character in Sanskrit drama.

**Kandavina**

Kāṇḍavina was used in the recitation of Sāman as an Upagānam (accompaniment), played by the wives of the priests. Another instrument used on the occasion was Pichchhola or Pichchhora, collectively called 'Apaghātila'.

**Kangula Hasta**

This is a single hand gesture in which the ring finger is curved inside in *Padmakosha*. This is used to denote *Lakucha* fruit (grapes), tiny bells worn by children, bell, a partridge, a betelnut, breast of a young girl, white water-lily, *chataka* bird and a cocoanut.

This gesture in Indian dance also represents, angry words of women, seeds, grapes etc.

**Kanistha see Adhama**

**Kānti see Gunas**

**Kanya**

This refers to unmarried girl. She falls under the main class 'Arya or Parakiya Nayika', as stated by later theorists of drama.

*Rasarnavasudhakara* defines her as an unmarried young girl, as bashful and under the care and protection of her father; she is quite open when she is playing with her female companions, but generally she represents the mugdha type (ie young and new to the exprience of love).

Such a heroine may appear either in a principal or subordinate role in a dramtaic story such as Malati and Madayantika in the Bhavabhuti's 'Malatimadhava' illustrates *Rasarnavasudhakara*.

**Kapisirshtya**

This is an instrument with the face of a monkey played on the occasion of Mahavrata ceremony.

The instrument Kapisīrshtya is mentioned in the Latyana Shrauta Sutra and in the Drāhyayana Srauta Sutra.

The latter says that this instrument was played by the Vīṇa player at the command of the Sdhvāryu who were seated in a 'Sadomaṇḍapa' in the easter inside of the sacrificial hall.

**Kapittha Hasta**

A single hand gesture in which the index finger should be curved down to touch the tip of the thumb in the *Shikara*. This is one of the symbols of Lakshmi and Saraswati also denotes milking cow, applying *kajal* to the eyes, sporting, holding flowers, grasping the veil, opening the door and offering of incense or lamp *(deepa)*.

**Kapolabheda**

This means the movements of the check and are of six kinds as follows:-

(1) **Kshama** (sagging week of cheeks):To depict 'sorrow, separation'.

(2) **Phulla** (spread):Used to depict 'full happiness'.

(3) **Ghūrṇa** (raised):To show 'enthusiasm, arrogance.

(4) **Kampita** (fluttering and trembling):To portray 'anger, joy and excitement'.

(5) **Kunchita** (narrowed):To show 'sudden cold, fear, sight, touch'.

(6) **Sama** (natural position):To depict 'anger, joy, excitement'.

**Kapota Hasta**

This is a double hand gesture in which the palms are curved outside in Anjali. Used to express "salutation, addressing a preceptor, respectful acceptance or agreement."

This gesture is also used in Indian dance to express the approach with modesty, conversation, with elders etc.

**Karanas**

Karana is a combined unit of prescribed positions (Sthāna-s), stage - walks (Chāri) and hand gestures (Nriṭṭahasta-s).

The term implies act of doing or producing any action. There are a wide variety of Karanas employed in Indian Classical dances. Bharata in his '*Natyashastra*' defines Karanas as the combined movements of the hands and the feet. *Natyashastra* prescribes Karanas or (Cosmic Shiva) 108 Bharata poses as follows:-

(1) Thalapushpaputa

(2) Varthitam

(3) Valithorukam

(4) Apaviddha

(5) Samanakha

(6) Lina

(7) Swasthikarechitha

(8) Mandalaswasthika

(9) Nikuttaka

(10) Ardhanikuttaka

(11) Katicchinham

(12) Ardharechitha

(13) Vakshasvasthika

(14) Unmattha

(15) Svasthika

(16) Prishtaswasthika

(17) Diksvasthika

(18) Aalathaka

(19) Katisama

(20) Akshiptarechitha

(21) Vikshiptashipthakam

(22) Ardhasvasthika

(23) Anchitha

(24) Bhujangathrasitha

(25) Urdhvajanu
(26) Nikunchitha
(27) Matthalli
(28) Ardhamatthalli
(29) Rechithanikuttitham
(30) Padapaviddhaka
(31) Valitham
(32) Khoornitha
(33) Lalitha
(34) Dandapaksham
(35) Bhujangatrasitham
(36) Nupuram
(37) Vaisakharechitham
(38) Bhramaraka
(39) Chathura
(40) Bhujanganchitha
(41) Dandakarechitha
(42) Vrischikakuttitha
(43) Katibhrantha
(44) Lathavrischika
(45) Chchinna
(46) Vrishchikarechitha
(47) Vrischika
(48) Vyamsitha
(49) Parsvanikuttitha
(50) Lalatatilaka
(51) Krantaka
(52) Kunchitha

(53) Chakramandala

(54) Uromandalam

(55) Akshiptha

(56) Thalavilasitham

(57) Argala

(58) Vikshipta

(59) Avartham

(60) Dolapada

(61) Vivruttha

(62) Vinivrittha

(63) Parsvakrantha

(64) Nisumbhitha

(65) Vidyuthabhrantha

(66) Athikrantha

(67) Vivarthitham

(68) Gajakriditha

(69) Thalasamsphoditha

(70) Garudaplutha

(71) Gandasuchi

(72) Parivrutta

(73) Parsvajanu

(74) Gridhravalinaka

(75) Sannatha

(76) Suchi

(77) Ardhasuchi

(78) Suchividdha

(79) Apakrantha

(80) Mayuralalitha

(81) Sarpitha
(82) Dandapada
(83) Harinaplutha
(84) Prenkholita
(85) Nithambam
(86) Skhalitha
(87) Karihastha
(88) Prasarpithaka
(89) Simhavikridatha
(90) Simhakarshitha
(91) Udvritta
(92) Upasruthaka
(93) Thalasanghattitham
(94) Janitha
(95) Avahitthaka
(96) Nivesa
(97) Elakakriditha
(98) Urudrittam
(99) Madaskhalitha
(100) Vishnukrantha
(101) Sambhrantha
(102) Vishkambha
(103) Udghattitha
(104) Vrishabhakriditha
(105) Lolitha
(106) Nagapasarpitha
(107) Sakatasya
(108) Gangavataranam

**Karangulibheda**

This denotes the movements of the fingers and are of seven kinds:-

(1) *Samyuta* (joined together)

(2) *Viyukta* (separated)

(3) *Vakra* (bent inside)

(4) *Valita* (curved sideways)

(5) *Patila* (pointing downwards)

(6) *Kunchamula* (bent at the roots)

(7) *Prasarita* (extended)

**Karkari**

This is a musical instrument perhaps the lute which occurs from the Rigveda (II, 43, 3) onwards and in the Atharva Veda. The Maitrāyaṇi Samhita (IV. 2, 9) describes cattle branded on the ears with a mark which resembles a lute.

**Karkata Hasta**

This is a double hand gesture in which the fingers of the two hands cross each other in *Anjali hasta* and the two wrists are kept apart.

This is used to denote "arrival of crowd, showing the belly, filling the conch-shell with wind, twisting or stretching of limbs and pulling down a branch of tree." This gesture is also used in Indian dance to indicate massaging of the limbs in love condition, a crab etc.

**Karṇe**

Conventional speech in Sanskrit drama where words are spoken in another person's ears preceded by words 'evam, evam' - like this to avoid repetition or to maintain secrecy.

**Kartarimukha Hasta**

A single hand gesture first to adopt Ardhapataka and take the index finger backward and the middle finger slightly forward.

This gesture is used to express overturning, opposition, plundering, corner of an eye, death estrangement, lightning, sleeping alone, separation, falling and creepers.

The term means a face of the arrow shaft. This is used to express opposition, disagreement, separation of lovers, etc.

**Kartari Svastika Hasta**

This is a double hand gesture in which the hands in *Kartarimukha* are crossed near the wrist.

In Indian dance, this gesture indicates trees, the summit of a hill, branches etc.

**Kartikeya**

He is the God of war. Son of Shiva, Kartikeya is one of the presiding deities of the theatre and according to *Natyashastra*, he should be worshipped with offerings and sacrifices.

**Kārū**

This female characters as seen in the Sanskrit dramas are artisans, women skilled in some craft or profession, like a washer - woman (as stated in '*Dasharupaka* of Dhananjaya).

**Karuka**

According to *Natyashastra*, poets (playwrights), directors, stage managers, musicians, scene designers and painters fall under the category of Natyacharyas. There are others Acharyas and artisans seem to have been necessary in the presentation of Sanskrit drama.

The Karuka is one who prepares things out of lac, stone, iron and wood. He is an artisan who prepares different items of stage paraphernalia.

**Karuna Rasa**

Karuna means 'Pathos, Tragic, Sad' etc. Karuna or the Pathetic is the sentiment of Pathos. According to *Natyashastra* Karuna results from sorrow or grief, and therefore Karuna has *Soka* as its permanent state.

*Dasarupaka* makes Karuna consist in grief even at the suffering of some misfortune. Dhanika, the commentator, refers to the binding of Sāgarika in Ratnavali as an illustration of this type.

It is aptly stated that it requires great skill and literary power to depict Karunarasa successfully. It bringout the subtleties of the human heart, and has been a forte of many classical playwright. Uttararamacharitam of Bhavabhuti is a fine specimen of Karuna which shows Rama's tragic grief after exiling Sita.

The Vibhavas required for this sentiment are curse, death or loss of dear one, loss of wealth, disaster etc.

The Vyabhicāribhāvas or the transient states for Karuna are tears, despondency, dejection, pangs of death, worry, illness, fatigue etc.

Pathos is represented in acting by weeping quietly, fainting, lamenting, bewailing and exerting the body or striking it.

*Varna* : Kapota (Dove)

*Mukharaga :* Prasanna (Pleased)

*Hasta* : Pataka

*Svaras* : Gandhara, Nishada

*Raga:* Rakthi Ragas usually dominate in this rupture like Bhairavi, Mukhāri, Thodi, Varāli, Punnāga, Sāveri, Sahāna, Kānada, Āhiri, Ghantā, Hindola, Mānji, Shanmukhapriya.

**Kārya**

An effect, necessary result of a cause, the motive or an object in a drama finally attained by the hero.

**[see also : Upsamhara - Samdhi]**

**Kāryapreṣya Duta**

This refers to one of the three kinds of messenger represented in Sanskrit drama. He is only an errand - boy, deputed to deliver a specific message or carryout a specified work.

**Katakamukha Hasta**

This is a single hand gesture as follows:-

(1) The middle finger is also bent alongwith the index finger in the *kapittha* and rest are stretched out.

(2) In *kapittha,* stretch the last and the ring finger.

(3) The thumb, the index and the middle fingers are joined together straight and the last two fingers are stretched out.

The gesture is used to denote plucking flowers, holding a pearl necklace or garland of flowers, drawing the string of the bow, offering betel leaves, preparing the paste of musk, sandal etc. by rubbing them against something, applying perfume, speaking and glancing.

**Kāshṭaviṇa (Mānushi) see Viṇa**

**Katakavardhana Hasta**

This is a double hand gesture in which the two hands in *Katakamukha* are crossed near the wrist to denote coronation, worshipping and wedding.

**Katha see Itivritta**

**Katibheda**

This denotes the movements of the waist and are of five kinds such as Chhinna, Nivritta, Rechita, Kampita, Udvahita.

(1) **Chhinna:** In Chhinna, the middle portion of the waist is turned obliquely and diagonally.

(2) **Nivritta:** In Nivritta is the return to the original position from Chhinna. In the latter, middle position of the waist is turned obliquely and diagonally.

(3) **Rechita:** Moving the waist in all the direction is called 'Rechita'.

(4) **Kampita:** Moving the waist sideways in quick motion is called 'Kampita'.

(5) **Udvahita:** Raising the waist and hips towards the sides slowly is called 'Udvahita'.

**Katicchinham**

Bharata's *Natyasastra* gives this eleventh and one of the 108 Karanas or Cosmic Shiva Bharata Poses. Here the hip is to be moved gracefully to the left and right. The hands are in the Pallava mudra. This should be repeated two or three times.

**Kāvya**

This is a minor type of drama (Uparupaka) having one-act and is a comedy (Hāsya). There are amorous speeches and a varied forms of songs like Bhagnatala, Dvipadika and Khandamatra are prescribed for it. The *Avaloka* on the *Daśarupa* states that the Kāvya is a sort of imitative dance and is an inter-play of song and dance.

**Kavyarthasuchaka**

Adibharata states that the Nandi verse should include apart from Ashirvachana, words of blessings, Namaskriya, ie, Salutation and Kavyarthasuchaka, ie, it must suggest the plot of the play and the benediction must be of eight or ten pādas.

**Khanda**

The combination of three Karanas is called a Khanda, according to *Natya Shastra*. The combination of three or four Khanda make up a Mandala. Sthanaka is a posture taken before the body movement starts.

**Khandita Nayika**

Bharata's treatise offer us eight varities of Heroine - in - love. Khandita Nayika is one of them. *Dasarupaka* describes Kandita Nayika as one who is also jealous (like Kalahantarita), as she has also sensed the other woman in her life. But here, she is portrayed as a powerful woman rather aggressive who does not wish to tolerate such betrayal on the part of her lover and regards it as disgraceful and feel insulted. Such Heroine may not experience helplessness, but inspite of her show of determination she weeps at heart for her lover whom she loves and still longs for him.

**[see also 'Nayika']**

**Khatwa Hasta**

This is a double hand gesture in which the two hands in *Chatura* are joined together with the index fingers and the little fingers pointing straight downwards. It is used to express cot and palanquin (*palki*).

**Kilaka Hasta**

This is a double hand gesture in *mrigasheersha,* the little fingers of both the hands are curved and interlocked in opposite direction is Kilaka Hasta. It denotes affection and sportive conversation.

**Kiṃchit Sadrisi (Simile of Partial Likeness) see Alankaras & Upama**

**Kinnari**

This is a kind of stringed instrument, one of the ancient plucked zithers. It is now vanished from the classical music and can be seen with such tribes like the Chenchus and the Raj Gonds of Andhra region.

**Kirāta**

It refers to mountaineers such characters are also represented in the Sanskrit drama. They are the retinue (paricchada) of the Hero who serve him in his Harem (Antaḥpura).

**Kolambaka**

This is the unstrung body of Vina, a string instrument (Tata).

**Kritanta**

One of the presiding deities of theatre who should be worshipped with offerings and sacrifices, tells *Natyashastra*.

**Kriyā**

It means an action, especially in music a Tāla gesture.

**Krodha**

It refers to 'Anger, Displeasure, Retaliation'. Krodha or "Anger" is the permanent state produced by means of conflict, insult, quarrel, abuse, differences, opposition and the like.

This fourth Sthayi Bhava is shown on the stage by raised nostrils, fierce look, bitten lips and the like.

**Krouncha**

This is one of the tonal qualities mentioned in the Chandogya Upanishad Kroucha refers to voice that has an effect of creating pathos (Karuna), like the bird 'Krouncha'.

**Ksatriya Nayika**

Bharata's fourfold division of Nayikas (Heroines) are Kulaja, Divya, Ksatriya and Panyakamini. Unlike later theorists, only *Natyadarpana* reverts to this categorization and divides each into further categories according as they possess the qualities of fortitude (Dhairya) grace (Lalitya) or nobility (Udāttatva). According to it a Ksatriya type should show all the three different qualities separately.

**[see also 'Nayika']**

**Kulaja Nayika**

Bharata's four fold division of Nayikas (Heroines) are Kulaja, Divya, Ksatriya and Panyakamini. Unlike later theorists, only Natyadarpana reverts to this categorization and divides each into further categories according as they possess the qualities of fortitude (Dhairya), grace (Lalitya) or nobility (Udāttatva). According to it, Kulaja is to be Udātta.

**[see also 'Nayika']**

**Kulajāṅgana** see **Lalita Prakriti Nayika**

**Kurma Hasta**

This is a double hand gesture in which the two hands should

be in *chakra* with middle three fingers folded and the little fingers are kept straight. It denotes "tortoise".

**Kushilava**

Though it may denotes a singer, a bard, or an actor. But specifically in accordance with *Natyashastra* "Kushilava is an expert in the arrangement of musical instruments and also in playing them." It says "Poets (playwrights), directors, stage managers, musicians, scene designers and painters fall under the category of Natyacharyas. These Acharyas play pivotal role in the presentation of Sanskrit drama."

**Kutapa**

Musical orchestra, also a place where the musicians sit.

More precisely Kutapa or Brinda denotes the instrumental ensemble. In Sanskrit drama, one can notice that it has been given much importance than the theatrical songs. Instrumental ensemble was very essential in those days to heighten the effect of the drama. Such ensemble were either small, medim, or large, ranging from five singers, two flutes, and three drums to twelve male and female voices, twenty-six flutes and nine drums.

In connection with gait, such musical ensemble or musical instruments played an important part in undertaking the different styles of walking of the dramatic characters. *Natyashastra* has prescribed the rhythmic syllables for the instrumentation which is suitable to the gaits of the four types of heroes; for other varities of characters, divine, human and demonic, and for different situations and emotions.

According to *Natyashastra,* the musicians sit in the following way : The Mardangika facing the east between the two doors of the greem room, the Pāṇavika to his left, Gayakas to the south of the Rangapitha, facing the north, Gayikas to his front on the north facing the south, Vainika to their left and two Vaṁshikas to their right. They occupy a place in the Rangashirsa between the two doors.

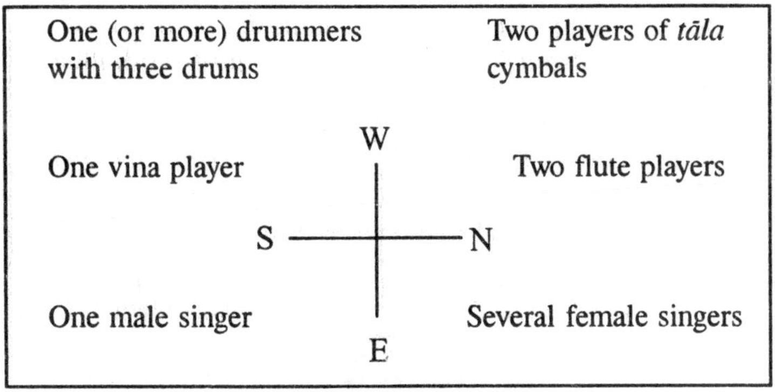


**Forestage**
**(Audience)**

**Kutilaka**

A crooked staff with three bends, usually carried by the jester in a Sanskrit drama.

# L

**Laghu**

A short duration in music and poetry is termed 'Laghu'.

**Laghu (Tala/Rhythm) see Laya**

**Laksana**

This is the secondary meaning of the word which is indicated or indirectly expressed, connotation.

**Lakṣanas see Alankāras**

**Lalita Prakriti Nayika**

Heroines, when are of exalted type, may be herself gracious and trained in arts (Lalitā), full of fortitude and capable of confidence or secrecy (nibritā). Such traits may be expected in a girl from noble family, ie, Kulajāṅgana. A courtesan and other women trained in arts and crafts will naturally be full of grace and charm (Lalita) and worthy of sharing confidence. Such Nayikas are called 'Lalitā Prakriti Nayika'.

**[see also 'Nayika']**

**Lasya**

This gentle dance with abhinaya of the poetic composition

set to music is said to have been created by Parvati who taught it to Usā.

After performing the pure dance 'Tandava', Shiva realised that without the soft expression, the dance was incomplete. This led him to teach soft lasya dance to Parvati. This two styles, ie, Tandava and Lasya became the basis components of dance. Thus Shiva's consort Parvati was the first to receive his blessings in the shape of a full knowledge of both Tandava and Lasya, including the nuances of Bhava, Raga and Tāla. Next in order to receive this knowledge from Lord Shiva were Hari, Brahma, Indra, Nandi (His gana), Tandu and other devas.

Parvati produced the Lasya form in front of Shiva comprising of the Rasa bhava (expressions), Samyuta, Asamyuta Hasta, Lasya, Sukhumara Lasya, Kramas, five Jatis, six Angas, seven Svaras.

After receiving Lord's blessings, she preached the art to her sons.

Ganapati and Subrahmanya and also to Usha, wife of the Sun God. The latter learnt Nritta, Subhachari, Akashachari, Bhumichari, Desichari from Viravallabhachari. From Ushadevi this art form got transmitted to Kshatriya women from north, Vaishya from middle, musicians from South and Gopika from Dvaraka.

When the sages enquired why the dance is included in the domain of drama when it neither relates to its meaning nor reflects its spirit. Abhinaya is enough to perform their functions, Bharata replied that "Dance does not meet specific needs, it has come into use simply because it creates beauty. It is loved by almost all people and is eulogised as being auspicious and the source of amusement. That is why the dance of love, ie, lasya dominates the dance of war in the field of dramatic art. Bharata has given twelve constituents of Lasyas which Abhinavagupta calls 'Lasyangas' their knowledge, the latter feels helps the playwrights and the players create a variety of pleasantness (Ranjana - vaicitrya) in drama.

In this twelve subdivisions of Lāsya called Lasyanga-s, the state of love (rati) is expressed through abhinaya.

The classical Lasya was therefore worked out into a series of items of dance called 'Lasyanga'. Though mostly musical, it has patches of very brief story narration interspersed. These twelve varities of Lasyangas are:-

Asina

Bhavika

Chitrapada

Dvimudhaka

Geyapada

Pracchedaka

Pushpagandika

Saindhava

Sthitipathya

Trimudhaka

Uktapratyukta

Utamottamaka

**[see also 'Nritta, Nritya' etc.]**

**Latabandha**

In dance idiom, it denotes a creeper formation where all the dancers put their arms around each other.

**Laya**

**Laya** in rhythmic system, is the rate of gestural succession, that is, "tempo".

Laya is the timing of musical events in terms of the interval that separates them, ie, tempo.

Bharata has dealtwith not only the melodic aspect of music, but also on the rhythmic side. Dhruva songs in a drama were all in specific Tālas or time - measures and such time - measures were analysed by Bharata from the point of view of situation and feeling. To quote V. Raghavam. "Not only was the tempo of the *dhruvā* set so as to promote the *rasa*, but even when there was no *dhruvā* song, and the actor moved or bent himself down or did something, there was pure instrumental playing intended to underline the mood. The different kinds of tempo, *layas,* of both the songs as well as of pure instrumental accompaniment, can be seen; for example, in the musical version of act IV of the *Vikramorvaśīya* referred to, where we come acros the *layas* called Dvipadikā, Valantikā, Jambhalikā, Carcarikā and Khaṇḍadhārā. In the *Mālatīmādhava* as the main Act opens, the hero Mādhava who has fallen in love is seen, in a dragging gait, vacant look and not quite all right in appearance; the direction is seen in Jagaddhara's commentary that the gait is to be in *Dvipadī laya* which is a slow measure composed of long *mātrās*. The gait and bearing, the very manner in which a character walks in, being most important for producing the first impression of the character and situation in the minds of the audience. Bharata devotes much attention to the fitting of suitable instrumental rhythmic accompaniment to the movements. Kohala made much contribution to this study and Abhinavagupta, while explaining this part of Bharata, naturally quotes Kohala frequently. In chapter XII when dealing with gait of characters as such and again in chapter XXXIII while dealing with drum-accompaniment, Bharata gives detailed instructions as to the "layas" and the drum - music suitable to the movements of different characters and moods. An example of this is the entrance-*dhruvā* which should be in *madhya laya,* what Kohala would call *Valita* or *Valantikā.* All exalted characters of noble bearing should adopt the *Dvipadī laya.* The slow tempo, *Sthita-laya,* with the rhythmic beats at longer intervals should characterize the invalid, the fatigued, those in austerities, the fear-stricken, the amazed, those in longing, love, or grief or going at ease. Kohala calls this *laya Ullasana.*"

Apart from the Raga, the most important element of Indian music is the system of musical time which is the buis of Indian rhythm patterns set to different and complex beats of 4, 6, 7, 9, 10, 12, 14 and 16 etc are called 'Talas'. The essential characteristic of Tala is its cycle or repetition nature. That is, a set of rhythmic units are juxtaposed in a cycle called 'Avarta' and repeat themselves the whole concept of Tala is fitted into a scheme of temporal divisions.

The basic part of the scheme is the quantification of time taken "to pierce with a pin one hundred lotus leaves placed one above another". 16384 *ksanas* is one *anudruta* and *aksara*, the practical unit of musical time and the brick out of which all further sections are constructed. (An *anudruta* is obtained as follows: 8 *ksanas* = *1* lava, 8 *lavas* = *1* kashta, 8 *kashtas* = 1 *nimisha,* 8 *nimisha,* = 1 *kala,* 2 kalas = 1 *chaturbanga,* and 2 *chaturbhagas* = 1 *anudruta*).

The further combinations of immediate practical use to us are the druta (2 *aksaras*), laghu (4 *aksaras*) and guru (8 *aksaras*). Now, the aksara (and hence the other groupings) have no objective time measure. That is one cannot measure it in terms of a watch or a metronome. It is purely subjective, though a certain traditional habit has given it an accepted time length. Depending, therefore, on its duration the *aksara* can have three degrees of tempo or *laya*. So, there are the *vilamba laya* (slow) *madhyama laya* (medium) and *druta laya* (fast) and each is twice as fast as the preceding one. Thus *madhyama laya* is double (in speed) of *vilamba*, and *druta* double of *madhyama.* (In the parlance of a Karnataka musician *laya* is often called *kala: vilamba laya* is, hence, *chowka kala*).

A *tala* is constructed out of a choice of three limbs or sections known as *anga.* These are different in duration. The three *angas* are *anudruta, druta and laghu.* The first is of one *aksara* and the *druta* of two. The third, laghu, is of a variable duration of 3, 4, 5, 7, or 9 aksaras. *Anudruta* is counted by a beat; *druta* by a beat and a wave of the hand; laghu by a beat and count of fingers: say, a *laghu* of five units by a beat + counting of four fingers. These three - *anudruta, druta, and laghu* have their signature thus.

Anudruta: druta: 0 laghu: 1

Since the laghu is of five kinds (*jati*) with varying numbers of aksaras, it is shown as : $1_3$, $1_4$, $1_5$, $1_7$, $1_9$.

The five are given individual names:

1. $1_3$ = *Tisra laghu (3 aksaras)*
2. $1_4$ = *Chaturasra laghu (4 aksaras)*
3. $1_5$ = *Khandu laghu* (5 *aksaras*)
4. $1_7$ = *Misra laghu* (7 *aksaras*)
5. $1_9$ = *Sankeerna laghu (9 aksaras)*

Like melody Tala, laya etc *have been raised to a high degree of sophistication.*

**Lesha (Wit) see Vagyabhinaya**

**Lina**

Bharata in his *Natyasastra* has given 108 Karanas or cosmic Shiva Bharata Poses. Lina is the six in the list. Here both hands in Pathaka mudra are placed on the chest as in Anjalihasta. Neck is slightly bend forward with both shoulders bent a little.

**Lingi (Vidusaka) see Vidusaka**

**Lingini**

They are religious women, nuns in a Sanskrit drama; *Dasarupaka* mentions about them as associates of the Heroine.

**Lokadharmi**

Lokadharmi denotes realism in drama and Bharata states that as the drama is a representation of the world and therefore, emphasizes propriety in the presentation of life on the stage.

Once a play is chosen, the next thing is to decide how to present it and the famous *Natyashastra* prescribes two way to take the play to an audience as Lokadharmi or a Natyadharmi. Bharata states "if it is to be read as it was written, with no modifications of any kind, without bodily movements and just like any piece of news or information, with many men and women looking and behaving in the usual everyday manner, then it is called a Lokadharmi and if it is rendered with long sentences, facial expressions, bodily movements and voice intonations, with heavenly as well as human being then it is a 'Natya dharmi [Natyashastra (XIII, 66-69).]

In Lokadharmi, each act produced, word uttered and dresses and costumes worn must all be in conformity with what is actually found in life. Thus when the representation of life on the stage by the dramatist is realistic it is Lokadharmi.

**[see also under "Dharmi"and "Natyadharmi"]**

**Lokapālas**

He is the 'Guardians of the world. Bharata mentions him as one of the presiding deities of the theatre who should be worshipped with offerings and sacrifices.

# M

**Ma (Madhyama)**

This is the fourth scale degree.

**[see 'Madhyama'(Ma)]**

**Mada**

It denotes 'Intoxication, Lust' etc. Mada (Intoxication) is the fifth mutable state (Vyabhichari Bhava) which should be represented on the stage by a show of drunkenness and rolling eyes, arms drooping or restlessly thrown about and irregular with an unsteady gait. It relates to the persons of the middle class.

**Madhurya see Gunas**

**Madhya Natyamandapa see Ranga**

**Madhya Nayika**

Generally there are three kinds of Heroine, according to later theorists. Madhya is one of the three sub-groups of the main class 'Sviya or Sva Nayikas'. Unlike Mugdha who is very young, Madhya is a little advanced in age and experience. She is in passionate love with her beloved and is capable of enjoying the sport of love till exhaustion sends her into a swoon.

Madhya Nayika is of three kinds:-

(1) Dhira

(2) Adhira

(3) Dhiradhira

Dhira kind is patient and bold, is a woman who can indulge in crooked or indirect speech directed with resentment against an offending love; the Adhira is inpatient and uses harsh words in anger to cause sorrow to her lover; The Dhiradhira is one who balances patience and impatience and speaks to her lover with indirect taunts, but is unable to check her tears caused by an inner hurt.

This Madhya - Nayika can be again divided into two sub-groups according as the Nayika has the status of a Jyestha or Kaniṣtha. *Bhavaprakashana* identifies further sub-varities of it according as they happen to be Udātta, Lalita or Shanta.

**[see also 'Nayika']**

**Madhya Nāyaka see Madhyama Nayaka**

**Madhyama**

According to *Amarakosha*, it denotes the medium paced dance, also called *'Ghana'*.

**Madhyama (Ma)**

This is one of the seven Svaras (Notes) and according to *Ragavibodha, Sangitaparijata, Sangitamakarandah* etc, the sounds of music are first perceived as relative pitches or intervals and then from the twentytwo Shrutis (Main Intervals) come the seven Svaras, namely Ṣaḍja, Ṛṣabha, Gāndhāra, Madhyama, Pañcama, Dhaivata and Niṣāda.

It is intersting to mention here that our authorities on music refer each Svara or Note to the sound of some animal.

Madhyama is said to represent the cry of the Heron.

**Madhyama Nayaka**

Classical theorists classify male characters into three classes of Jyestha, (Uttama) Madhyama (Madhya/A-mukhya) Kanistha (Adhama, Hina, Nicha). This applies to the Nayaka, Neta or the leader of the principal dramatic action as well. *Natyadarpana* of Rāmachandra and Guṇachandra states that A-mukhya or Madhyama Nayaka is slightly inferior to the principal hero in qualities, behaviour and achievements.

In drama, the Pataka - Prakari - Nayaka, ie, the leading character of the sub-plot or an incident fills this role. The Pratinayaka or the counter hero may also be either Madhyama or Adhama, according to the nature of the dramatic plot. The Madhyama type of characters, on the whole, lacks two, three, five or six desirable qualities, says *Bhavaprakashana*.

**Madhyama Nayika see Madhya Nayika, Nayika Madhyama - Prakriti Pramadā**

**Madhyama - Prakriti Pramadā**

A female character which possesses most of the qualities of Uttama-Prakriti woman, but in lesser proportion and has some minor faults too are Madhyama - Prakriti Pramadā.

**Magadhi**

This is one of the seven principal Prakrit dialects used in the Sanskrit plays.

According to *Dasharupa*, this is the language of the low people. It is spoken by inmates of the Royal harem, by diggers of subterrarean entrances, inn-keepers and watchmen. It is sometimes used by the Hero in self defence.

**Mahachari**

In the context of drama, this is one of the twenty constituent parts of Purvaranga (preliminaries in a play) which is performed on the stage. Mahachari is preceded by an item called 'Chari' and the latter is again preceded by 'Rangadvara' Rangadvara is when the play [abhinaya] begins, the sutradhara recites a new verse and vows before Jarjara (Indra's banner). Then follows Chari, in which different paces and gestures with an erotic sense features. Mahachari comes next, similar paces, but more impetuous in degree.

**Mahadevi**

In a Sanskrit play, there are women who are associated with a royal Hero. Mahadevi is a crowned queen devoted to her royal husband, acting always in his interests and in that of the harem; she is usually a mature woman, capable of anger but free from natural jealousy and willing to share happiness or sorrow with her husband.

**Mahakala**

According to Bharata's *Natyashastra* (6, 45), Mahakala is the God of Abhorrence (Bibhatsa rasa). This deity is regarded as a form of Shiva, who is destroyer, black and terrific.

**Maharaja**

This denotes 'Great King'. The *Natyashastra* has given a set of words for calling the different characters according to their position. A king is usually addressed as *'Maharaja'*.

**Maha Vina**

This musical instrument was played in the time of Mahavrata ceremony. It is stated that in the western sides of the Yajñaśālā, the Mahavina and the Pishilavina were played.

The *Drāhyāyana Shrauta Sutra* mentions about Mahāvina.

**Mahendra see Indra**

**Maheshvara see Shiva**

**Makara Hasta**

This double hand gesture is given by *Natyashastra* in which both the hands in *pataka*, facing downward with their thumbs raised are placed on each other.

It denotes "lion, snake, crocodile, shark, fish and other such animals, *Abhinaya Darpanam* has not mentioned to this gesture.

**Make-up see Angarachana**

**Mālā (Series of Offers) see Vagyabhinaya**

**Malyakrit**

The Natyashastra refers to some Acharyas who are expert in preparing materials for the stage. Thee are many types of artisans seem to have been necessary in the presentation of plays.

Malyakrit is one of who makes garlands for the characters.

**Mancha**

It means the stage or performance arena.

**Mandala**

Mandala is a mystic circle being used in Tantric meditation. A magical, consecrafed area which must be kept pure for ritual end.

In dance form, it denotes a circular movement.

This is one of the six standing positions of men; a movement formed by a group of charī-s. Part of the 'Bodily Acting' or 'Angika Abhinaya', Chapter XI of *Natyashastra* doctrine deals with 'Mandala'. If Chari is a pose, then Mandala is a movement resulting from a number of Charis. (XI, 1). To represent fights, battles and such incidents involving movements, Mandalas are to be exploited (XI, 63), if necessary to the accompaniment of musical instruments.

Mandala bheda denotes static position. Cheshtakrita which comes under Angikabhinaya, comprises the movement of the entire body. Mandala, the static posture falls under this head. According to *Abhinaya darpanam,* mandala bheda are of ten types:-

(1) **Sthanaka** (standing straight): This means standing in *samapada* (natural) with the feet in natural position and *Ardhachandra hasta* placed on waist.

(2) **Ayata** (Stretched): Placing both feet half a cubit apart with knees bent sideways and assume chaturasra pose.

(3) **Aleedha** (stride): Left foot is placed before the right, one and half cubits away. The left hand in *Shikhara* and the right in *Katakamukha*.

(4) **Pren khana** (swinging): One foot is placed by the side of the heel of the other foot holding Koorma in both the hands.

(5) **Prerita** (Impelled): One foot is put on the ground force fully, one and half cubit apart from the other foot with bent knees. One held near the chest, in *Shikhara* and the other in *Pataka* stretched out.

(6) **Pratyaleedha** [Opposite to Aleedha (stride)]: This is the reverse position of Aleedha, the right foot takes the place of the left and the same is the case with the hands.

(7) **Svastika** (Crossed): The right foot is put across the left and the right hand, across the left.

(8) **Motita** (Grinding): The toes of both the feet rest on the ground with each knee touching the ground alternately. Both the hands in *Tripataka*.

(9) **Samasūchi** (pointed): The toes and the knees of both the legs touch the ground.

(10) **Parshvasūchi** (pointed level to one side): The toes of both the feet and knee of one leg touch the ground.

*Natyashastra* furnishes two types of Mandalas namely Akashiki (Aerial) and Bhumi (Earthly) Each of them have ten forms as follows:-

(i) **Akashiki :** Ten varities are Atikranta, Vichitra, Lalitasanchara, Suchividdha, Dandapada, Vihrita, Alataka, Vamaviddha, Lalita, Kranta.

(ii) **Bhumi :** Ten kinds are:-

Bhramara, Askandita, Avarta, Samotsarita, Edakakridita, Addita, Shakatasya, Adhyardha, Pishtakutta, Chasagata.

**Mandala see Khanda**

**Mandalasvasthika**

Bharata in his *Natyasastra* prescribes this eight and one of the 108 Karanas or cosmic Shiva Bharata Poses. Here standing in the Mandala posture the hands holding Svasthika mudra with the palms turned up at the same time facing front.

**Mandapa see Rangamandapa**

**Mandra**

It means 'the low', the lowest note permitted.

**Manibandha bheda**

This means 'movements of the wrist and are of five types as follows:-

(1) *Nikunchita* (bent outwards as in presenting a gift) .

(2) *Akunchita* (bent inwards as in pushing away something)

(3) *Chala* (repeatedly moved inwards and outwards as in calling, opening etc)

(4) *Bhramita* (wrist is moved around as in weilding swords and knives)

(5) *Sama* (straight as in holding or accepting something)

**Manodharma**

This refers to an actor's own jugement in selection of the conventional techniques to create a fresh performance.

**Manodharma Sangita**

It denotes 'spontaneous music in its purest form. In this form the singer has to create the melody of the concerned Raga according to his own ability and imagination.

**Manoratha (Indirect expression of desire) see Vagyabhinaya**

**Mantra**

It means ' pious thought, prayer, hymn; Vedic hymn, sacred text; mystical verse etc.

Mantra is sacred evocation, incantation.

It is to be noted that the entire edifice of the Sanskrit play production has a fundamental religious basis. Offering, sacrifices, mantras, herbs, recitation and food are offered on the Natyamandapa. An elaborate forms of worships with proper chanting of mantras are followed at every turn right from the erection of theatre to the presentation of a play. The day before and on the day of festivity, different deities are invoked with different mantras.

**Marana**

It denotes 'Death, Cessation' etc. Marana (Death) is the thirty first Mutable State/Vyabhichari Bhava which according to Bharata, should be represented in acting by loose body, motionlessness, closed eyes, hiccups, unnatural breathing, vacant looks towards relations and indistinct speech.

**Mānushi Viṇa see Viṇa**

**Mārdava**

This is one of the six techniques employed in singing the svaras of the Vedic scales. It refers to the 'Singing of the lower notes from Chaturtha that to atisvārya without stress, included in the avashepiṇi opposite of Daruṇya.

**Mārga**

It means 'path' and denotes :-

(1) The ancient musical system.

(2) In rhythmic system, Mārga is the relative density of events within a given span of time.

**Marga Sangita**

Traditional music authorities show two main distinctions in the theory and practice of Saṅgita. There are two styles called 'Marga' and 'Deshi'.

Marga Sangita is the high style practised by the celestial musicians or by sages who knew the theory of divine music.

This Gandharva or celestial music is no more present. But it is significant to add here that the word 'Marga' should not be considered to have derieved from the root Mṛg, ie, to search for, but should be traced back to Marga (path) and then the Marga Sangita could accord to the ancient path, ie, classical, as opposed to Deshi Sangita.

**Mārgasārita**

This is the eight constituent parts of Purvaranga (preliminaries of a play), taken up behind the curtain. Margasarita means 'Playing together of different instruments'.

**Margi**

Denotes a tradition of art which is rigorously learnt by initiated disciples from a teacher - an exclusive system.

**Māriṣa**

It means a venerable man, a respectable mode of address in Sanskrit drama.

**Marutas**

God of wind; relating or belonging to the Marutas or Storm - gods. Marutagana (air) symbolises ventilators that keep the playhouse airy and help to avoid suffocation and heat. Marutas are among the presiding deities of the theatre, who should be worshipped with offerings and sacrifices.

**Mati**

It denotes 'Resolution, Determination, Intention' etc.

Mati (Resolution) is the twenty-eighth Mutable State/ Vyabhichari Bhava which according to Bharata, should be represented on the stage by preaching, sacred speech, explaining and clearing doubts and so on.

**Mātra**

It refers to a time unit in a music or verse and also denotes a phrase or line within a larger formal component.

In rhythmic system, Mātrā is a phrase or line, typically consisting of four padabhāgas; It also denotes a time duration (mora), as in verse.

**Matsya Hasta**

This is a double hand gesture in which the two hands in *pataka* are placed one above the other with the thumbs pointing outwards.

It denotes "fish".

**Mattavarani**

Some refers it to a varandah or a wing located at both the sides of a Rangapitha. Some refers to it as a balcony, a corridor, a room etc. Some modern scholars interpret the term as a railing which is provided at the top of the stage so to form a fence to protect actors and actresses from the intoxicated men from the audience hall.

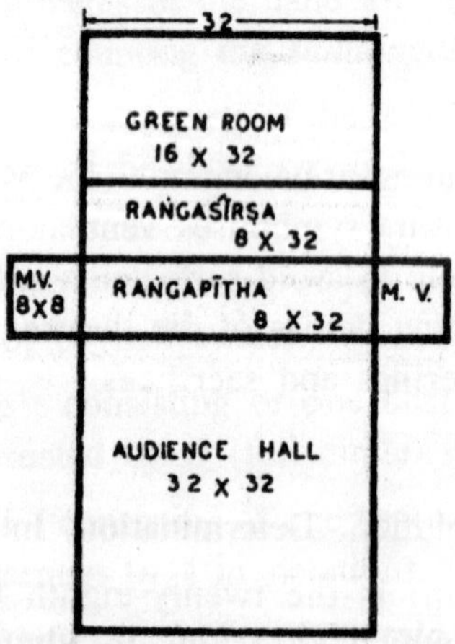


**Mattavaranis (Square Shaped) <According to Abhinavagupta>**

It is a wooden railing 1-1/2 hastas in height and located on the top of the Rangapitha and along its edge that is towards the audience hall. It is provided with four columns. It serves to protect actors and actresses from the attack of intoxicated persons from the audience hall.

**Mayura Hasta**

This is a single hand gesture first adopt *Pataka* and let the thumb and the ring finger touch the tips of each other. Mayura is used to express peacock's neck, creeper, bird, vomiting, removing of hair, an ornamental mark on the forehead (*tilaka*), scattering, river water, discussing the *shastras,* a famous thing etc.

**Megha**

It is said that the Megha (clouds) guards the musical instruments in a performance (A presiding deity of theatre).

**Melāpaka**

It refers to the second component of a prabandha, (art song) usually an ornamental interlude.

**Melāpaka see Dhatus**

**Mitartha Duta**

This refer to one of the three kinds of messengers represented in Sanskrit drama. Mitartha type of messenger carries a message of limited import faithfully and correctly.

**[see also 'Duta']**

**Mitra**

According to Bharata 'Mitra' is one of the presiding deities of the theatre to be worshipped with offerings and sacrifices.

Mitra (sun) symbolises brightness of the jewelled costumes etc.

**Mleccha**

It refers to 'Barbarions'. Such characters are represented in the Sanskrit drama and are the retinue (Paricchada) of the Hero who serve him in the Harem (Antahpura).

**Moha**

It denotes 'Delusion, Confusion, Perplexity'. Delusion is the tenth Mutable State / Vyabhichari Bhava which should be shown in acting by staggering, falling, reeling and not seeing properly and so on.

**Mridangam**

The *Natyashastra* describes music as an indispensable adjunct of Sanskrit drama. It mentions instruments such as Mridanga, Paṇava, Dardura, Dundubhi, Muraja, Jhallari, Paṭ aha, Vamsha, Shaṅkha and Ḍakkinī.

Mridangam is a vocative instrument to maintain Tala, Gati, Laya and the varied aesthetic syncopations to enliven a concert, is of superb charm and is believed to be invented and played by Shiva's sacred bull Nandikeshwara.

Someshvaradeva's *Manasollasa* provides details of craftsmanship of Mridanga, the percussion instruments in the verses 687 to 701.

The Mridangam is a percussion instrument. Presently this South Indian instrument has a barrel-shaped hollow wooden body bulging in the middle and tapering at the ends. The two ends are covered with parchment. At the centre of the right head there is a black circular patch made with a paste of manganese dust, boiled rice and tamparind juice.

**Mridu slakshaṇa**

This is one of the tonal qualities mentioned in the '*Chhandogya Upanishad*' Mridu Slakshana denotes soft, sweet and brilliant voice.

**Mrigashirsha Hasta**

This is a single hand gesture in which either in the *Sarpashirsha*, the little finger and the thumb are straightened or in the *Pataka*, the middle three fingers are stretched and bent forward and the thumb stretched outward.

This is used to denote "women, cheek, a wheel, limit, fear, quarrel, background, calling, *tripundraka* made on the forehead, a deer's head, drawing on the floor (*rangoli*), massage of the feet, entire, joining, birth place, holding an umbrella, communicating, calling the beloved etc."

**Mrityu**

One of the presiding deities of theatre, (according to Bharata) and should be worshipped with offerings and sacrifices.

**Mudras**

Denotes hand gestures. (Hast a mudras) Each basic hasta mudra is used in different ways depending upon the context in performing arts. Mudra denotes a hand gesture in dance, pantomine, vedic recitation, chant etc. A mudra is a definite identification and provides a symbolic representation of a person, place or thing through the manner in which the palms, the thumbs and the fingers are arranged in different formations. Mudras can be formed with one or both hands, each mudra hving a separate significance or meaning A performer, usually a dancer, synchronises the facial expressions with the hasta and the mudras to portray the particular items, emotions or objects depicted in the text.

**[see 'Hasta Mudras']**

**Mugdha Nayika**

According to later theorists, there are three types of Heroines. Mugdha is one of the three sub-groups of main class Sviya or Sva Nayikas.

Mugdha Nayika is a very young and inexperienced or new to the experience of love; being untrained she is not straight in the practice of love; she strives to learn the activities of love secretly, but is shy and appears all the more charming on account of her bashfulness; when offended by her lover she merely looks on, weeps; but she is soft in anger and does not say a word, pleasant or unpleasant; but her youth is bursting out and rising passion and shyness seem to compete with each other in her case.

**[see 'Nayika']**

**Mukhabilam**

This refers to the 'belly of the stringed instrument named Vāṇa. Synonyms are Chama (in Sanskrit) and Chamma and Pokkara in Pali.

**Mukhabilam see Vāṇa**

**Mukhaja**

This is expression through the facial features such as drishti bheda, Bhrubheda, Puta bheda, Tara bheda, Kapola bheda, Nasa bheda, Adhara bheda, Jihva bheda, Dashana, Chibuka and Hanu bheda, Vadana bheda.

**Mukharaga**

The expression 'Mukharaga' denotes natural change of the colour of the face according to the Rasa-bhava and Varna refers to the colour artificially applied to produce a certain effect. According to Bharata's *Natyashastra,* there are four types of facial colours. They are:-

(1) **Svabhavika (Natural):** It expresses natural mood and Shanta Rasa (peace).

(2) **Prasanna** (Pleased): Prasanna colour expresses Shringara, Karuna, Hasya and Adbhuta Rasas (love, kindness, humour and surprise).

(3) **Rakta** (Red): Rakta colour expresses Karuna, Vira and Raudra Rasas (Sadness, Valour and Anger).

(4) **Shyama (Dark):** Shyama expresses Bibhatsa and Bhayanaka Rasa (Hatred and Fear).

**Mukha - Samdhi**

According to Sanskrit treatise on dramatics, the plot of a drama is divided into five divisions which it terms 'Samdhi' or Junctures. Mukha-Samdhi or the opening Juncture is the beginning where the process of germination takes place. It embodies a trace of the sentiment which is going to be the predominant rasa of that particular drama. Therefore, 'Bija' or the germ having come into existence, the drama is on its way to unfold itself. Bija is a very important element of the plot which occurs in the Mukha-Samdhi.

As we know that Samdhi is made up of Arthaprakriti (an essential element of the plot) and Avastha (stage of developmnet of the plot).

Here 'Bija' is the Artha-prakriti and 'Avasta', ie, the stage is the initial one and, hence, called Arambha which *Natyashastra* defines as an eagerness aroused about the final attainment of the result with reference to the Bija (germ). In Mudraraksasam of Visakhadatta, the policy of Chanakya to defeat Raksasa is the Bija of the play. The action of the play commences as Chanakya, by chance, gets Rakshasa's signet ring - the technical Arambha.

**Mukhavina**

A clarion like wind instrument.

**Mukhya see Adhikarika Vritta**

**Mukula Hasta**

This is a single hand gesture in which the tips of all the fingers and the thumb touch one another in a bud formation.

This is used to express food, the five arrows of the god of love, holding of a signet or seal, the navel and a banana flower.

It also represents offerings to gods and dieties, bud of lotus or water lily, taking meals and applying religious mark etc in Indian dance form.

**Mukutakara**

The *Natyashastra* refers to some Acharyas who are expert in preparing materials for the stage. There are many types of artisans seem to have been necessary in the presentation of plays. Mukutakara is one who makes crowns (Mukutas) for the characters with the help of different materials as discussed in traditional doctrines.

**Maraja Drum**

This is a kind of covered instrument (Avanaddha). According to *Abhinaya darpana,* in the Nandi verse (Benediction), charming tunes are performed in honour of Ganapati, the god of the Muraja drum and other gods.

The *Natyashastra* helds music, an indispensable adjunct of Sanskrit drama. It mentions some musical instruments such as Mridanga, Paṇava, Dardura, Dundubhi, Muraja, Jhallari, Paṭaha, Vaṁsha, Shaṅkha and Ḍakkinī.

**Mūrcchanā**

It means 'expanding, spreading', as in

(a) the rotations of the basic scales; and also

(b) with reference to ornamental melodic clusters or multiple instrumental finger strokes.

*Brihaddeshi* describes that which spans (mūrccha) the scale of a mode is called 'Murcchanā'. The term Varna (melodic movement) refers to the act of singing and is of four kinds viz Sthayi (level), repetition of the same sound; Arohi (ascent); Avarohi (descent) and Sañcārī (wandering or ascent and descent combined). The 12 notes, seven major and five minor, constitute the octave. According to *Sangitaratnakara,* the ascent as well as the descent taken in regular order begining and ending with a particular note of the octave is called Murcchana.

**Mushti Hasta**

A single hand gesture in which all the four fingers should be folded and thumb placed on them.

Mushti is used to denote steadfastness, grasping one's hair, holding things and the fighting mood of wrestlers etc.

This also represents fights, blows, holding a sword, victory, valour and like emotions in dance.

# N

## Nāda

Dhvani means 'sound' and the sound of music is termed as 'Nādā', intelligible sound, and is said to be result from the union of physical breath with the fire of intellect. All music is based upon relations between sounds. Traditional treatises on music put forth that the sounds of music are first perceived as relative pitches or intervals and then from the 22 main intervals called 'Shrutis' come the seven notes 'Svaras' namely, Sadja, Ṛṣabha, Gāndhāra Madhyama, Pañcama, Dhaivata and Niṣāda.

*Pāṇini Siksha* deals with the origin of sound or Nādotpatti, which is the prime factor for speech as well as for music. The ātma wishing to speak stirs the mind which in turn strikes the anala or fire abiding in the body. The prāṇa or wind stimulated in turn by the agni rises up to the heart which is the *mandrasthāna* appropriate for singing in the morning and is in the gāyatri metre (chhandas). Coming to the throat it is madhya sthāna producing medium sound suitable for the mid-day and is in the trishṭub metre, and when it reaches the head it is *tārasthāna* in jagati metre and is appropriate for singing in the evening time. In the final stage the wind, after reaching the head comes down and finds an outlet through the mouth. Then it becomes articulated sound and assumes the form of *Nāda or*

*Dhvani*. This articulated sound has five elements called Svara (musical sound), Kāla (time or duration), Sthāna (Appropriate seats for producing sound), Prayatna (efforts taken to produce sound), and Anupradhāna. The sthānas or seats of sound production are heart, throat, head, palate, teeth, nose, lips and jaws.Sangitaratnakara speaks of nida (sound) an a finer form prior to its being audible.

According to Saṇgitaratna kara (I.II. 1-4) The articnter sound (vagṇa) is manifested by nāda. Work (vāk) is manifesfed from Varṇa and language from words and the a chining in the world (vgura hara) is through language. The world therefore is dependent on Nada. And it .is thin nāda which be comes manifers in the body of Man.

**Nāḍi**

This denotes a musical instrument, a reed flute. In the *Rig Veda* as well as in *Kāthaka Samhita* where in one passage it is describes alongwith the Tuṇaka.

**Nadika**

This a measure of time equal to 24 minutes, also called a Ghatika.

**Naga**

A serpent - demon or semi-divine being, having the face of a man and the tail of a serpent and inhabiting the Pātāla. One of the presiding deities of the Ancient Indian Theatre.

**Nagabandha Hasta**

This is a double hand gesture in which the two hands in *Sarpasirsha* are crossed near the wrist. It denotes *Nagabandha* (snakes coiling round each other).

In Indian dance, this gesture also indicates pairs of hands, creeper etc.

**Nagaraja**

One of the presiding deities of theatre, the serpent-king

who should be worshipped with offerings and sacrifices, states Bharata.

**Namaskriya**

It means 'Salutation'.

(I) *Natyashastra* mention that Rangapuja should involve Namaskriya. At one place it mentions that when a theatre-house is built; cows should live there for a week and mantras be recited by the Brahmanas. The director be initiated and after keeping fast for three days must salute with folded hands major gods, divine beings, kings, sages and dramatic obstacles and success.

(II) Adibharata states that in addition to Bharata's Ashirvachana, ie, the words of blessings, the Nandi [Benedictory] verse should include Namaskriya, ie, salutation.

**Nakshatrahasta**

It means Hastas for stars.

Twentyseven stars and their hastas are:-

**Ashvini :** *Tamrachooda hasta.*

**Bharani :** Shaking *sukatunda* with stretched thumb.

**Krittika :** Shaking *tripataka.*

**Rohini :** *Ardhapataka* with thumb touching the two bent fingers.

**Mrigasheersha :** *Kangula.*

**Ardra :** Middle finger and ring finger are bent alongwith the thumb.

**Punarvasu :** With the index finger bent, the second finger and thumb are joined.

**Pushya :** Shaking *mrigasheersha* with extended index finger.

**Ashlesha :** Thumb and little finger stretched.

**Magha :** *Kangula* with spread fingers.

**Purvaphalguni :** *Tamrachooda hasta.*

**Uttaraphalguni :** Shaking *shikhara.*

**Hasta :** *Pataka* is shaken.

**Chitra :** *Sandamsha hasta.*

**Swati :** *Katakamuka* with forefingers touching the middle of the thumb.

**Vishakha :** *Padmakosha* slightly shaken.

**Anuradha :** Stretch the index finger in *mushti*.

**Jyeshtha :** *Padmakosha* facing downwards.

**Mula :** *Ardhapataka* with slightly curved tips of index and middle finger.

**Purvashadha :** *Pataka* with index and middle fingers curved into palm.

**Uttarashadha :** *Ardhachandra* and the third and little finger curved or bent inwards.

**Shravana :** *Mayura* is shaken.

**Dhanishtha :** *Mukula* moving horizontally.

**Satabhishaka :** *Soochi hasta*.

**Purvabhadrapada :** *Pataka* with middle finger curved.

**Uttarabhadrapada :** *Soochi* in both the hands crossed at the fore fingers.

**Revati :** Shaking *Gajadanta hasta*.

**Nāli**

This is a kind of wind instrument, a flute. *Apassthamba-Shrauta Sutra* mentions 'Nāli' as a musical instument being played in the Mahāvrata ceremony.

**Nandi**

This is a prayer recited at the beginning of the play proper, a verse or verses in praise of a deity.

It means 'Benediction', an auspicious ritual supposed to be capable of eliminating obstacles in the presentation of a drama. All later writers on the science of drama and dramaturges treat 'Nandi' in a practically uniform manner as prescribed by Bharata.

*Bhavaprakashana* mentions that the term 'Nandi' comes from Nandi, the bull of Shiva. The dance of the bull in a particular manner became worthy of representation. Its worship in that manner is called 'Nandi'. It is also known as Nandi because it delights the spectator. In this context, the word 'Nandi' is drawn from Nand, to please. This denotes a benedictory stanza in a Sanskrit drama. Here before the actual drama commence, a series of introductory performances called 'Purvaranga' is customary; comprising of music, songs, dances etc and also some ritual acts of worship and prayers to the gods etc. These comes to an end with nāndi or benedictory stanza and after which the Sutradhara appears on the stage.

Nandi is the distinguished feature of Sanskrit drama in which the play begin with such invocation, usually to god Siva who is the presiding deity of dance and drama. Critic M.L. Varadapande pointsout that in the *Natya Sastra* there are various Indian deities deputed to protect different dramatis personae where they are performing on the stage. A verse says: Let Indra protect the actor playing the role of hero, Saraswati assume the role of heroine, Onkara the Vidushaka (Jester) and Shiva rest of the characters.

This is one of the twenty different constituent parts of Purvaranga (preliminaries of a play) performed on the stage.

Nandi praise or a benediction is recited when the preceding item 'Parivartana' is over (ie the stalking round the stage with praise of the guardians of the world 'Dikpalastuti and adoration of Indra's banner Jarjara puja'.

According to *Abhinaya darpana*, after many kinds of charming tunes have been performed in honour of Ganapati, the god of the Muraja drum and other gods, the dancing girl should have the permission of her preceptor to begin dressing herself suitably. Then to destroy evils, to protect living creatures, to please gods, to bring edification to the spectators, welfare to the leader of the nata group, protection to the dancing girl and to make the teaching of her preceptor fruitful, she begins offerings flower to gods.

*Natyadarpana* informs that the Nandi may be composed by the poet, or the troupe manager and that it may be recited by the Sutradhara, Sthapaka or Pariparshvikas.

*Nātaka - Laksana - Ratnakosa* feels that the Nandi should be recited by the stage - manager. Nandi is recited by the Sutradhara in a middling tone. It comprises of twelve or eight pādas and after each pāda, both the Paripārśvikas say 'Evamastu [so be it].

According to the *Rasarnavasudhakara*, there may be eight, ten or twelve pādas. *Bhavaprakashana* opines that there should be eight or twelve pādas or sentences. According to *Prataparudriya,* it may have eight, twelve eighteen or twenty two Padas.

The *Sahitya darpana* states that the Nandi should have words signifying sacred objects such as Shankha (Conch), Chandra (Moon), Abja, Koka and Kairava (different types of Lotuses) and should have eight or twelve pādas.

It is stated in the *Natyashastra* that if Nandi is properly executed, Chandra (moon), one of presiding deities of theatre is pleased. It should please gods, Brāhmanas, the kings or be done in honour of them.

**Narma - Sachiva see Dharma - Sachiva**

**Nartaḥ**

Means 'dancing', 'a dance' etc.

**Nartaka**

This denotes a male dancer; a dancing master.

An actor, an actor in a farce in which scenes from actual life are represented by gestures; a master; a buffoon.

**Nartaki**

This means a female dancer, a nachaki; a singing girl; an actress.

**Nartana**

A dancer

Gesticulation, dancing, dance.

**Nartit**

It refer to "Danced", made to dance.

"Dancing", "moving to and fro" etc.

**Nasabheda**

This means 'movements of the nose' and are of six types as follows:-

(1) **Natā** (breathing heavily, bringing the nostril in and out): Used in distress, sighing.

(2) **Mandā** (normal breathing is maintained): Used in 'resting'.

(3) **Vikrishta** (wide open): To show anger, heroism, a strong smell.

(4) **Succhhvāsā** (taking a deep breath):To express 'inhalation, smelling desirable objects'.

(5) **Vikūṇita** (twisting the nose to one side): To show 'disapproval, jealousy and disgust'.

(6) **Svabhavika** (natural position of the nose): Used to denote 'natural conditions'.

**Nata**

The 'Nata' is the performer of Natya. He is called 'Nata' because he represents and imitate the actions of men. He is an expert in the representation of sentiments, feelings and courage.

It, therefore, denotes an actors. In old day the actors formed a distinct caste of their own and literary evidences show their social status were not very high, though some enjoyed the friendship of distinguished personages. They were mostly itirerant, moving in groups from one city to another seeking patronage and worked under the leadership of a sūtradhara.

**Naṭagāmaṇi**

This means a leader of actors.

**Nātah**

Means "Dancing", "Acting".

**Nātaka**

This is an important type of Sanskrit drama, based on mythological or heroic tales, the chief character being again a divine person or a king. One of the major genres (Rupaka), *Natyashastra* of Bharata states : 'When the peculiarities of society were sought to be linked with certain gestures or when the actions of gods, rishis, kings or of the members of a society were copied, they came to be known as a Nataka."

Dhananjaya's *Daśarupa* prescribes that in this kind of play, the Hero must be endowed with high qualities, in other words self controlled and exalted, ie, Dhirodatta type and ought to be glorious, desirous of winning fame, very energetic, trayi (a preserver of the three Vedas), a ruler of the world, of famous lineage, a royal seer or a good and above all, the incident for which he is popular be made the main story of the drama.

All Vrittis should be in their proper place in a Nataka and the plot should contain the five elements of action corresponding to the five dramatic stages and be divided into five *Samdhis* (Junctures) and these Junctures should further be divided into sixty four sub groups.

In it, the Patāka, Prakari and Viskambhaka should be used.

The dominant sentiment (rasa) is either Sringara (Love) or Vira (Heroic). Having five to seven acts in length, not exceeding ten.

According to traditional dramatic norms, only one sentiment should be predominant, either the Heroic or the Erotic. Other sentiments should be made subordinate and towards the end the Marvellous sentiments could be employed.

Kalidasa's Abhijnanasakuntala and Bhattanarayan's Venisamhara are two examples of Nataka variety.

**Natakamandali**

It refers to 'Theatrical company, troup etc. The Arthashastra gives us some invaluable information on the existence of Natakamandalis, their maintenance and way of working. He informs at one place, that if any Natakamandali came from another country to produce a play, it was required to pay five paṇas [a particular coin equal in value to 80 cowries] to the King.

Each king employed natas, dancers, singers, musicians, story-tellers, actors and aindrajalikas (jugglers) and their salary were fixed. A Nata (Kushilava) was given 350 panas annually, while high class instrumentalists were paid 700 panas. It was king's duty to provide teachers for women artists to make them proficent in singing, dancing, acting, writing, playing on instruments, particularly Vina, Venu and Mridanga, preparing garlands, ornamenting the body with different materials and to spend on the above-mentioned items from the treasury of the Rajamandala (Government). The sons of ganikas (Courtesans) and the principal Natas were appointed head Teachers or Acharyas for all other stage-players of the Natakamandali. Such troupes were sometimes acted as spies who would try to reach the enemy-king, reports Arthashastra.

**[see also "Siddhis"]**

**Natakīvritam**

It means 'dramatic treatment'.

**Natakiya**

The Natayakiya is a beautiful woman who can sing and

has the capacity to rouse sentiments. She is familiar with the different kinds of musical instruments and has knowledge of rhythm and tune.

**Nātakiya**

Pertaining to a drama.

**Natana Bheda**

According to *Abhinaya darpanam* Natana (Tandava and Lasya) comprises of Nritta, Nritya and Natya.

In our ancient classics the performing arts were classified as Nritta, Nritya and Natya.

**Natarah**

The son of an actress or a dancing girl.

**Nataraja**

Dance is a divine creation, declare the HIndu Shastra. It relates back to Shiva's role as Nataraja, the lord of dance. His dance symbolises an ecstasy of motion which with its vital rhythm holds the universe together while perpetuating the cosmic activities of Creation, Preservation and Destruction. He dances the *Tandava* (the vigorous, masculine dance), as his consort Parvati performs the graceful, feminine *Lasya*.

Lord Shiva as the fountain-head of dance and all the various dance forms flowed from Him to the Gods and devas and through them to he sages and seers who transmitted the composite performing art to the people.

**[see "Ranga - devata" and 'Shiva']**

**Nata - Sutras**

It means concise rules about acting.

**Naṭavākya**

This refers to an actor's benediction; Bharata Vākya.

**Natayati**

Means enacts, a stage direction connoting enactment with fourfold abhinaya.

**Nati**

Refers to an actress or an actor's wife, a natiya a nartakiya, ranga stri or natabhārya. Though *Natyashastra* expressly admits of 'Rupanusarini' as a mode of representation of female role by a male actor and the assumption of women's roles by men has very early evidence. But this was not the normal practice. On the contrary, it was the 'Nati who usually played the female role as in the Karpūṛamanjari. Even in the Kuttanimata; where an actual representation of the first act of the Ratnavali is discussed, a woman is found to be in the role of the princess.

**Nāṭī see Nātika**

**Nāṭika**

The *Natyashastra* has at one place mentioned about a kind of play which it calls the Nāṭi or Nāṭika. This is a minor type of drama (Uparupaka), which is discussed in the *Dasarupa*. According to it 'The plot is taken from the Pakarana, and the hero is; like Nātaka, a wellknown king, selfcontrolled and light hearted type. The main sentiment (Rasa) is the erotic (Sringara), with its various characteristics.

This is one such variety of Sanskrit drama which resemble the 'Nataka' in many ways, slighter in subject and extant and usually depicts the hero's amorous adventures.

In Natika, the heroine is near the hero because of her link with the harem. Through her hearing and seeing him, a newly awakened passion arises in the hero in regular stages. The hero is apprehensive of the queen.

The Natika contains the four sub-classes of the Kaishiki Vritti (The Gay style) which are represented by the four acts. Under the category of Uparupaka, only the Natika alongwith 'Trotaka' could exercised some influence upon dramatic literature.

Sriharsha's Ratnavali and Priyadarshika are Natikas. Viddhashalabhanjika is another significant drama in this genre.

**Natya**

The word may denote many things as follows:-

* Dancing;

* Dramatic representation, gesticulation, acting;

* The science or art of dancing or acting;

* The costume of an actor.

**[For details see Itivritta, Nritta, Nritya, Natyaveda etc.]**

**Natyacharya**

It means 'A teacher of dramatic art.

According to *Natyashastra*, Poets (playwrights), directors, stage managers, musicians, scene-designes and painters fall under the category of Natyacharyas.

**[see 'Acharya']**

**Natya dharma**

It means 'Dramatic Conventions'.

**Natyadharmi**

This is one of the practices of abhinaya presentation with a stress on stylisation.

Bharata says that the representation of life on the stage by the dramatist is realistic, it is lokadharmi. But he adds that it is also his duty to see that his truths are imaginate truths and not actual truths, that his representations are ideal and not photographic. The whole process of selection and reticence, dialogue, music, dancing and each meticulous details of gestures and expressions and other devices on the stage make-up adopted by the artist to idealise facts and help the spectator to imagine things of his experience and things outside it-all these come within the scope of the Natyadharmi (conventional). Besides, if anything used by people, appears in a drama as endowed with a corporal form and speech, we have what is called Natyadharmi.

**[see also Lokadharmi]**

**Natya - dharmika (Natyadharmi)**

Refers to the 'Rules of dramatic representation"

**Natyaka**

It means 'Office of a dancing or drama master'.

**Natyakara**

According to *Natyashastra*, poets (drama composers), directors, stage - managers, musicians, scene-managers, musicians, scene - designers and painters fall under the category of Natyacharyas. The Natyakara plays a pivotal role in the presentation of Sanskrit drama. It is he who leads the characters in a play by directing them in the representation of feelings.

**Natyalankaras see Alankaras**

**Natyamandapa**

Refers to a theatre, play house in Bharata's Natyashastra (2-3).

**[see "Ranga"]**

**Natyarāsaka**

A minor form of drama (Uparupaka), the Natyarāsaka is a sort of ballet and pantomime. *Sahityadarpana* defines it as one-act piece with changing time and rhythm (Bahutālalaya sthiti).

**Natyarasas see Rasas**

**Natyartha**

The inner meaning of the play; the rasa (sentiment) content of a play.

**Natyashala**

A theatre or a play house, also called a Natyamandapa, Natya shala, Natyaveshma, Preksagriha, Ranga etc.

**[see "Ranga"]**

**Natyashastra**

In general, it applies to the dramatic science, dramaturgy;

A work an dramatic representation etc.

*Natyashastra* is the earliest known treatise on Indian dramaturgy, ascribed to Bharata and dated around the second century A.D.

**[see "Natyaveda"]**

**Natyavatarana**

It means 'Descent of Drama to Earth'.

**Natya - Veda**

Myth attributes the genesis of drama in India to divine beings. It is believed that Lord Brahma, in compliance with the request of gods created the fifth Veda, the Natya Veda.

Manmohan Ghosh in his introduction to the English renderation of *Natyashastra* opines that Bharata flourished in the c. 5th century B.C. and is believed to have written *Natyashastra*. However the author, ie, Bharata himself admits in the very first chapter of this dramaturgy that he is relating the *Natyashastra*, as uttered by Brahma, the first in the divine trinity and only then goes to narrate the legend. In Kṛtayuga, ie, the Golden Age, there was no need of any kind of entertainment, as the blissful state that prevailed at that time ruled out any sorrow. With the beginning of Tretayuga (the Silver Age) the people came in contact with sensual pleasures and eventually this pleasure got mingled with pain. Jambudvipa was now inhabitated by gods, demons, Gandharvas, Yaksas, Nagas etc. So some leading gods approached Brahma and requested some sort of entertainment for them which should be both audible and visible. As the Sudras were not allowed to listen to four existing Vedas, so a new Veda may be created to be enjoyed and shared by all.

This led Brahma to compose a fifth Veda who first went into yogic trance and recalled to his mind four vedas. He took some ingridient from each of them.

Natya Veda took speech, song, abhinaya and rasa, from the four Vedas, namely, Rig, Sama, Yajur and Atharva respectively.

This new Veda became 'Nātya' by name with Itihasa (i.e. semi-historical stories which shall conduce to Dharma (Duty), Artha (Wealth) as well as Yasha (Fame), will contain good counsel and collections (of old maxims), will provide guidance to people of the future as well, in all their actions, will be enriched by teaching of all Shastras (Authoritative works) and will give a review of all arts and crafts.

When Brahma asked Indra to pass it on to learned gods, the latter confessed that to comprehend, assimilate and preserve this drmatic science, can only be practised by the erudite sages who are well versed with the mystery of Vedas. So the task fell on Bharata who learnt the new art and passed it on to his hundred disciples. It is pertinent to mention here that every member of the Hindu Trinity directly participated in the creation of Natyaveda. Lord Shiva contributed the Tandava, his spouse Parvati created the Lāsya form of dance and Lord Vishnu, the four styles essential for effective performance.

Visvakarma, the divine architect was commissioned to build a theatre-house where the veda of the dramatic art could be performed. The music was set by sage Narada and the *gandharwas* namely Swan, Aprat, Angari, Bambari, Hasthaha, Chuhasthaha, Kruchanu, Viswashu, Murthanvan, Suryavarchas and Sruti sang. The orchestra was conducted by sage Swati, the play was choreographed by Bharata, Bharata's sons were the actors and the dancers were the *apsaras* of Indra Sabha namely Ghanasthani, Ramba, Bumjisusthali, Menaka,

Sahajanya, Premalochana, Anulochana, Trudashi, Viswashi, Urvashi, Purvasidriya and Tilottama.

Brahma's composition 'Amrita-manthana', a Samavakara play on the story of the churning the nectar out of the ocean milk and also Dima (a play with Raudra as the dominant rasa) were presented in front of Lord Shiva in Kailasa.

Lord Shiva's Tandava dance may be taken to be the first form of Nritta.

Parvati's Lasya may be regarded as the origin of Nritya.

Brahma's play 'Amrita-manthana may be regarded as the begining of the Natya or dramatic tradition.

Thus, the fifth Veda (Natya Veda) was imparted to Bharata by Brahma to stage the first play Amrita manthana which dealt with the triumph of gods over the demons (Asuras).

This Natyaveda came to be known as '*Natyashastra*', the earliest, treatise on the theory and practice of drama comprising all facets of theatre including erection of theatres, composition and production of plays, dance, music, costumes.

In one of the verses in Chapter VI of *Natyashastra*, Bharata has furnished eleven elements of Drama which collectively called the *'Digest of Natyashastra'*. These significant dramatic components are:-

Rasa (Sentiment)

Bhava (Emotion)

Abhinaya (Acting)

Dharmi (Modes of representation)

Vritti (Styles of expression)

Pravritti (Local usages)

Siddhi (Success of production)

Svara (Note)

Atodya (Musical instruments)

Gana (Song)

Ranga (Theatre)

**Natyaveshma**

The term denotes a theatre, playhouse in Bharata's *Natyashastra* (2.2).

**[see 'Natyamandapa]**

**Natyavyaḥ**

Means an actor.

**Natyoktis**

Natyoktis are special dramatic speeches employed by damatic characters, having particular manner of delivering these special speeches, and are really the dramatic conventions that govern them and the kind of Abhinaya in order that their full import be conveyed to the spectator as required in the interest of the dramatic story. In this sense, the Natyoktis are to be treated as a Natyadharma. (Dramatic Conventions)

Bharata discusses 'Natyoktis', under the head 'Chitrabhinaya' governing the vachika kind. While later theorists treat it as a division of the dramatic plot (Vastu) and presented according to dramatic conventions (Natyadharma).

Natyoktis are related to Vastu, because the plot of a drama is carried to the spectator only through dialogue and dramatic speeches and the Natyoktis, being a part of the dramatic dialogue and speeches, are obviously a part of the Vastu or dramatic plot. A playwright while building and in the process of developing his story, may desire that some speeches may be heard by all (Prakasha) and Akashabhasita (Aerial). Some may be restrictively heard, ie; Janantika 'Aside'. Apavarita (Excluded), Karne (whispered in ear' and some many not supposed to be heard, ie, Svagata or self-addressed. All these speeches are 'Natyoktis'.

**Natyopakarana**

Natyopakarana are the accessories of a dramatic production and used to create a scene according to sequence. These the objects can be mobile or immobile, such as vehicles, palaces, houses, huts, caves and gardens and are made by experts.

**[see 'Pusta']**

**Navagrahahasta**

It denotes Hastas for planets. They are :-

(1) **Surya** - Sun: *Alapadma* and *kapittha* are held near the throat, the former suggesting the orb and the latter the rays of the sun.

(2) **Chandra** - Moon: *Alapadma* in the left and *pataka* in the right hand, suggesting the light of the moon.

(3) **Kuja** - Mars: *Soochi* in the left and *mushti* in the right hand.

(4) **Budha** - Mercury: *Mushti* in the left and *pataka* in the right hand.

(5) **Guru** - Jupiter: Both hands in *Shikhaa,* the left hand above the left shoulder and the right hand placed on the right thigh after moving it from left shoulder indicating the sacred thread.

(6) **Shukra** -Venus: Both hands in *mushti* held near the chest one above the other.

(7) **Shani** - Saturn: *Shikhara* in left and *trishoola* in the right hand.

(8) **Rahu** : *Sarpasheersha* in the left and *soochi* in the right hand.

(9) **Ketu** : *Suchi* in the left and *pataka* in the right hand.

**Nayaka**

Sanskrit term meaning "Hero". In ancient times, in a play the Nayaka or Hero usually used to be a king or other exalted personage, noble, handsome, brave etc.

In a Sanskrit dramatic composition, the Hero is the principal character, who directly by his own efforts or through the endeavour of his ministers and helpmates, stands as the leader of an action and obtains its fruit, (Phala), which is Purusārtha (Dharma, Artha, Kāma). A drama, therefore ends with a successful and happy note.

*Dasarupaka* has categorised the hero according to he qualities the possesses and another basis is in relation to the sentiment of love. According to the first criteria, the hero will be of four varities, namely, Dhirodatta, Dhiralalita, Dhirasanta and Dhiroddhata.

The Dhirodatta Nayaka is patient, unshakable, serious, forgiving and of firm resolution.

The Dhiralalita Nayaka is free from worries, devoted to some artisatic pursuits, happy and tender - hearted.

The Dhirashanta Nayaka must possess all the standard qualities of a hero.

In Dhiroddhata Nayaka, arrogance, envy, anger, deceitfulness are at sixes and sevens with others around him.

According to the second parameter the *Dasarupaka* gives us four types of Nayaka (according to his dealings with the object of his love) He could be a Daksina Nayaka, Shatha type, Dhrista or Anukula. Daksina Nayaka is courteous one who is sympathetic towards his love which he later neglects; the Shatha Nayaka, a rogue hero does something unpleasnat in a secret manner; the Dhrista Nayaka betrays tell-tale signs of his dalliance with another woman, and Anukula Nayaka, the Agreeable hero is the loyal one.

There are some innerqualities or natural merits of a Nayaka, enlisted by traditional theorists. *Daśarupaka* gives ten such qualities. Some of which are: Shobha, Gambhirya, Tejas etc.

According to *Natyashastra*, there are eight different qualities attributed to the male temperament. Male character therefore, ought to be of brilliant character, graceful appearance, self possession, steadiness, gravity, sportiveness, nobility and spirit.

Again, as prescribed by Bharata's treatise, a hero of royal descent should be strong, intelligent, truth loving, dextrous and brave, having great courage and control over his senses.

*Bhavaprakahana* of Sharadatanaya categorize Nayaka in the context of love, implying the attitude and behaviour of the Hero in regard to the matters of love. Its fourfold distinctions are Anukula, Daksina, Shatha and Dhrista. This is followed by *Sahityadarpana* of Vishvantha and *Rasarnavasudhakara* of Singha Bhupala.

*Rasarnavasudhakara* gives us another division, according to which the 'Hero' in the context of love appears to be of three kinds: Pati, Upapati and Vaishika. It further suggests among these three kinds a further grouping into high, low and middling.

**Nayika**

Sanskrit term denoting 'Heroine'. In ancient Sanskrit drama, the Heroine used to be either a lady of noble birth or in some cases, a courtesan of great virtue, beautiful and accomplished. Theoretically there can be as many as 384 varities of Nayika in a Sanskrit drama. First we have Bharata's wellknown "Asta - Nayikah".

*Natya Shastra* has furnished various stages of love and *Daśarupaka* discusses these stages while explaining Ayoga. According to Bharata's treatise a lady in love generally passes through longing, anxiety, recollection, enumeration, distress, lamentation, insanity, sickness, stupor and death. These are the ten main states or situations to which she is likely to be go through while in love.

Bharata's wellknown categorisation of Heroine into eight types also represent the stages of love to which she may belong. This ramification is based on the amorous relationship of the heroine with the hero, and depends on the variety of treatment and attention bestowed upon her by her lover.

These are:-

(1) Vasakasajja

(2) Virahotkanthita

(3) Svadhinapatika

(4) Kalahantarita

(5) Khandita

(6) Vipralabdha

(7) Prositabhartrika and

(8) Abhisarika

The heroine figure practically only in a drama having an erotic theme. In Sanskrit drama Sringara rasa is the main sentiment when ladies take part in it. So traditional Indian dramatic theory dwells at length upon the subject of heroine - in - love. She is the main character among the female roles.

*Natya Shastra* has also dealtwith another aspect of Nayika's nature as *Dhira, Lalita* and *Udatta.*

*Natyashastra* has categorized the heroine on the basis of varied factors. If it is done according to their nature, heroine could be *Uttama*, ie, of superior type who is patient and dignified; *Madhyama*, ie, an ordinary type who has some faults, and *Adhama*, ie, of lower type just like an Adhama type of hero.

According to the general threefold classification, the female characters may be of three types

(1) Uttama - prakriti Pramadā

(2) Madhyama - prakriti Pramadā

(3) Adhama - prakriti Pramada

Bharata recognizes four varities if we classify them as Divya, Nripapatni, Kulastri, Ganika.

According to Bharata, there are also women of differnt kinds associated with a royal Hero. They may be Mahadevi, Devi, Svamini, Sthapita, Bhogini etc.

According to later theorists, Nayikas are of three kinds:-

(1) Sva or Sviya

(2) Anya or Parakiya

(3) Sadharana or Samanya

Dhananjay provides three kinds of heroine, as shown in the diagram, numbers indicate the sixteen varities, if we classify them as Sva, Anya and courtezan or a common woman (Sadharanastri).

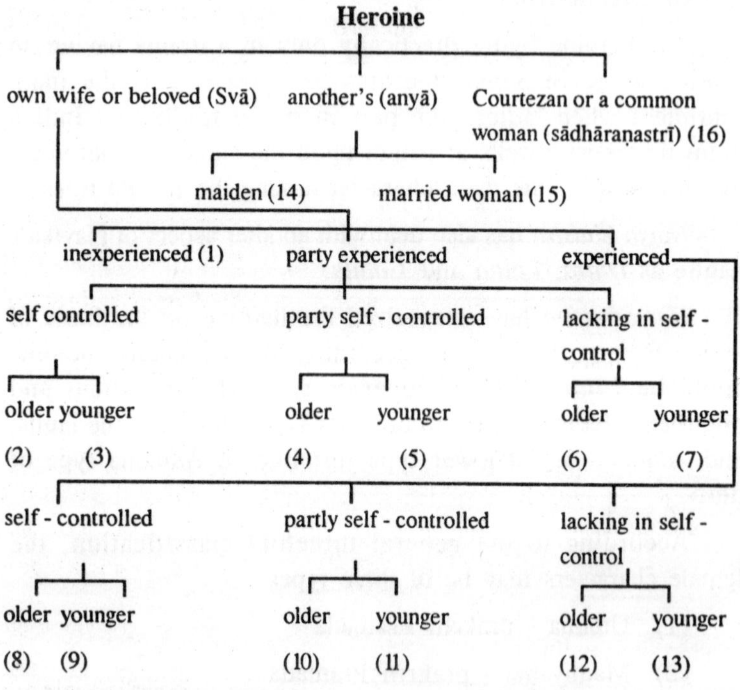


Dasarupaka treats various types of Heroines in more detailed manner. They are:-

(1) Sviya (one's own wife)

(Shilavati, Arjavadiyogini, Lajjavati)

(2) Mugdha

(Vayomugdha, Kamamugdha, Ratavama)

(3) Madhya

(Yauvanvati, Kamavati)

(4) Dhira

(Dhiradhira, Madhyadhira)

(5) Pragalbha

(Bhavapragalbha, Ratapragalbha)

(6) Parakiya

(Sadharanastree, Anyastree).

Theorists when classify the Nayika into Sviya, Anya (or Parakiya) and Sadharana (or Samanya), we have further sub groups as follows:-

(1) **Sviya:-** 13 varities (Mugdha 1; Madhya, according to Dhira, Adhira, Dhiradhira division, or Udāttā, Lalitā, Shanta division, 3; each Jyestha or Kanistha; so 3x2 = 6; Pragalbhā, like Madhya, 6. In all, 1+6+6=13).

(2) **Anya (Parakiya):-** 2 varities (Uḍhā or Kanya)

(3) **Sadharana (Samanya):-** 1 variety.

Thus, we have sixteen varieties that represent the major kinds and types of Nayikās.

Combined with the former number with Bharata's Asta - Nayikah, we have 128 varities (ie, 16 x 8).

Again if one more principle of social status is taken into consideration that divides women into three classes Uttama, Madhyama and Adhama, we have 384 types (128 x 3).

*Bhavaprakashana* and *Sahitya Darpana* mention of 384 kinds of Nayika in dramatic composition.

**Nayika Sahayikas**

This denotes female characters supporting the heroine, according to traditional dramatic theory.

In most of the Sanskrit plays, a heroine is being seen

accompanied or attended upon by one or more female characters, loyal to their mistress, take up some responsibility and try always to help the heroine. Collectively they are called 'Nayika Sahayikas.

Nayika Sahayikas could be maids, ascetics, friends, foster mothers, women well versed in the art of painting and messengers on secret errand etc.

*Dasharupaka* mentions the following, 'Associates of the Heroines' namely Dasi (Ceti), Sakhi, Karu, Dhatreyi, Prativeshika, Lingini, Shilpini, Duti (Svayam) etc.

*Bhavaprakashana* adds few more in the list of *Dasarupaka* while discussing the Associates of the Heroine, they may be woman who is skilful in entertaining by telling stories and anecdotes; a professional actress or dancer (Rangopajivini); Preksanika (a woman who arranges spectacular shows for entertainment; young unmarried girls or princesses female heretics etc.

**Nepathya**

Broadly it denotes, 'Decoration', 'an ornament'; 'Dress', 'Costume'; Costume of an actor etc.

Aharya, the third kind of abhinaya, according to Classical Dramatic Treatise, is defined as that which is produced through Nepathya and make-up, painting, costume, ornaments, accessories of characters all togethers are called 'Nepathya' Bharata broadly categorize them as Pusta, Alankara, Angarachana and Sanjiva.

**Nepathyagriha**

It refers to a green-room. A tiring room, the space where the actors attire themelves which is always behind a curtain, mentioned in Bharata's *Natyashastra* (2-35).

Bharata's stage is divided into three compartments

(I) The Nepathyagriha

(II) The Rangashirsa

(III) The Rangapitha.

According to Bharata's prescription, there are two doors from Nepathya griha to the stage. One is used only for actors coming right up to the front on the Rangapitha (characters low in status) and the other exclusively as an entry to the Rangashirsa for higher characters like the Hero and the Heroines etc. In the centre of these two doors, musical instruments are placed.

**Nepathya-ukti**

This is the lines delivered from behind the curtain or from the Green-room. The Nepathya speeches and letters etc are other dramatic devices, besides Akashabhasita, to achieve economy in stage business and avoid the appearance of a character for a trivial purpose. *Natya - Laksana - Ratnakosha* prefers this technique.

**Nepathya - Vidhanam**

It denotes the arrangements of the Tiring room (Green-room).

**Netā**

This denotes 'Hero' and according to Sanskrit Dramatic Theory, Netā (Hero), Vastu (Story) and Rasa (Artistic enjoyment) constitute the three essential ingredients of a dramatic composition. Furthermore, according to the difference in these respects the ten varieties (Daśarūpakas) are to be recognised.

**[see 'Nayaka']**

**Netri**

This is the synonym of 'Nayaka', the hero of a drama.

**[see 'Nayaka']**

**Ni (Niṣāda)**

This is the seventh scale degree.

**[see Niṣāda]**

**Nibaddha Gāna**

Sharangadeva in his *Sangitaratnakara* states : The sages have declared Gāna to be two fold, namely. Nibaddha (composed) and Anibaddha (Improvised). That which is composed of Dhātus (Sections) and Aṅgas (Limbs) is called Nibaddha...... Nibaddha has three names, viz, Prabandha, Vastu and Rūpaka.

**Nicha see Adhama**

**Nidarshana (Unfavourable Precedent) Vagyabhinaya**

**Nidra**

It denotes 'Slumber, sleep' etc.

Nidra or 'slumber' is the twenty first Mutable State/ Vyabhichari Bhava which according to Bharata, should be shown on the stage by a heavy face, stretching of limbs, rolling of eyes, yawning, laziness, deep breathing, relaxing the body and closing the eyes.

**Nigraha see Dharma**

**Nikuttaka**

According to *Natyasastra*, Nikuttaka is the ninth and one of the 108 Karanas or Cosmic Shiva Bharata poses where the performer should touch the floor with the heels and the hands must move between the head and shoulders.

**Ninda (Simile of Censure) see Alankaras and Upama**

**Nī-rasa vastu**

It refers to essential incidents in the plot without rasa which are lengthy or forbidden by tradition for enactment on stage. They are usually narrated or depicted with the aid of linking devices.

**Nirgita**

This means singing with meaningless syllables imitating the sounds of the instruments - employed in the preliminaries.

**Nirgitavādya**

Bharata in the chapter on 'drum', speaks of pure drumming to accentuate action. The music in which there are no words or songs but only the rhythm-syllables like Jhuntum, Dhen, Dhi, Dhan, Ti, Kita - what are now called Jati, Sol or Bol which were played on the instruments only is termed in the Natyashastras as 'Nirgitavadya' and as the contribution of the Asuras to the Sanskrit theatre. Even now the memory of this ancient tradition survives in a high degree of instrumental proficiency being acclaimed in musical parlance as "Asura - sādhakam".

**Nirukta**

In music, it denotes a tone quality.

This is one of the tonal qualities mentioned in the *Chandogya Upanishad.* Nirukta represent definite, identifiable voice.

**Nirukta (Convincing Explanation) see Vagyabhinaya**

**Nirvahana - Samdhi**

According to Sanskrit dramatic theory, the plot of a drama consists of five divisions which it terms 'Samdhis' or Junctures, a blending of Arthaprakriti (essential element of the theme) and Avastha (stage of development of the plot). Also known as Upasamhara Samdhi, Nirvahana Samdhi is the last juncture or in otherwords end or final stage of the journey.

*Natyashastra* defines it as "All element starting from Bija and directed towards the same purpose as well as those that are related to the fruit arc brought to a harmonious end in this juncture. Nirvahana, according to *Dasarupaka* is a stage where all the tendrils or threads grown up from the laying of the seed, and which had spread as desired, are brought together in a successful tie-up, ie, brought to a point of harmonious convergence.

Here 'Phalagama' is the Avastha and 'Karya' is the Arthaprakriti. *Natyashastra* describes *Phalayoga* as the achievement of the desired result at the end and *Karya* as that which has been previously mentioned as the leading purpose, and that for which Arambha has been made. Thus, Karya is the primary action, very essential to the Bija (Germ) for attaining the Phalaprapti.

**[see also Upsamhara - Samdhi]**

**Nirveda**

It means 'Detachment, Discouragement, Apathy' etc.

Nirveda is the first Vyabhichari Bhava, or Mutable State. It should be represented by means of remorse, deep breathing, deliberation, etc.

**[see Shantarasa]**

**Nīṣāda**

This is one of the seven Svaras (Notes) and according to *Ragavibodha, Sangitaparijata, Sangitamakarandah,* etc, the sounds of music are first perceived as relative pitches or intervals and then from the twenty two Shrutis (Main Intervals) come the seven Svaras, namely Ṣaḍja, Ṛṣabha, Gāndhāra, Madhyama, Pañcama, Dhaivata and Nīṣāda. It is interesting to mention here that the traditional authorities on music refer each Svara or Note to the sound of some animal.

Niṣāda represents the trumpeting of the elephant.

**Nishadha Hasta**

This is a double hand gesture, mentioned in *Natyashastra* in which one hand in *mukula* is encircled by the other hand in *kapittha* or with left hand in *shikhara* and right hand in *mrigasheersha*.

It is used in collecting and donating something, abadonment, rule, speaking truth, precision, pressing something, fear and terror (also man and women). This Samyuta Hasta is not given in *Abhinaya Darpanam.*

**Niṣkrāma**

This is one of the four silent Tāla gestures (right palm down with fingers extended).

**Niskramana**

It means 'exit from the stage'.

**Nisristartha Duta**

This refer to one of the three kinds of messenger, represented in Sanskrit drama. Such a duta is the most intelligent messenger who comprehends the intention of his master without much briefing, speaks to the expected person and answers all his queries or doubts on his own. Nisristartha Duta can read the minds of both between whom he acts and achieves his mission successfully. He is wise and patient, firm in mind and thought, courageous, devoted to the master and bent on fulfilling the entrusted mission, and is ready, if situation demands, to exhibit his heroic powers.

**Nīyatapti see Avamarsa - Samdhi**

**Niyati**

One of the presiding deities of theatre, according to *Natyashastra* and should be worshipped with offering and sacrifices.

**Nritta (Nṛtta)**

It is pure dance, dependent on rhythm (laya, tala).

Nṛtta and Nṛtya comes from Nṛt. There is reference to Nṛt in the Rigveda, while the earliest use of Nat (from where is derieved 'Natya' is found in Panini. This shows that Nṛt was an earlier form. Nat is found to have been used in the senses of dancing and acting.

Nritta is nonrepresentational dance while Nritya is representational dance.

Nritya is a more evolved form of Nritta. The latter is the original form of entertainment on which Nritya was an improvement. Nritta involved Tāla (Rhythm) and Laya (Tune) only and not Bhāva (Emotion) while Nritya was essentially linked with Bhāva (Emotion), and producing Bhāva (Emotion) in the spectator's mind is an art far more advanced than mere 'Gatravikṣepa' (Bodily movement). Nritta, therefore, is dance, while Nritya is Mimetic Art (the gestures added to it). And Natya has speech too. Natya covers all the three items Dance, Music and Speech. Therefore both Nritta and Nritya are different from Natya, while Nritta is quite distinct, but Nritya is useful in Nātya, stātes 'Abhinavabharati'.

The Natyaveda emerged out of four Vedas. After having forged this fifth Veda, Brahma commanded Bharata to learn it and pass it on to his disciples. Lord Shiva, commended Tandu to teach Nritta to Bharata so that he could employ it in his dramatic presentations. Tandu being the first instructor of Nritta, dance came to be known as Tandava. Shiva gave a performance of this dance which is virile and violent, after the destruction of Daksa's sacrifice. Later its gentler form Lasya came into being with Parvati who too gave a performance after seeing the dance of her Lord Shiva.

Nritta is rhythmic dance movement which has symbolic significance in Indian dance idiom.

Nritta or pure dance, according to Indian tradition is an expression of body movement where Nritya as said before combines pure dance with the expression of emotion. Natya is the art of drama, through which (in case of dance) a dancer develops a theme or tells a story. Abhinaya means literally to carry forward, ie, present a theme to the audience, natya in its fullest development. Further there is a two-fold division of Nritta and Nritya into Lasya and Tandava, the graceful and virile aspects.

**Nritta Hastas see Hastamudras**

**Nritya**

Nritya is an 'Expressive dance.

Amarakosha gives six symonyms for dance. These are Tāndava, Nātana, Natya, Lāsya, Nritya and Nartana. In general Nritya is an art of dance. But the concept is quite different from Nritta. The latter is pure dance, according to Indian tradition, an expression of body movement alone. While Nritya combines Pure dance with the expression of emotion. An evolved form of Nritta, an amalgation of Tala, Lala and Bhava (Rhythm, Tune and Emotion respectively) thus far more advanced than bodily movement (Gatraviksepa).

It combines nritta and natya, ie, foot work and Abhinaya. (according to Indian tradition). Nritya is 'representational dance, while Nritta is 'nonrepresentational' dance.

The origin of dance in India is attributed to divine being. It is said that the fifth Veda was imparted to Bharata by Brahma to enact the first play, Amrita manthana which dealt with the triumph of gods over the demons Myth further tells as that Shiva saw the drama and introduced the *Tandava* dance with energetic movements, and had it taught to Bharata, by Tandu, while Parvati taught the Lasya, the gentler and graceful variety to Usha, the daughter of Bana, later Usha handed down the art to the Gopis of Dvaraka that was spread to Saurashtra and other part of the country. Thus, the tradition of the art of dance (Nritya) was established in the country.

Bharata has given due place to Dance in Drama. According to him, Dance is primarily of two types - Tandava (The Virile), the dance of war and Lasya (The Gentle), the dance of love the latter got more importance in Drama than the former. Bharata, therefore, discusses in detail the twelve constituents of the gentle dance. He explains one hundred and eight Karanas, thirty-two Angaharas and four Rechakas which only the students of this art can appreciate.

Bharata opines that the position of different limbs of the body - fingers, hands, feet, neck, waist, flanks, thighs, abdomen etc, is vital in Dance and combined movements of these limbs are 'Karanas'.

Nritya or dance, according to *Natyashastra* and other ancient Indian texts on dramaturgy, music and aesthetics was a part of "Natya" (acting) and Sangeetha (music) Dance was treated as an essential part of drama and formed part of all celebrations and was performed before every undertaking as it is calculated to make the occasion auspicious.

The ancient Hindu dramas or Rupakas (visual representation) were an admixture of dances, songs and costumes as the chief medium. In the Vishnu Purana dates back to the 200 A.D. informs that *the actors danced a play* "Natakam Nanruth". This clearly indicates that dance as an art form existed long before the period of Bharata's treatise on dramatugy called "*Natyashastra*".

**[see 'Nritta'. and 'Natya']**

**Nrityashala**

Means a dancing hall.

**Nrityasthanam**

It denotes stage, dancing room.

**Nruta**

This is one of the six techniques employed in singing the svaras of the Vedic Scales. Singing of the lower notes from Chaturtha to Atisvārya without sharp intonation; included in the Avashepini, opposite of Anuta.

**Nyāsa**

According to traditional musical theory, there are three important notes in the Rāga. *Sangita Ratnakara* of Sharaṅgadeva mentions Nyāsa as the ending note. The Graha is the starting note and Amsha, the predominant or main note. Nyāsa is the final note.

**Nyāyād-apeta see Dosas**

# O

**Odra - Māgadhi**

It refers to regions/provinces such as Aṅga, Vaṅga, Kaliṅga etc. *Natyashastra* of Bharata explains four Pravrittis or Local Usages to the producers of plays to give realistic touch or in other words, to create ambiance to the production by reflecting in their performances the locales of the various regions of this vast land. Odra-Māgadhi is one such Pravritti which takes into consideration the practices, peculiarities, costumes, languages and manners of this region.

**Ogha**

In the actual playing of the instruments, there are different methods. Three major styles are: Tattva, Anugata and Ogha. Ogha is the play of the instruments in a crescendo.

**Ogha see Drutam**

**Ojas see Gunas**

**Onkara**

He is one of the presiding deities of theatre and according to Bharata, should be worshipped with offering and sacrifices.

**[see 'Ganapati']**

# P

**Pa (Pañcama)**

This is the fifth scale degree.

**[see pañcama]**

**Pada**

It means 'word', in the sense of (a) text in general; or

(b) a passage of music set to a meaningful text (as opposed to nonsense syllables).

**Pādabhāga**

In rhythmic system, Pādabhāga is one formal unit (measure, phrase) of a group of four, literally "a division into [four] paws" (as of a quadruped).

**Padabheda**

This refers to the movements of the foot and according to Bharata, they are of five kinds namely Udghattita, Sama, Agratala-sanchara, Anchita, Kunchita.

(1) **Udghattita :** In Udghattita, the heel is brought down after the fore-part of the sole placed on the ground.

(2) **Sama:** Here the foot placed on the ground naturally.

(3) **Agratalasanchara:** In Agratalasanchara, the toe is placed on the ground and the heel is raised up.

(4) **Anchita:** In Anchita, the heel is placed on the ground with forepart of the foot facing up.

**Padabheda : (Anchita)**

(5) **Kunchita:** In Kunchita, toes pressed on the ground with the middle of the foot is bent.

Some other foot movements are:-

(i) **Suchi (Soochi)**: This is also a foot movement where only big toe of the right foot is placed on the ground while left is kept naturally.

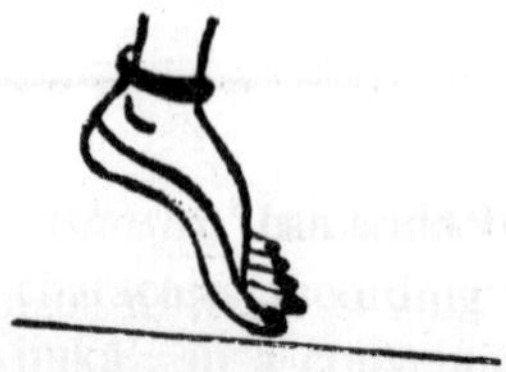

**Padabheda : (Suchi)**

(ii) **Tryasra:** This is also a foot movement in use where heel of one foot is brought and placed near the middle of the other foot like 'T'.

**Padangulibheda**

This denotes the movements of the toes and are of five types:-

(1) **Adhahkshipta** (toes are constantly falling down wards): Used to express haughtiness and amorous agitation.

(2) **Utkshipta** (toes bent upwards): Used to express bashfulness of newly wed woman.

(3) **Kunchita** (toes are bent down): Used to express cold, fainting, fear and possession by evil.

(4) **Prasarita** (toes are extended): Used to express 'paralysis, sleep; relaxation of limb.

(5) **Samlagna** (by joining the big toe with other toes): Used to depict 'dragging something'.

### Padas

It means movements of feet in Indian dance.

### Pādas (Nandi)

It denotes 'feet'. The fourth part of a Shloka or strophe. *Natyashastra* has prescribed that the significant Nāndi verse of a drama (one of the twenty constituent parts of Purvaranga or preliminaries), in the form of benediction be of eight or twelve feet 'Pādas', should be poetically beautiful and should be sacred and approved by gods. The Sutradhara recites the Nandi n the middle tone, while his Paripārshvikas say 'Evamastu' (so be it) at the end of every foot (Pada).

Prataparudriya opines that it may have eight, twelve, eighteen or twenty two pādas in a benedictory part of Parvaranga called 'Nandi'.

According to the *Rasārnavasudhakara*, there may be eight, ten or twelve pādas in Nandi.

*Bhavaprakashana* feels that there should be eight or twelve padas or sentences in a Nandi verse.

### Padmakosha Hasta

This is a single hand gesture in which all the fingers are stretched and brought close but not touching one another.

The gesture is used to express:- "fruits, *'bel'* the wood-apple, round breasts of a woman, a circular movement, a ball, cooking-pot, food, a flower-bud, scattering flowers, *'japakusum'* flowers, bell, an anthill, a lotus and an egg."

This gesture in dance also indicates lotus bud, Kapittha and bilva fruits, mango flowers, cluster of flowers etc.

### Padoccaya (Multiplex Prediction) see Vagyabhinaya

### Paishaci

This is a sub-dialect of Prakrita used in the Sanskrit plays. Pīshācas or goblins as dramatis personae spoke this dialect of Prakrita known as 'Paishaci'.

**Paṇava**

The *Natyashastra* helds music as an indispensable adjunct of Sanskrit drama. It mentions of following musical instruments: Mridanga, Paṇava, Dardura, Dundubhi, Muraja, Jhallari, Paṭ aha, Vaṁsha, Shaṅkha and Ḍakkinī.

**Paṅcāli**

It denotes province/regions contiguous to the Himalayas or the northern bank of the Ganges. *Natyashastra* of Bharata explains four Pravrittis or Local Usages to the producers of plays to give realistic touch or to create ambiance to the production by reflecting in their performances the locale of the various regions of this vast land. Paṅcāli is one such Pravritti which takes into consideration the practices, peculiarities, costumes, languages and manners of this region.

**[see also 'Pravritti']**

**Pañcama**

This is one of the seven Svaras or Notes and according to *Ragavibodha, Sangitaparijata, Sangitamakarandah* etc, the sounds of music are first perceived as relative pitches or intervals and then from the twentytwo (Main Intervals) (*Shrutis*) come the seven Svaras, namely Ṣaḍja, Ṛṣabha, Gāndhāra, Madhyama, Pañcama, Dhaivata and Niṣāda.

It is interesting to mention here that traditional authorities on music refer each Svara or Note to the sound of some animal. Pañcama is said to be the note of the Cuckoo (Kokila).

**Pāṇi**

Refers to a measure of the synhchronization of melody and accompaniment.

In rhythmic system, Pāṇi is the principleof synchronization by which the entrances of the various performers are regulated.

**Pānisanghātam**

This denotes one who keeps time clapping both the hands.

In the Purushamedha Prakayana of the Taittiriya Brahmaṇa (3rd Ashtaka and 4th Prashna), names of professional artists and musicians are mentioned whose services were required in the sacrificial hall and it includes the name of 'Pānisanghātam'.

**Panyakamini Nayika**

Bharatas fourfold division of Nayikas (Heroines) are Kulaja, Divya, Ksatriya and Panyakamini. Unlike later theorists, only *Natyadarpana* reverts to this categorization and divides each into further categories according as they possess the qualities of fortitude (Dhairya), grace (Lalitya) or nobility (Udāttatva).

According to it, Panyakamini or courtesan should be graceful (Lalitā) and Udāttā.

**[see 'Nayika']**

**Parakiya Nayika**

According to later theorists of drama, there are three varities of heroines. Parakiya or Anya Nayika is one of these. She is either a Kanya (young and unmarried girl) or Ūḍhal Parodha (a married woman).

**[see under 'Kanya' and 'Paroḍhā and Nayika']**

**Paravritya see Apavaritaka**

**Paricchada**

This denotes the 'Retinue' of the Royal Hero, both men and women who serve him in his Antaḥpura (Harem), and are assigned different duties in the Royal Harem and occasionally figure in minor roles in Nataka and Natika varities such as Eunuchs (Varṣavara) Mountaineeers (Kirata), Deaf-mutes, Dwarfs, Hunch back (Kubja), Barbarions (Mleccha), cowherds, Shakara.

Some unique characters, moulded by convention are Kanchuki (The Royal Chamberlain) Pratihāri (King-Hero's Attendant) are other belong to the Royal Harem.

This dramatis personae fall in the category of 'Artha - sachiva', if we classify the Associates of Hero according to *Bhava-prakashana*.

**Paricharika**

It refers to the maids and female servants employed in the King's harem. Such characters from the Royal Harem figure in the Sanskrit drama. One prominent attendant who continuously figure is the Pratihari.

**Parighaṭṭanā**

This is the six constituent parts of Purvaranga (preliminaries of a play) taken up behind the curtain. It means tuning of the stringed instruments (Tantri).

**Parikramā**

This is the technique of going around the stage to establish Natyadharmi Zonal Divisions.

**[see 'Parikramana']**

**Parikramana**

In Ancient Dramatic Treatise, it is stated that the change of place, time etc in a drama should be conveyed by the conventions like Parikramana, Kaksa arrangements and by the characters themselves and thus, Bharata regards gestures, poses, movements very significant elements in drama. He employs them as stage techniques. Adha Rangacharya exemplifies in the following way:-

On the Rangapitha, as required by a particular scene, one side (or end) may represent the back door of the palace and the other one the palace garden. But this different is not conveyed by any special device lika a curtain or any other object; it is the actor who by his movements tells us that just coming out of the palace back door he (or she) is gong to the palace garden. Thus the distinction is establihed by further going n a circular movement (Parikramana) and moving to the new spot (Kaksa). The distinction between different Kaksas shall be conveyed by a circular movement on the Ranga-pitha; by the Parikramana another Kaksa may be said to have been established (XIII, 3)...... the Parikramana is also used to denote nearness or distance between two spot (e.g., with 2 or 3 very quick Parikramanas the character can say that it has come the whole distance from one town to another (XIII, 17).

**Pariparshvaka**

Refers to 'Assistnat to Sūtrādhāra'. He is a deputy or right hand man of 'Sutradhara' in the production of Sanskrit drama in age old days.

**Parivarta**

In rhythmic system, Parvarta is a prescribed repetition of a formal unit.

**Parivartana**

In all there are twenty items in a Purvaranga [Preliminaries] of a play. Parivartana is one such constituent parts which is taken up on the stage. Here is performed Parivartana, stalking round the stage with praise of the guardians of the world (Dikpalastuti) and adoration of Indra's banner (Jarjarapuja).

**Paroḍhā Nayika**

According to *Rasarnavasudhakara*, she is a married woman who may appear as a heroine in compositions of a lower order. *Dasarupaka* cautions that a married woman must not be represented as a heroine in the principal sentiment of a play, that means, the married woman (Ūḍhā) may appear not as a Pradhana - Nayika, but only as an Upanāyika or a subordinate heroine in a secondary role or in a sub-plot *Sahitya Darpana* refers to her as a woman devoted to religious pilgrimages etc.

Paroḍha Nayika falls under the main class 'Anya or Parakiya Nayika'.

**Parshnibheda**

It refers to the movements of the heel which are of eight types :-

Utkshipta (raised up)

Patita (brought down)

Utkshiptapatita (raised up and brought down alternatively)

Antargata (turned inwards)

Bahirgata (turned outwards)

Mithoyukta (joined together)

Viyukta (separated)

Angulisangata (heel of one foot touches the toe of the other foot).

**Parshvabheda**

According to *Natyashastra* this denotes the movements of the sides. They are of five types, namely, Nata, Samunnata, Prasarita, Vivartita, Apasrita.

(1) **Nata:** In Nata, waist is bent one side alongwith the respective shoulder. Nata is used in showing "to approach or reach somebody."

(2) **Samunnata:** In nata position, the other raised side consists of waist, arm and shoulder is Samunnata (In Nata, the waist is bent one side alongwith the respective shoulder). Samunnata is used to show "in going backwards."

(3) **Prasarita:** Here side is stretched towards its respective direction. It is used to show "great joy."

(4) **Vivartita:** Turning side ways is called 'Vivartita', used for turning towards the side.

(5) **Apasrita:** This is the last of the five kinds of movements of the sides (Parshvabheda). Vivartita is 'turning side ways', while return to the original position from Vivartita is called 'Apasrita'.

**Pasha Hasta**

This is a double hand gesture in which the index fingers of both the hands in *soochi* are curved and interlocked in opposite direction. It denotes "a mutual quarrel, a string and a chain."

**Pashu-Pakshi Hasta**

It means Hastas for Birds & Animals.

They are :-

(1) *Aja* - goat : *Shikhara* hands facing each other.

(2) *Ashwa* - horse : Hand stretched in front with *tripataka.*

(3) *Baka* - crane : The little finger is bent towards the palm in *hamsasya.*

(4) **Bhalu** - bear : *Pataka* in the right hand is held at the back of the left hand which is in *padamkosha.*

(5) **Bhramara** - bee : *Bhramara hasta.*

(6) **Chakravaka** - rudy goose : The two hands in *alapadma* are fluttered.

(7) **Chakravaka** - yak : *Mushti* in the left and *mudra* in the right hand touching at the wrists.

(8) **Chataka** - bird : *Kangula* is fluttered.

(9) **Dhenu** - cow : Middle finger is bent while the other fingers are stretched.

(10) **Dundunbha** - non poisonous two headed snake : *Kartaree* in the right hand facing upwards the *katakamukha* in the left hand also facing upwards.

(11) **Gaja** - elephant : *Arala* is placed at the ear by the left and *kari* by the right hand.

(12) **Gardabha** - donkey : *Mukula* bent in front of the face.

(13) **Garuda** - king of birds: *Garuda hasta.*

(14) **Girika** - mouse : The first finger is bent and stretched obliquely in *mukula.*

(15) **Godha** - iguana : *Pataka* with separated thumb and little finger. It is *tala-pataka.*

(16) **Gokarna** - mule : *Nagabandha* are moved upwards.

(17) **Hamsa** - swan : *Hamsasya hasta.*

(18) **Hastini** - female elephant : *Ardhachandra* is extended downwards and then the fingers are separated.

(19) **Kapi** - monkey : The thumb and second finger are joined in *mushti.*

(20) **Kapota** - pigeon : *Kapota hasta.*

(21) **Kattu** - forest-fly : *Hamsasya hasta.*

(22) **Khadyota** - firefly or glow worm : Thumb is touching the middle finger.

(23) **Kokila** - nightingale or cuckoo : *Arala* is fluttered.

(24) **Krauncha** - curlew : The little finger is bent towards the palm in *alapadma.*

(25) **Krishna Sara** - antelope : *Mrigasheersha hasta.*

(26) **Kukutta** - cock : *Bhramara hasta.*

(27) **Kulira** -crab : The left hand is placed on the right and the fingers are interlocked in *karkata.*

(28) **Kuranga** - antelope : *Mrigasheersha hasta.*

(29) **Maan** - dear : *Mrigasheersha hasta.*

(30) **Makara** - crocodile : *Pataka* hands are joint and then separated.

(31) **Marjara** - cat : The thumb and the third finger are joined in *mushti.*

(32) **Mayura** - peacock : *Mayura hasta.*

(33) **Meen** - fish : *Matsya hasta.*

(34) **Mūshika**- mouse : Stretch slightly the fore fingers from *mukula.*

(35) **Paravata** - dove : *Kapota is fluttered.*

(36) **Puzhu** - worm : *Sandamsha hasta.*

(37) **Sarasa** - Indian crane : The little finger is bend in *mukula.*

(38) **Shalya** - porcupine : Index finger is raised in *mrigasheersha.*

(39) **Shashanka** - hare : *Pataka* hands are moved obliquely.

(40) **Shuka** - parrot : *Shukatunda* fluttered.

(41) **Shunaka** - dog : The little finger in *pataka* is bent.

(42) **Simha** - lion : *Simhamukha hasta.*

(43) **Sukara** - boar : *Matsya* facing downwards and the fingers are stretched and shaken seperately.

(44) **Uluka** - owl : *Gajadanta* hands are held facing each other.

(45) **Ushtra** - camel : Move the thumbs up and down in anjali.

(46) **Vanara** - monkey : *Mukula* near the face and knee shaking.

(47) **Varaha** - wild boar : *Varaha hasta.*

(48) **Vayasa** - crow : *Katakamukha hasta.*

(49) **Vrishabha** - bull : In *Simhamukha hasta,* the second and the third fingers are bent towards the palm and the thumb is placed upon them.

(50) **Vrishchika** - scorpion : *In ardhapataka* the forefinger and the middle are bent or curved slightly.

(51) **Vyaghra** - tiger : *Vyaghra hasta.*

**Pāta**

In rythmic system, Pāta is an audible gesture, usually a clap.

This is an audible Tāla gestures.

**Pāṭa**

A passage of recited drum syllables (one of the aṅgas of a prabandha).

**Paṭaha**

The *Natyashastra* helds music, an indispensable adjunct of Sanskrit drama. It informs about some musical instruments like Mridanga, Paṇȧva, Dardura, Dundubhi, Muraja, Jhallari, Paṭaha, Vaṁsha, Shaṅkha and Ḍakkinī.

**Pataka**

This hand gesture is used at the beginning of a Indian dance to denote clouds, heaven, sword, peace etc.

**Pataka (Garva Samdhi)**

**[see 'Garva-Samdhi]**

**Patāka**

It denotes 'Banner' a kind of trouphy which in ancient times was awarded by the king to a winning team, in a drama competition.

**[see under 'Siddhis']**

**Patāka Hasta**

A single hand gesture in which four fingers are stretched close together with a bent thumb.

This is used at the beginning of *natya,* the clouds, forest, forbidding things, bosom, night, river, heavens, horse, cutting or rebutting, wind, lying down, exiting, prowess, favour, moonlight, strong sunlight, opening the doors, meaning of seven case -endings, wave, entering a road, equality, anointing the body, for oneself, taking an oath, silence, palmyra leaf, shield, touching things, blessing, a king, denoting such and such place, the sea, succession of good deeds, addressing a person, going forward, holding a sword, month, year, rainy day and such other purposes.

**Pātāka Nāyaka**

Denotes the leader of the subsidiary plot.

He is the Hero of the sub-plot. Pithamarda, an associate of Hero in the context of love matters is a Patakanayaka. He is also called a Upanayaka, a secondary Hero. An efficient helpmate of the Hero, Patākānāyaka is just a little inferior to the Hero so far as qualities and achievements are concerned. He is a camp-follower of the Hero, his bosom friend and companion, his Kāma-sachiva.

A fine example of pure pataka or upa-nayaka is to be traced in Bhavabhuti's characterization of Makaranda in the play Malatimadhava where he shows his sincere devotion to his friend, the Hero 'Madhava' and brilliant heroic qualities as well, worthy of a true Hero.

**[see also 'Pitha marda']**

**Paṭa-paṭi**

Means 'Stage curtains', same as hand-held Javanika (Yavanika).

**Pāṭhya**

It denotes

(1) Recitation

(2) The male singer in the theatre ensemble.

In the description of the genesis of 'Natyaveda, it is stated that this fifth Veda was a creation from the four Vedas, the components of Natya suggested are : Pathya, Gita, Abhinaya and Rasa. The Sanskrit dramatic theory leans heavily on Anukriti (Mimetic representation) carried out by appropriate Abhinaya (Acting). Natya is an admixture of experience of sorrow and happiness of all humanity rendered by Abhinaya The Rasa element (emotional experience) maybe referred to the pleasure the spectators derieve from the performance; and the Gita, if it comes as an accompaniment, may be yet another source of enjoyment.

The Pathya element that remains may either be prose speeches (dialogues), or maybe even a series of songs or narraitive recitations that carried the gist of the story and the dramatic action to the spectator, while the actors acted the drama.

**Pathyaguna**

This denotes the attributes of musical rendering. The Shastras have given six factors that govern the rendering of music. They are :-

(I) Svara (musical notes)

(II) Sthana (voice location)

(III) Varna (Ascent)

(IV) Kaku (Effective Modulation of Voice)

(V) Alankara (Embellishment)

(VI) Anga (Speech delivery)

**Pati**

*Rasarnavasudhakara* gives us a categoorization of Nayaka (The Hero) in the context of love into three types: - Pati, Upapati and Vaishika. Pati is one who is married to the woman (or Heroine) according to prescribed religious rites. In his behaviour of love with his wedded wife he may be Anukula, Shatha, Dhrista or Dakṣina.

**[see Nayaka]**

**Pātra - Pravesha**

First entrance of an important dramatis personae.

**Pātrāni**

This cannotes 'Dramatic characters. *Nataka - Laksana - Ratnakosha* mentions that all those who make their appearance on the theatre - stage for some woork or purpose and take their exit from it, are to be termed as 'Pātrāni'. Apart from the Nayaka and Nayika, there are other dramatis personae in secondary, minor or negligiable roles and are somehow associated with dramatic action and thus, make a stage appearance. *Bhavaprakashana* categorize them into three divisions as Dharma - sachiva Artha-Sachiva and Kāma Sachiva.

**Pekkhā**

A show put upon a stage

**Pekkhaghara**

It denotoes 'a theatre House'.

**[see 'Ranga']**

**Phala**

This is the 'fruit' which the leader (neta) or hero desires to achieve for himself in a play or which a playwright designs for the hero's achievement. It could be anything connected with the goals of human life, ie, Purusartha.

**[see also 'Purusartha' and 'Adhikarika Vritta']**

**Phala bhokta**

Hero who is competent to enjoy the fruit of the efforts in a drama is called 'Phala bhokta'.

**Phalagama see Upsamhara - Samdhi**

**Phalaprapti**

Attainment of the fruit of one's desire (in a drama) is called 'Phalaprapti'.

**Pichchhola (Pichchhora)**

This is a wind instrument played by blowing the air through the mouth into the pipe. This device of producing sound in this instrument is technically referred to as 'Upamukha' in the *Shrauta Sutra* of Drahyayana and Lātyāyana.

Pichchhola was used in the recitation of Sāman as a Upagānam, played by the wives of the priests. Another instrument used in the occasion was Kāṇḍavina, collectively called 'Apaghātila'.

**Piṇḍibandha**

Patterns in dance formations made by dancers is 'Pindibandha'.

**Pishaca**

Refers to a goblin, devil, who finds representation in a Sanskrit drama.

Pishachas are also the presiding deities of theatre, according to *Natyashastra*, who should be worshipped with offerings and sacrifices.

**Pishia Vīṇa**

This musical instrument was played in the time of Mahavrata ceremony. It is stated that in the western sides of the Yajñaśālā the Mahaviṇa and Pishilaviṇa were played.

The *Drāhyāyana Shrauta Sutra* mentions about Pishīa Vina.

**Piṭhaka**

This means 'a seat'.

**[see 'Ranga']**

**Pīthamarda**

This denotes a typical type character in a Sanskrit drama who used to be the friend or hanger-on of the hero.

Pithamarda is a bachelor too poor to be a citizen, expert in the art of pleasure, hero's assistant in love

Traditioonal Sanskrit damatic theory attaches more importance to Rasa (or sentiment) than either plot or character. But still it has meticulously dealt with different kind of dramatis personae. Pithamarda refers to the character supporting the hero. He is therefore a friend or ally of the Nayaka (Hero) and the character attributed to him resembles that of the Nayaka.

Generally, the Pithamarda belongs to the Uttama class.

Pithamarda is just a little inferior to the hero so far as qualities and achievements are concerned. He is a camp-follower of the hero, his bosom friend and companion, and for all practical purposes, the equal of the hero or only next to him. That is why he is regarded as a Pataka nayaka, the hero of the sub-plot or Upanayaka, a secondary hero. He is in the forefront as hero's Kama-Sachiva (an associate in love affairs).

*Sahityadarpana* says that a Pithamarda can really be an efficient helpmate of the hero.

According to *Bhavaprakashana,* he is trust worthy, enjoys the confidence of the Hero and he may often play the role of negotiating on behalf of the hero and work to appease the anger of the heroine.

*Nataka - Laksana - Ratnakosha* states that when a Vita attains the position of being a preceptor to a courtesan in the arts of love and those of entertainment he is called Pithamarda. Therefore a playwright, if wishes, can keep the roles of a Pithamarda and a Upanayaka (having brilliant Heroic qualities that makes him a secondary Hero) distinct.

**Plot see Saṁdhīs (Junctureṣ), Vastu, Itivritta etc.**

**Pluta**

In means a protracted duration in music or poetry.

**Prabandha**

This refers to an art song.

**Pracheya see Svaras (Vedic)**

**Prachya**

This is one of the seven principal Prakrita dialects used in the Sanskrit plays.

Thc Vidusaka (Jester) and others speak Prachya, which is hardly different from Shauraseni.

This sub-dialect 'Prachya' was employed by Śudraka in his magnum opus 'Mṛcchakatika'.

**Pragalbha / Praudha Nayika**

According to later theorists of drama, generally there are three types of Heroines.

Pragalbha or Praura Nayika is one of the three subgroups of the main class 'Sviya or Sva' Nayika. She is a mature woman who is in full glory of her youth, is excessive in her passion and thoroughly experienced in the ways of love; in the sport of love she loses herself in the body of her lover, and even the beginning of love-overtures sends her into a swoon of delight. The element of pride makes her also emerge in three further types like Dhira (patient), Adhira (impatient) and Dhiradhira (who balances between patience and impatience).

Nayikas of this class can be again divided into two groups, according as the heroine has the status of a Jyestha or Kaniṣ tha. *Bhavaprakashana* identifies further sub - varities of Pragalbha Nayikas, according as they happen to be Udātta, Lalita or Shanta.

**[see 'Nayika']**

**Prahasana**

This is one of the ten forms of drama, as stated in Traditional Sanskrit Treatise; containing imaginary story. This farcical comedy is categorised into two varities.

(I) **The Shuddha prahasana:** The pure one and the characters include Shaiva gurus (Bhagavat), Brahmins and person belonging to various strata of society appear, each speaking his special dialect or devoting himself to his special calling.

(II) **The Saṅkīrna prahasana:** The dramatis personae in this mixed type comprise of Courtesans, Slaves, Eunuchs, Vita (Parasites), Dhurtas (Rogues) etc. Besides, there is a third kind of Prahasana as follows:-

(III) **The Vikritaprahasana:** This is the distorted type (Vikrita) where Eunuchs and Chamberlains appear as gallants.

Prahasana, or bourgeois comedy in Sanskrit drama focussed on less exalted persons such as ministers, Brahmins, merchants each. It is, infact, a short dramatic piece depicting the tricks and intrigues of various low-class characters.

Mṛcchakaṭika of Sudraka is the most excellent example of this variety.

In this form, the playwright borrows the story from the every day life and incorporates all sorts of illusions, wordy disputes and dissensions between rogues and worthless persons.

The drama *'Hasyacudamani'* is a Prahasana.

**[see also 'Prastavana']**

**Prakarana**

It cannotes two thing, it applies to an introduction, prologue etc and is also a species of drama with invented or fictitious plot.

Prakarana is, infact, one of the major genres of drama (Rupaka) which has close affinity with the Nataka form so far as the junctures, introductory scenes and sentiments are concerned.

Dhananjay's *Daśarupaka* states that the action in Prakarana should be invented and should take place on the earth.

In the Prakarana, all the Vrittis can be employed. The Hero should be a minister, a Brahmin, or a merchant, of the type known as self-controlled and calm (dhira praśanta), undergoing misfortunes and having virtues, the search for pleasure and wealth being his chief objects in life. The story is therefore, conceived by the playwright; the Hero is a Brahmana or a Minister or a Merchant; Sringara (Love) is the dominant rasa; having five to ten acts. The Heroine in prakarana maybe of two types : the high - born wife of the Hero or a courtesan. In some dramas, there is only the high - born woman; in some, only the courtesan; and in some cases, both. High - born women remain indoors, the courtesan outside, and the two should never meet. Due to these varities of Heroine, the Prakarana is of three types.

(I) Shuddhaprakarana (The wife as Heroine)

(II) Vikritaprakarana (The courtesan as Heroine)

(III) Saṅkirnaprakarana (Includes both)

The third mixed category abounds in rogues.

Mṛcchakatika of Śudraka and 'Malatimadhava' of Bhavabhuti are two fine examples of Prakarana variety.

**Prakaraṇa (Music)**

Means "production", a collective term for the *Gītakas.*

**Prakaranika**

This is a minor type of drama (Uparupaka) and according to *Sahityadarpana,* it is a Natika with the Hero and Heroine taken from the rank of Sarthavahas.

**Prakari**

It cannotes various meanings. An interlude or episode inserted in a drama to explain what is to follow is Prakari. It also refers to "Theatrical dress" and may be a "kind of song".

**[see Avamarsa - samdhi]**

**Prakari Nayaka**

He is the 'Leader of the episode' in a drama.

**[see 'Nayaka']**

**Prakasha**

This is an 'open speech', a kind of Natyokti, usual dialogues in a drama which maybe open to all the audiences as well as the characters who are present on the stage at the time are termed as 'Prakasha'.

Prakasha is described in theory as 'Sarvashravya'. *Bhavaprakashana* states that Sarva here refers to 'Sadasyas', ie, the audiences in the theatric house.

**Prakrita see Bhasavidhanam, Vibhasas etc.**

**Prakriti Hatas**

This means Hastas for Nature ; They are:-

(1) **Agni** - fire : *Sandamsha* with one hand touching the body and *chatura or triparaka* at the level of the chest.

(2) **Amalaka** - tree : *Samputa* followed by the *vriksha hasta.*

(3) **Arjuka** - teak tree : *Simhamukha* followed by the *vriksha hasta.*

(4) **Ashoka** - tree : *Pataka* in *swastika* position followed by the *vriksha hasta.*

(5) **Ashvattha** - big tree : *Alapadma* in both hands followed by the *vriksha hasta.*

(6) **Champaka** - flower tree : *Kangula* followed by the *vriksha hasta.*

(7) **Deva-Mantrini** - japakusum flower tree : *Pataka and chatura* crossed at the wrists followed by the *vriksha hasta.*

(8) **Dadhi sagara** - ocean of curds : *Tripataka* in both the hands waving upwards and downward.

(9) **Ganga** - river : *Tamrachooda* followed by the *nadi hasta.*

(10) **Hintala** - palm tree : *Kartareemukha* followed by the *vriksha hasta.*

(11) **Ikshu sagara** - ocean of sugarcane syrup (sweet) : *Alapadma* hands waving upwards and downwards.

(12) **Jambu** - tree : *Ardhapataka* followed by the *vriksha hasta.*

(13) **Kadali** - banana plant : *Mukula* in movement followed by the *vriksha hasta.*

(14) **Kamala** - lotus : *Alapadma hasta.*

(15) **Kapittha** - Elephant apple : *Alapadma* hands joint at the wrists.

(16) **Kaveri** - river : *Chatura* followed by the *nadi hasta.*

(17) **Ketaki** - screw - pine tree : *Pataka* and *chatura* in *swastika* position followed by the *vriksha hasta.*

(18) **Khadira** - thorny tree : *Tamrachooda* bent downwards followed by the *vriksha hasta.*

(19) **Ksheera sagara** - ocean of milk : *Sarpasheersha* in both the hands waving upwards and downwards.

(20) **Kuruvaka** - amarani tree : *Kartareemukha and tripataka* followed by the *vriksha hasta.*

(21) **Lakucha** - grapes : *Kangula hasta.*

(22) **Lavana sagara** - ocean of salt : *Mukula* held upwards and downwards.

(23) **Maha-Meru** - great mountain meru : *Chatura* facing upwards are crossed at the wrists.

(24) **Mandara** - flower tree : *Chatura* in both the hands followed by the *vriksha hasta.*

(25) **Mount Chakravala** - mountain chakravala : *Shikhara* with the left hand held high and revolved round and round the right hand showing *soochi.*

(26) **Mount Kailash** - mountain kailash : *Sikhara* by the left hand extended and ardhachandra with the right hand moved round below.

(27) **Mount Mandara** - mountain mandara : The right hand high showing *pataka, ardhachandra or tripataka and sikhara* with the left hand raised to the same height.

(28) **Mount Meru** - mountain meru : *Kartaree* with the left hand held and *ardhachandra* with the right hand moved round below.

(29) **Nadi** - river : *Hamsasya* brought from above with the movement like waves towards down to indicate river.

(30) **Narangi** - orange tree : *Padmakosha* followed by the *vriksha hasta.*

(31) **Narmada** - river : *Ardhapataka* in movement followed by the *nadi hasta.*

(32) **Nimba** - *neem* (margosa) tree : *Shukatunda* are crossed followed by the *vriksha hasta.*

(33) **Palash** - tree : *Ardhachandra* followed by the *vriksha hasta.*

(34) **Parijata** - flower tree : *Pataka* twisted upwards followed by the *vriksha hasta.*

(35) **Papanashini** - river : *Shukatunda* followed by the *nadi hasta.*

(36) **Phansa** - tree of Jackfruit : *Chatura* followed by the *vriksha hasta.*

(37) **Punnaga** - tree : *Chatura and pataka* followed by the *vriksha hasta.*

(38) **Rasala** - mango tree : *Tripataka* followed by the *vriksha hasta.*

(39) **Samudra** - ocean : *Kataka* at the left chest with the left hand and *tripataka* at the face level with the right hand.

(40) **Saraswati** - river : *Pataka* and *chatura* followed by the *nadi hasta.*

(41) **Sarayu** - river : *Alapadma* followed by the *nadi hasta.*

(42) **Sarpi sagara** - ocean of ghee : *Chatura* hands held upwards and downwards.

(43) **Shala** - sal tree : *Shukatunda* in *swastika* followed by the *vriksha hasta.*

(44) **Shuddhodaka sagara** - ocean of pure water : *Pataka* hand held upwards and downwards to indicate waves.

(45) **Sindhuvara** - tree : *Mayura* in both the hands inter locked followed by the *vriksha hasta.*

(46) **Sura sagara** - ocean of nectar : *Arala and pataka* held upwards and downwards.

(47) **Suvarnamukhi** - river : *Ardhachandra* followed by the *nadi hasta.*

(48) **Tintrini** - tamarind tree : *Kangula hasta* followed by the *vriksha hasta.*

(49) **Tungabhadra** - river : *Hamsasya* followed by the *nadi hasta*.

(50) **Vakula** - crane : *Sandamsha hasta*.

(51) **Vata** - banyan tree : *Pataka* followed by the *vriksha hasta*.

(52) **Vayu** - air : *Arala* in the right hand and *ardhapataka* in the left.

(53) **Vetravati** - river : *Soochi* followed by the *nadi hasta*.

(54) **Vilva** - wood apple : *Chatura hasta*.

(55) **Vriksha** - Tree : *Tripataka* in both the hands facing each other raising upwards from the middle and stretching the hands on sides above the head showing the trunk and the branches.

(56) **Yamuna** - river : *Chandrakala* followed by the *nadi hasta*.

**Praksepya**

This is one of the four kinds of ornaments according to the method of wearing them, states *Natyashastra*. Praksepya covers Nupura (anklets) and such other ornaments. Other kinds are Avedhya, Bandhaniya and Aropya.

**Pralaya**

This refers to "Fainting" (Eighth Sattvika Bhava/Emotional State) which Bharata says, should be simulated by an actor by loss of consciousness, still body, suspended breathing and falling on the ground like dead.

**Pramatha**

According to *Natyashastra* (6, 44), Pramatha is the God of Humour (Hasya rasa), This deity is regarded as an attendant of Shiva.

**Praṇata**

In music, it refers to 'passing from dvitiya svara to tritīya svaras'.

**Prapti (Discovery) see Vagyabhinaya**

**Praptya's see Garbha-Samdhi**

**Prarochana**

It refers to the 'Announcement of the contents or intimations of the contents of a drama.

This is 'Laudation', a part of the prologue.

Infact, the last item of Purvaranga (preliminaries of a play) which is performed on the stage and is preceded by Trigata, an item in which conversation between the Sutradhara, the Vidushaka and a Pariparshvika in which the Vidushaka speaks all kinds of nonsenses. Once 'Trigata' is over, Prarochana, the final item of the twenty constituent parts of Purvaranga commences.

[see also **"Prastavana"**]

**Prasāda see Gunas**

**Prāsaṅgika**

The dramatic plot, according to Bharata, is of two types:

(1) Adhikarika (Principal), and

(2) Prāsaṅgika (Incidental or Subsidiary)

Prāsangika Vritta or the subordinate plot is that which lacks the capacity of the principal plot and only serves as an instrument for the principal accomplishment of the desired fruit (Phala) which the hero desires to achieve for himself, or which a dramatist designs for the hero's achievement in a drama.

Later theorist calls it 'Anga'.

**Prashamsa (simile of Praise) see Alankaras and Upama**

**Prashnikas**

An assessor in the drama competition is called 'Prashnika'.

Prashnikas are 'Critics of dramatic performance', the arbitrators [Pañca].

*Bhavaprakashana* has added two names in the list of the judges as prescribed by Bharata. These are *Nripa* and *Istartha*. *Nripa* is included to assess the royal qualities of greatness, the King's pleasures in love, heroism, activities in the harem and the King's life. *Istartha* denotes a Bard to judge the praises and songs addressed to the Royal hero. *Bhavaprakashana* has omitted '*Astravid*, ie, the expert in missiles and weapons, given by Bharata.

**[see "Siddhis"]**

**Prasiddhi (Celebrity) see Vagyabhinaya**

**Prastavana**

It denotes the 'Prologue' of the play. Bhārativritti or in otherwords the constituents of prologue are Prarochana (Inducement), Prahasana (Comedy) Vithi (series and Amukha (Commencement). In Prarochana audience is invited to witness the performance which would minister to their delight, is process of stimulation of expectancy in the spectator by the glorification of the dramatist or the theme of the play to be enacted.

The second element adopted in Bharatavritti is Prahasana which is figured in the introduction of the play contains only some jocular remark or witty dialogue or satrical expression to provide comic relief.

All the authors in the field of science of drama recommended that Vithi be included int he Prastavana. In all there are thirteen sub-divisions of Vithi called the Vithyanga. Notable are:-

(1) Asatpralāpa (Useless chatter)

(2) Vakkeli (Repartee)

(3) Adhibala (Over - powering)

(4) Chala (Deception)

(5) Mridava (Softening or mild interchange)

(6) Trigata (Triple explanation or known to three)

(7) Ganda (Abrupt remark)

Amukha denotes 'commencement', the last element of Bharatavritti. In old plays, Amuka was in existence as Sthapana. But in later period, it came to be designated by the more familiar term 'Prastavana' (prologue). This Amukha or Prastavana, according to *Natyashastra*, is a piece of delibeations between either Nati or Pariparsvaka on one side and Sutradhara on the other.

It gives information about the ensuing drama. The Amukha can be categorized into five divisions:-

(1) **Kathodghata:** (An abrupt opening of the story; here a reference is made to a point in the story of the drama by the Sutradhara which is taken up by a character who enters and the actual drama starts.

(2) **Udghatyaka (Opener)**

(3) **Avalagita (Link)**

(4) **Prayogatisaya: (Excellent contrivance)** This is the employment of a Prayoga (Science, situation, theme) when another is already on made by Sutradhara, leading to the entry of an actor.

(5) **Pravrittaka (Induction):** In this type of Amukha a situation relevant to the matter in hand is being told by the Sutradhara and the same is taken up by actor who immediately enters to commence the play proper.

## Prasthana (Prasthanaka)

A minor form of drama (Uparupaka), the Prasthana or Prasthanaka contains two acts. The *Avaloka* on *Dasharupa* states that the Prashthana is a kind of imitative dance (Nrityabheda).

## Pratihari

In Sanskrit dramas, they denotes the female guards of the royal harem.

They are the prominent attendants of the Royal Hero in the Sanskrit drama in which they appear as a guard of the entrance to the Royal Chamber, whether in the Palace or outside in a temporary camp. A Pratihari reports and announces all the arrivals to the King, deliver and carries informations and remains ever alert at her post at the entrance - gate.

According to of Bharata, the principle duty of a Prathari is to inform the King about all happenings relating to the political matters of war and peace and issues arising out of social dealings and religious or cultural connections.

**Pratimukha - Samdhi**

According to Sanskrit dramatic theory, the plot of a drama is divided into five divisions which it terms 'Samdhi' or Junctures. Pratimukha - Samdhi is the second Juncture that occur after Mukha - Samdhi. Bharata describes this juncture as the disclosing of; the seed visible and now invisible. The Bija (seed) which gets deeply embedded in the previous Samdhi is now brought to view in this juncture, ie, the seed of the plot has to grow in order to develop towards its fulfilment which calls for possitive effort or Yatna which may or may not be successful. Here the Artha - prakriti (essential element of the plot) is *Bindu* serves to continue the main theme, arises either as a result of anger (Mānaja or Krodhaja) or some misfortune (Vipattija).

**Pratinayaka**

Denotes a villain in a Sanskrit drama, the character use to be courageous and resourceful, is none the less violent, stubborn and wicked.

According to traditional Sanskrit treatises, Pratinayaka is the rival of the hero. In modern context, he can be called a villain, being greedy, haughty, stiff, an addict and sinful. The Nayaka or hero has to struggle against the viles and the strategems and all other resources of this hostile rival. Therefore, the most important male character after the hero is Pratinayaka.

**Pravesha**

This means 'entry on the stage'.

**Praveshaka**

This is a linking device, introductory scene of an act.

**[see "Anthopakshepakas"]**

**Prativeshika**

Dhananjaya in his '*Daśarupaka*' defines this female character as neighbour, married matron from the next house (as associate of the Heroine).

**Pratyāhara**

This is the first constituent parts of a Purvaranga (Preliminaries of a play) done behind the curtain. Bringing in of the Kutapa (the musical instruments) is called 'Pratyāhāra'.

**Pratyanga**

This denotes expressions through other limbs of the body. According to *Abhinaya Darpana*, they are Skandha bheda, Bahu bheda, Prishta bheda, Udara bheda, Jangha bheda, Uru bheda, Manibandha bheda, Jagu bheda, Janu bheda and Griva bheda.

**Pratyutkrama**

Means 'leaving one note in between two notes in the ascending order; similar to dhātu svara of Karnatic music. One of the Avantara svaras.

**Pravesha**

This refers to one of the four silent Tāla gestures (right palm down with fingers closed).

**Pravistakam**

Means 'Entrance on the stage'.

**Pravrittakam**

It means 'Entrance on the stage'.

**Pravritti**

It refers to local colour in drama. Bharata prescribed that the dramatists should make his players follow the speech, dress, manners and conduct that are theirs.

Literally it cannotes Appearance, manifestation, conduct; behaviour etc. In stage production, Bharata has stressed that there is a fourfold distinction in the way of people which he termed 'Pravritti'. People of different countries are distinguished by the dress, language, costume etc. So he categorized them into four as Southern (Daksinatya), Western (Avanti), Northern (Panchali) and Eastern (Goudramagadhi) therefore a performance must follow the style and the Vritti current in the customs of people of the region in which the drama is to be enacted.

Chapter XIV of *Natyashastra* deals with this Pravritti or the local usages.

Even in one of the verses in Chapter VI of *Natyashastra*, Bharata has furnished eleven elements of Drama which can be collectively called the 'Digest of Natyashastra. These significant dramatic components are :-

Rasa (Sentiment)

Bhava (Emotion)

Abhinaya (Acting)

Dharmi (Modes of representation)

Vritti (Styles of expression)

Pravritti (Local usages)

Siddhi (Success of production)

Svara (Note)

Atodya (Musical instruments)

Gana (Song)

Ranga (Theatre)

Pravritti is, therefore, a very essential element in dramatic representation and classical theory gives stress on this 'Regional modes of a play production'.

**Prayoga**

It denotes 'production'. In the context of drama, Bharata asks "what is Prayoga?" He himself answers 'It is the union of song, instrument and action', if one has to produce a drama.

A combination of vocal music, instrument accompaniment and dance is known as 'Prayoga'. The song should begin first, followed by instruments and the dance movements follow thereafter.

**Prekṣhagriha**

Denotes a theatre, mentioned in Bharata's *Natyashastra* (2.7)

**[see "Ranga"]**

**Prekṣaka**

It denotes 'Spectator' of a drama.

**Preṅkhaṇa**

This is a form of minor drama having one - act with no Sutradhara (Stage - Manager) in it. According to *Sahityadarpana,* the Nandi and Prarochana are sung behind the curtain.

**Priccha (Interrogation) see Vagyabhinaya**

**Prishtha and Udara bheda**

This denotes the movements of the belly and back and are of three types :-

(1) **Kshama** (pulled inside): To express 'laughing, weeping, deep breathing and yawning.

(2) **Khalva** (bent): To express 'sickness, meditation tiredness due to penance and hunger.

(3) **Purna** (full belly): To express 'inhaling, fatness, sickness.

**Priye**

This means 'My dear'. Bharata in his Natyashastra has given a set of words for addressing the different characters according to their position. The wife is often called 'Priye' in an erotic sentiment, a convention followed in Sanskrit plays.

**Priyokti (Compliment) see Vagyabhinaya**

**Prologue see Prastavana**

**Prositabhartrika Nayika**

Bharata's treatise mentions eight varities of Heroine - in - love and Prositabhartrika Nayika is one of them. *Dasarupaka* defines her as 'one separated from her husband who is away on a journey'. The Hero might have gone on the journey in order to earn, or to fulfill his duty towards the King or his master. So such type of Heroine is not engulfed by doubt or jealousy and is in a better stage, but the separation makes her sad. She cannot enjoy anything, and passes her time in great anguish.

**[see also 'Nayika']**

**Purohita**

This refers to a King's official or family priest, an important associate of the Royal hero in a Sanskrit drama. He is called 'Dharma-sachiva' and *Bhava - prakasana* also describe him as Narma - sachiva.

**Purusartha**

Four main goals of human existence recognised by ancient Indian society (Artha, Kāma, Dharma, Mokṣa), also known as 'Chaturvarga sādhana'.

*Agnipurana* and *Nataka - Laksana - Ratnakosha* state that Natya is a means of achieving the three goals : piety (dharma) wealth or prosperity (Artha), and pleasure or love (Kāma). This achievement ie the goal of human life or Purusartha is shown through the plot or the story of a drama and by means of the actions the hero under takes or which some one executes for him.

**[see also: "Nayaka" 'Dharmaphala", "Kama" and "Artha"].**

**Purvaranga**

This is the pre-performance rituals of a dramatic troupe; preliminaries.

Bharata's *Natyashastra* has laid down that a dramatic presentation should always be preceded by a set of preliminaries (preliminary rituals) most of which are of a religious or devotional nature. This entire set of ceremonies is called 'Purvaranga' which is intended to propitiate various gods and also to entertain the spectators, on the whole an altogether external preliminary to the stanging of a dramatic composition.

Purvaranga, therefore, refers to these series of introducing items before the actual presentation of a Sanskritd drama. Usually the play proper is preceded by a session of instrumental music, songs and dances, sometimes very lengthy and complicated including certain ritual act of worship and prayers to the gods.

According to Bharata, there are twenty different constituent parts of a purvaranga, the first nine are presented off stage (behind the curtain) and the rest on the stage. They are the part of a regular Purvaranga.

These are:-

(*Pratyāhāra,* bringing in of the musical instruments [*kutapa*]; *avataraṇa,* placing of singers [*gāyaka*]; *āraṁbha,* beginning of the rehearsal song of the chorus; *āśrāvaṇā,* tuning of instruments which are played upon the striking [*ātodya*]; *vaktrapāṇi,* tuning of the wind instruments [*vādya*]; *parighaṭṭ anā,* tuning of the stringed instrument [*tantrī*]; *saṁghoṭanā* meant for rehearsing the use of different hand poses for indicating the time-beat; *mārgāsārita,* playing together of different instruments; *āsārita,* entrance and practice of the dancing girls:- All these are done behind the curtain.

The parts of the *Pūrvaraṅga* performed on the stage are :- *gīta*, song in praise of gods and then *utthāpana*, song on the setting up of the banner of Indra [*jarjara*]. Here the *sūtradhāra* appears, followed by two *pāripārśvikas* who carry a water jug [*bhṛṅgāra*] and the banner of Indra. The *sutradhāra* strews flowers, brings in Indra's banner and cleanses himself with the water of the jug. After this, is performed *parivartana,* stalking round the stage with praise of the guardians of the world [*dikpālastuti*] and adoration of Indra's banner [*jarjarapūjā*]. *Nāndī,* praise or a benediction is next recited by the *sūtradhāra* in a middling tone. It consists of 12 or 8 *pādas* and after each *pāda*, both the *pāripārśvikas* say *evamastu* [so be it]. Then follow *vardhamāna,* an increasing intensity of *tāṇḍava* [manly dance]; *śuṣkāvakṛṣṭa,* an introduction in which the *sūtradhāra* recites some verses in a sonorous voice; the *jarjaraślokas,* in praise of the god whose worship is being celebrated, or in praise of a king or of Brahmā; *raṅgadvāra,* when the play [*abhinaya*] begins, the *sūtradhāra* recites a new verse and bows before Indra's banner [*jarjara*]; *cārī,* different paces and gestures with an erotic sense; *mahācārī*, similar paces, but more impetuous in degree; *trigata,* conversation between the *sūtradhāra,* the *vidūṣaka* and a *pāripārśvika* in which the *vidūṣ aka* speaks all kinds of nonsense; *prarocanā,* announcement of the contents.

These are the constituent parts of a regular *pūrvaraṅga* or a *caturasra pūrvaraṅga.* The *tryasra pūrvaraṅga* is similar but shortened, while in the *citra* [variegated] *pūrvaraṅga* strewing of flowers and dance of the gods etc. are included.

In short, Purbaranga denotes the performance of the preliminaries before the actual enactment of the play as prescribed by the classical texts an Sanskrit dramatic theory.

**Pushpaputa Hasta**

This is a double hand gesture in which the two hands in *sarpaseersha* are joined on the side with the palms facing upwards.

Used in the "offering of camphor to the imge of a god, an act of adoration, taking of water, fruit, etc. prayers (*sandhya)*, offerings to Gods, and a flower-offering with chanting of *mantra.*" This gesture in Indian dance also indicates carrying of corn.

**Pusta**

It means "the model work". Bharata regards Aharya as the third variety of acting (abhinaya) which is produced through nepathya and by nepathya he means four things, viz, Pusta, Alankara, Angarachana and Sanjiva. He explains apart from costumes, dresses and ornaments all that is required by character as distinctive of its individuality is called 'Pusta'. This comprises of masks, weapons, totems and such other stage objects that go and are naturally linked with a character. For e.g. a mace with Bhima or a bow and arrow with Arjuna in Mahabharata plays.

Therefore, objects like mountains, chariots, aeroplanes etc that are made from cloth or leather, etc, to be used in a drama are called 'Pusta' (XXI, 9).

Again, the Pusta should be of three kinds:-

(I) **Samdhima,** ie, where the mountains and cars, etc are made of cloth or leather.

(II) **Vyajima**, ie, the kind that are made by some kind of mechanical device, and

(III) **Chestima** means where these are shown by means of gestures.

Bharata opines that any object in the actual world, when represented in a drama, must be presented with all its characteristics (XXI, 101) Not only that, for the sake of sustaining the illusion that the object is real it must be made in proper proportion (XXI, 155).

Bharata admits that it is not possible to reproduce stage objects exactly as they are in real life though it is of utmost importance to make them look outwardly extremely similar to the original and they should be made of such material that on the stage it should be portable, ie, easy to carry them They could be made of hollow bamboos and cloth and never from iron or any heavy materials.

*Natyashastra* (XXI, 190 - 97) states that even objects like mountains, mansions, temples, idols etc, could be made out of lacquer or cloth or hollow bamboos or leathers, etc. Such objects must be light (Laghu)j and not heavy (Guru).

As for weapons, they are not meant for actual use like breaking or beating, etc, but are intended to be used symbolically (XXI, 212).

Pusta, therefore denotes 'Model work', small, light weight cutouts of artificial objects used in a dramatic performance.

**Pusya see Rangapuja**

**Putabheda**

This means the movements of the eyelid and are of nine kinds. They are :-

(1) Unmesha (separated)

(2) Nimesha (closed together)

(3) Prasrita (spread or expanded)

(4) Kunchita (contracted)

(5) Sama (natural)

(6) Vivartita (raised up)

(7) Sphurita (trembling)

(8) Pihita (closed)

(9) Vitadita (motionless)

**Putraka see Vatsa**

# R

## Raga

Rāga is a melodic frame work, mode a musical mode or sequence; harmony; melody ; a musical note (as falling within a particular Rāga). The woird Rāga comes from the Sanskrit verb 'Rañj', *i.e.,* which colours the mind, or in other words, which delights it. But besides this general meaning of the term Rāga, it has precise meaning as a musical term.

Raga is the basis of Indian melody. Indian music is built on the Raga and Tala concepts. The word Raga comes from the Sanskrit root meaning "to colour", the basic idea being that certain melodic shapes produce a continuity of emotional experience and "colour" the mind.

Since neither the melodic shapes nor their sequence are fixed precisely the Raga serves as a basis for composition and improvisation which is a characteristic of Indian music.

We may refer, in this connection, to the two versions of the story about the origin of music to be found in the old works on music. The first claims that Rāgas emanated from Śiva, who represents the transition from chaos, five emanated from the five mouths of Lord Śiva and one from that of his consort. The other version has a more significant implication. According to it Śrī Kṛṣṇa, who is the fountainhead of all Bhāvas and Rasas, once played his divine flute and the result was that every one of the innumerable Gopīs who represented one particular Bhāva and Rasa became inspired and song before the Lord, there by creating one particular Rāga. That Rāga is the representation in sound of a particular emotion giving rise to a particular feeling is amply supported by this mythological story.

Raga as said earlier is the basis of melody in our music. The notes which are to convey certain definite emotions or ideas must be carefully selected from the 22 intervals of the Shruti scale and then grouped to form a mode, a Rāga. According to *Sangitaratnakara* it is defined as an arrangement of sounds, which possesses Varṇa (melodic movement), furnishes gratification to the senses and is constituted by musical notes.

A combination of Svaras is called Grama. Raga (modes) necessarily depend upon two Gramas and are mainly produced from Sadja Grama.

According to traditional musical norms, there are three important notes in the Raga, namely, Graha, Aṁsha and Nyāsa. *Sangitaratnakara* describes Graha as the starting note, the Aṁsha as the predominant and Nyāsa as the ending note. Amsha is considered the most important and infact the soul of the Raga. Sharangadeva in this treatise identifies the Amsha, the main note, with the sonant, the Vādi. In his words : Because it is most used during a performance, the Vādī (sonant) is called Amsha main note. *Abhinavabharati* of Abhinavagupta exprresses the same view. The Amsha svara is the same as the Vādī. All the characteristics of the Rāga are embodied in its Murcchana or Ṭhāṭa.

In all, the sage Narada accepted 58 Ragas, out of which 21 are Masculine, 24 are feminine and the rest 13 are Neuter Ragas. These are :-

**Masculine Ragas are :**Darbari, Bangal, Soma - raag, Shree Raag, Bhoopali, Chhaya-Gaud, Andoli, Dombuli, Shuddha-Hindola, Gaud, Phadamamji, Suddha-Nati, Raagaranga, Maalabagaula,

Chhayanata, Kolaahala, Saurashtra, Vasanta, Shuddha Saaranga, Raagadwahni, Karanaat.

**Feminine Ragas are :** Thundi, Turashka-Tundi, Malwari, Maahuri, Pauralika, Kambhari, Bhallati, Saindhavi, Saalanga, Gaandhari, Devakri, Desi, Velavali, Bahuli, Gunkari, Dhurjari, Varaathi, Darbari, Hamsi, Gaudi, Naarayani, Ahari, Megharanjani, Mishra Nata, Bhairavi; and

**Neuter Ragas are :** Kaushiki, Lalita, Dhanashri, Kurunji, Saurashtri, Shuddha Darbari, Naagavarathika, Kamodi, Ramakri, Saaveri, Badahamsa, Saamavedi, Sankarabharanam,

According to him, Ragas that are to be sung **three hours before the sunrise** are :

Deshaakshi, Shuddha-Bhairavi, Varatika, Shuddha-Dravetika;

**Ragas in the morning are:** Gandhara, Devagandhara, Dhannyasi, Saindhavi, Naarayani, Gurjari, Bangal, Patamanjari, Lalita, Hindola, Shree, Saurashtra, Malhar, Saamavadi, Vasanta, Shuddha-Bhairava, Velavali, Soma-Raag;

**Ragas at mid-day are:** Shankaraa-Bharanam, Badahamsa, Desi, Manohaari, Saaveri, Dombuli, Kambhoji, Gopi-Kambhoji, Kaushiki, Madhumadhavi, Baahuli, Mukhari, Kaushiki;

**Ragas in the evening are:** Shuddha-Naata, Saalanga, Naati, Shuddha-Varatika, Gauda, Maalava-Gaula, Shree-Raag, Ahari, Raamakriti, Ramji, Chhaya, Sarva-Varatika, Varatika, Dravatika, Bhoopali, Desi, Naaga-Varatika, Karnaat, Haya-Gauda;

**Ragas that are sung three hours after sunset** are:- Malhaari, Maahuri, Andoli, Raamakriti, Chhayanat

His classification of Ragas are according to Hindustani style. He further devides Ragas into three groups, according to the use of notes in them such as

(I) *Sampurna,* a raga having all the seven notes. These are fourteen in number :- (Deshakh, Maddhayamadi, Vasanta, Bhairavi, Shuddha - Bhairavi, Shuddha Vasanta, Varatika, Nata Raag, Mālavi, Badahamsa, Mukhari, Ahari, Ramakriya, Gandhari)

(II) *Shadava* - a raga having six notes only; and

(III) *Udava* - a raga having 5 notes only.

Presently we have about three hundred varities in Raga of which a hundred are common. The Ragas are categorised in many ways. The time to sing (Time classification) is strictly followed in Hindustani style; and not so much in Karnataka style of music. Apart from this parameter Ragas may be classified by their aesthetic qualities, scientific capabalities, individual characters, pleasing capacities, seasons, regions and so on.

However the six basic Ragas are :-

(I) Bhairava (suitable for performance at dawn and is associated with awe and fear).

(II) Megha ( to be performed in the morning and is associated with peace and calm)

(III) Dipaka (to be performed in the afternoon; and is associated with love)

(IV) Striraga (to be performed in the afternoon and is associated with love)

(V) Kausika (to be performed at night and is associated with joy and laughter)

(IV) Hindola (to be performed at night, and is associated with love)

A *raga* is a melodic idea capable of elaboration and improvisation. The rules of grammar of a *raga* are:-

1. It has a definite set of notes which are its alphabet.

2. The minimum number of notes for a *raga* is five and maximum nine. There are however, exceptions.
3. It has a permitted manner of ascent (*arohana*) and descent, (*avarohana*).
4. A *raga* uses characteristic melodic units *(pakad, chalan, tan, sanchara or varna*).
5. Certain *svaras* in its alphabet find emphasis to varying degrees (*vadi, samvadi, anuvadi*). Melodic sections commence and end on defined notes (*graha and nyasa*).
6. While there are graces and accents common to all *ragas,* most of them have *gamakas* all their own, which give them distinctive qualities.

Even when two ragas have the same notes, they may differ in the use of the sharps and flats or the more delicately shaded microtonal variants.

**Ragas see also Jatis**

**Ragdari**

It means having, or following, Rāga : the Indian classical style of singing.

**Ragini**

It's a modification of a main musical mode or Rāga, thought of as a feminine personification.

Raginis are derived from six basic Ragas namely Bhairava, Megha, Dipaka, Sriraga, Kausika, and Hindola. They are personified as wives of the masculine Ragas.

**Rajajivi (Vidusaka) see Vidusaka**

**Rajaka**

The Natyashastra refers to some Acharyas who are expert in preparing materials for the stage. There are many typesof artisans seem to have been necessary in the presentation of plays.

The Rajaka is one who dyes the dresses for the characters in a play.

**Rajan**

It means 'King'. Bharata has prescribed a set of words for calling the different charactes according to their positions in Sanskrit plays Kings were called by Brahmanas at their pleasure by their names. Risis (sages) addressed them as 'Rajan'. He was called 'Deva', ie, Lord by servants and people in general, and as 'Bhatta' (Prakrit form of 'Bharata') (sire) by members of his harem.

**Rajasika**

Means 'Worldly', one of the three main types of characters in Indian drama. Other being Satvika (Godly) and Tamasika (evil-minded).

**Rakṣasa**

They are the descendent of non-Aryan seer Pulatsya, a non-Aryan class.

Rakshasa means 'Infernal, demonical' 'Rakshasah' is an evil spirit, a demon, a vampire, a fiend, but who appears to be of various descriptions, and is either a powerful Titan or enemy of the gods in a super human or incarnate form, as Ravana and others; an attendant on Kuvera, and guardian of his treasures; or a mischievous and cruel goblin or ogre, haunting cemeteries, animating dead bodies, and devouring human being etc.

In the context of drama, it denotes such characters represented in a dramatic composition. *Natyashastra* states that those who are fat and tall, whose voice was deep like thunder and who had terrifying eyes, eyebrows and faces, were selected for the roles of Rakshas, Danavas, and Daityas. The Aviddha type of performances which is full of war were to be done by them, as they were violent by nature and full of vigour. Such characters are seen in Dima, Samavakara, Vyayoga and Ihamriga etc.

**Rakṣasa Hastas**

It denotes the 'Hastas for demon' to depict any evil character. The *Shataka Hasta* are held on both sides of the face, near the eyes in Indian dance.

**Ranga**

Refers to stage, theatre, play house mentioned in *Natyashastra* (2.1).

Bharata used various terminologies while dealing with theatre-house. He uses words like

(1) Natya Vesma
(2) Natya - Griha
(3) Natya - Mandapa.

All the above terms denote an entire play house. Again he uses

(1) Ranga shala
(2) Ranga bhumi
(3) Ranga - mandapa.

Rangashala and Ranga mandapa would mean like an auditorium, while Rangabhumi would mean 'stage'.

He also employs the word 'Preksyagriha' it denotes an auditorium like Rangashala and Rangamandapa.

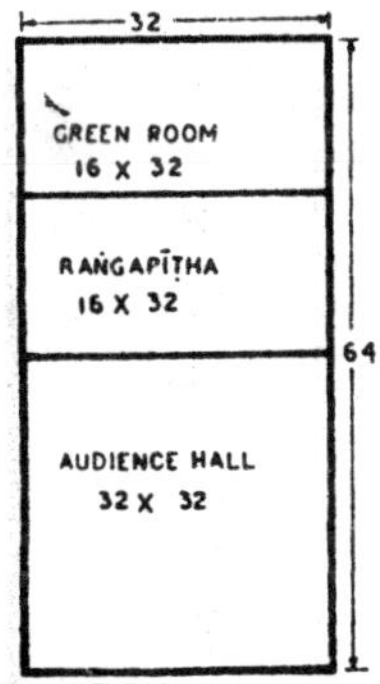


**Division of Theatre : (Bharata)**

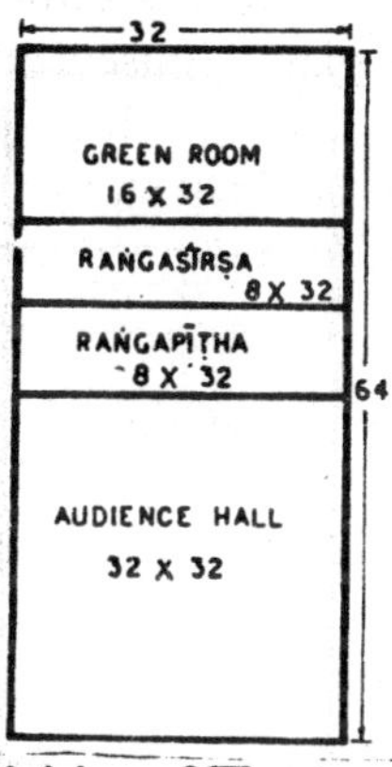


**Division of Theatre : (Abhinavagupta )**

According to *Natyashastra*, there are three types of play - house Vikrista [Rectangular], Chaturasra [Square] and Tryasra [Triangular]. Here we find two opinions about the varieties of theatres.

(I) According to one, Vikrista is Jyestha, Chaturasra is Madhya and Tryasra is Avara. Jyestha type is specially meant for gods Madhya for kings and Avara for ordinary people Jyestha theatre, Abhinayagupta opines, should be used for dramas where gods are Heroes, as in Dima, the Madhya when kings are Heroes, as in Prakarana, and the Avara when ordinary men are Heroes as in Bhana and Prahasana.

(II) Another school divides each of the first type into Jyestha, Madhya and Avara. ie,

| | |
|---|---|
| Vikrista | Jyestha |
| | Madhya |
| | Avara |
| Chaturasra | Jyestha |
| | Madhya |
| | Avara |
| Tryasra | Jyestha |
| | Madhya |
| | Avara |

In this we get nine types.

The *Shilparatna* and the *Bhavaprakashana* also agree that the play - house as made ready for performance maybe of three types, ie, Rectangular, Square and Triangular. The *Vishnudhamottara* states that the theatre might be of two types, Rectangular and square.

In one of the verses in Chapter VI of *Natyashastra*, Bharata has furnished eleven elements of Drama which collectively be called the '*Digest of Natyashastra*. These significant dramatic components are:-

Rasa (Sentiment)
Bhava (Emotion)
Abhinaya (Acting)
Dharmi (Modes of representation)
Vritti (Styles of expression)
Pravritti (Local usages)
Siddhi (Success of production)
Svara (Note)
Atodya (Musical instruments)
Gana (Song)
Ranga (Theatre)

Natyashastra has dealt elaborately with 'Ranga', one most essential component of dramatic art. Infact the whole second chapter of *Natyashastra* by Bharata contains one hundred and five stanzas giving an account of different types of theatres (Natyamandapa), its dimensions and layouts as well as information on the construction of walls, columns, roof, their decorations the seating arrangement in the audience - hall, numbers and locations of doors, etc

Bharata has dealt at length about the construction of a theatre house. The producers of a play must first scrutinize the site which should be "level firm, hard, black or white soil". The suitability of soils is further decided after examining its colour, smell, sound and temperature. The layout of the theatre should be given on as auspicious day for which a white cord be used (*Natyashastra* 2.27), made of cotton, barks of a tree or munja or Balbaja grass. Site should be cleared of all rubbish (like bones, skeletons, etc) and shrubber, and then measurement laid out. He furnishes a number of ritual ceremonies, superstitions omens, etc. After throughly observing all these, a plot 64x32 measures should be laid out. The length of 64 should be divided into two equal halves of 32x32 and another 32x32, one for the Auditorium and the other for stage purposes.

The theatre, according to *Natyashastra* is a Beam and Column structure. In all, there are 32 numbers of columns. If we adhere to the Bharata's specifications four columns should be placed at four corners of the theatre. They are the Brahmana column, Ksatriya Column, Vaishya Column and the Shudra Columns beginning at the South-East corner and ending at the North-West corner. The theatre should be enclosed by walls on all the four sides. The load of the roof is to be taken by columns and not by wall. In the stanza 2.95 of *Natyashastra*, Bharata states that columns should be strong enough to take load coming from Beams. As walls are not load-bearing, some columns are located in walls also.

Mattavarani (the Railing) divides the theatre in two equal divisions. There are four columns along the Mattavarani, out of which two are embedded in walls and the other two are located at the distance of Eight Hastas from walls. The distance between these columns is 16 Hastas. The Rangashirsa, thus, have a clear space 16 Hastas long and 8 Hastas broad, without any hindrance from columns. On the stage, there is an additional ten number of columns, as stated in the stanza 2.98 - 89-1/2 of the *Natyashastra*.

Bharata, further mentions that in the Audience - Hall, there should be 14 columns (Natyashastra 2.92-93). Of which 6 columns in the Audience Hall and 8 additional columns around them.

Bharata has given specification for the three different types of theatres. In a Rectangular theatre, there should be two doors for entering the Rangashirsa from the Green-Room (stanza 2.69). He, however does not, furnish information on the location of doors of this type. But there should be a door in the western wall for the entry of characters from outside into the Green-Room, as given in the case of the Triangular theatre (stanza 2.103).

For the Square-shaped theatre, one door maybe provided at the eastern wall for the entry of characters from outside into Audience - Hall. (Stanza 2.97). Thus there are four doors provided in the Rectangular theatre. For square type theatre, there should be only one door for entering the stage from the Green-Room. Therefore, there should be only three doors in this type. These minimum numbers of doors may also be provided to the Triangle - shaped theatre.

According to Abhinavagupta, there should be two doors linking the stage with the Green-Room; irrespective of the shape of the theatre.

Bharata's stage is, therefore, divided into three comparments.

(I) The Nepathya - griha

(II) The Rangashirsa

(III) The Rangapitha.

There are two doors from Nepathyagriha to the stage, one is used only for actors coming right up to the front on the Rangapitha (Characters low in status) and the other exclusively as an entry to the Rangashirsa for higher characters like the Hero or the Heroine etc. In the centre of these two doors, musical instruments are placed.

*Natyashastra* mentions that the height of the theatre should be equal to that of the two storeyed building. A second floor is not provided either above the stage or the audience - hall. The theatre should have two storeys (*Natyashastra* 2.80) According to Abhinavagupta "the ground on which the Rangapitha or the theatre is standing is one floor and the other floor is the surface of the Rangapitha ie Rangashirsa which is at the higher level than the ground. The theatre has one flour and another floor is that part of the stage where a small mandapa is located in which a dancer dances, or the step-like arrangement of seats in the audience-hall is the second floor.

Bharata's *Natyashastra* in the stanza 2.79-1/2 mentions that the shape of the roof of the theatre should be like that of a cave in a mountain. This means the roof should be flat being curved near the edge on all the four sides where it meets the walls; or may be it is shaped like a barrel-vault. This description fits very wells to the Buddhist chaityas excavated at Nasik, Ajanta, Ellora etc.

Auditorium (Natyamandapa) should be in the shape of a hillock or a cave and of two levels with lattices or small windows, without any strong breeze and one where the voice is loudly carried. Thus according to Bharata, like stage, the Auditorium too is equally important.

Bharata prescribes the step-like seating arrangement in the audience-hall and states that seats should be made of bricks and wooden planks (*Natyashastra* 2.90-1/2) seats in the audience-hall should be one hasta broad and one hasta in height and arranged like steps of a stair case, so that audience sitting on these seats should face the stage (*Natyashastra* 2.91-91-1/2). There should be the distance of eight hastas between the stage and the first step of the seating arrangement in the audience - hall. The total height of the step - like arrangement should be 8 hastas (2-94).

The seating arrangement, in the square-shaped theatre is 32 hastas long and 8 hastas Broad. The eastern most step is at the height of 8 hastas from the top of the plinth. Excepting the first row of steps, people sitting in the audience - hall should have their seats at a higher level than that of the Rangashirsa.

Measurement for the building of theatres, according to Natyashastra is based upon the conceptionof Hasta and Danda. It states that the smallest measure is Anu (Atom) and eight Anus make one Raja (Cardust), eight Rajas one Bāla (Hairend), eight Bālas one Likṣā (Nit), eight Likṣās one Yuka (Louse), eight Yukas one Yava (Barley), eight Yavas one Angula, 24 Angulas one Hasta, four Hastas one Danda. This list greatly matches with one mentioned in Kautilya's Arthashastra.

According to Bharata, A theatre should be divided in two main parts of equal length, the eastern and the western parts, the theatre being oriented along the east-west (*Natyashastra* 2.33). The sixteen hastas long and 32 hastas broad part at the extreme west end is meant for the 'Green-Room'. The remaining part 16 hastas long and 32 hastas broad is meant for a stage (*Natyashastra* 2.34-35).

The Audience-hall is a square of 32x32 hastas, on the east side.

Separate area is not alowed to the Rangasirsa other than meant for the Rangapitha. Therefore no space for Rangapitha and the Mattavarani (Fig.1).

Dimensions of theatres are given in Hastas (24 Angulas) as well as in Dandas (96 Angulas). But theatres are constructed in the measure of Hasta.

The following table gives dimensions in hastas, of all the nine varities of theatres alongwith the utility of each of them according to Vishveshvara as follows :-

**Dimensions of Theatres**

| Shape (stanza 8) | Type | Dimensions (Hastas) (stanzas 9-10) | Utility (stanza 11) |
|---|---|---|---|
| Rectangular | Large | 108x64 | for gods |
| | middle | 64x32 | for kings |
| | small | 32x16 | for public |
| Square | large | 108x108 | for gods |
| | middle | 64x64 | for kings |
| | small | 32x32 | for public |
| Triangular (equilateral) | large | 108 | for gods |
| | middle | 64 | for kings |
| | small | 32 | for public |

The following table furnishes dimensions of different types of theatres in the Hasta and the Danda measures as corresponding metre measure :-

**Dimensions of Theatres**

| Shape | Type | Hastas or Daṇḍas | meters (1 hasta = 24 angulas) | meters (1 hasta = 96 angulas) |
|---|---|---|---|---|
| Rectangular | large | 108.00x64.00 | 49.25x29.62 | 197.00x117.00 |
| | middle | 64.00x32.00 | 29.62x14.81 | 117.00x59.24 |
| | small | 32.00x16.00 | 14.81x7.40 | 59.24x29.60 |
| Square | large | 108.00x108.00 | 49.25x49.25 | 197.00x197.00 |
| | middle | 64.00x64.00 | 29.62x29.62 | 117.00x117.00 |
| | small | 32.00x32.00 | 14.81x14.81 | 59.24x59.24 |
| Triangular | large | 108.00 | 49.25 | 197.00 |
| (equilateral) | middle | 64.00 | 29.62 | 117.00 |
| | small | 32.00 | 14.81 | 59.24 |

**[see 'Rangashirsa', Rangapitha, Mattavarani, Rangapuja, Pusya etc].**

**Ranga - ājivah**

Denotes an actor.

**Ranga - anganam**

Arena an amphitheatre.

**Ranga - avataranam**

It denotes "Entrance on the stage" and also "An actor's profession".

**Ranga - avatarin**

Denotes 'An actor'

**Ranga - charah**

An actor, a player.

**Ranga - daivata - Pujana see Ranga-devata**

**Ranga devata**

Nataraja is regarded as the chief stage deity or Ranga - devata.

The entire edifice of the Sanskrit drama has a fundamental religious basis right from the construction of a theatre - house to the enactment of a play. It involves elaborate rituals and worshipping of devatas or deities. The major presiding deities of the theatre are Chandra (moon god), Lokapālas (Gudradians of the world) Marutas, Mitra, Agni (fire god), Varuna, Adityas, Rudras, Bhutas, Apsarasa, Yaksinya, the ocean god, Kritanta, Nagaraja, the Rod of Yama, Niyati, Mrityu, Indra, Vidyut, Yaksas, Pishachas, Guhyakas, Vajra, Jarjara, Brahma, Vishnu, Shiva, Kartikeya, Sarasvati, Omkara etc.

There are some deities who are the protectors of the playhouse or auditorium. According to Bharata, there are ten such gods and goddesses as follows:-

(1) **Chandra** (Moon) protects the main building of the playhouse and keeps it cool and peaceful.

(2) **Marutanga** (Air) symbolises ventilators that keep the playhouse airy and help to avoid suffocation and heat.

(3) **Mitra** (Sun) symbolises brightness of the jewelled costumes etc.

(4) **Varuna** (Rain) Controls the interior.

(5) **Agni** (Fire) protects the stage.

(6) **Megha** (clouds) guards the musical instruments.

(7) **Indra** protects the hero.

(8) **Sarasvati** protects the heroine.

(9) **Omkara** protects the jester.

(10) **Shiva** protects the entire lot of characters in the play.

It is to be noted that in early dramas, the elaborate Purvaranga was partly not just a musical and dance performance to entertain the assembled audiences; but it contained in good proportion the formal worship offered to the presiding deities of the stage and theatre.

Bharata himself believes that gods take their appropriated places in the theatre pandal to protect the dramatic performance from all possible impediments and dangers; so, no dramatic spectacle may be presented without first worshipping the stage deities. (Ranga - Daivata - Pujana).

**[see "Rangapuja", "Ganapati", "Saraswati", "Shiva", "Brahma" etc].**

**Ranga-dvara**

Denotes "A stage - door" and also the prologue of a play.

In the second context, this is one of the twenty constituent parts of Purvaranga (preliminaries of a play), performed on the stage and the item is preceded by Jarajarashlokas. Rangadvāra is an item in which the play (abhinaya) begins, the Sutradhara recites a new verse and bows before 'Jarjara' Indra's banner.

**Ranga-jivakah**

Refers to an actor.

**Ranga mandapa**

This refers to the 'stage proper'.

Rangamandapa or Mandapa is described by *Bhavaprakashana* as 'a place where the assembled members, the master of the musical assembly and his friends enjoy themselves passionately by the presentation of vocal and instrumental music and dance or drama.

**[see 'Ranga']**

**Rangapitha**

Refers to a stage, mentioned in Bharata's *Natyashastra* (2.63).

It denotes the stage and the surface of the stage is termed as the Ranga Sirsa. The term Rangapitha has been used by Bharata in his description of the stage while the term Rangashirsa occurs when the description of the surface of the stage is given. (*Natyashastra* 2.100). But he has only dealth with Rangapitha. If it would have been a separate part, different from the Rangashirsa, of the state Bharata would have dealt with the characteristics of the surface of the Rangapitha also ie, Rangashirsa which find mentions in stanzas 2.72, 73, 75. He states "Rangashirsa should not be convex like the back of a tortoise, nor should be concave like the back of a fish, but it should be level as the surface of the mirror".

Bharata's stage is divided into three compartments.

(I) The Nepathya griha

(II) The Rangashirsa

(III) The Rangapitha

There are two doors from Nepathyagriha to the stage, one is used exclusively for characters coming right up to the front on the Rangapitha for characters low in status.

**Rangapuja**

Ritual worship of the stage, as prescribed in the ancient Sanskrit dramatic treatises is called 'Rangapuja'.

Bharata devotes at length regarding the worship of the gods of the stage and an elaborate forms of worship are prescribed to erect the theatre-house as well as correct invocation while laying the foundation of the stage; rituals concering erection of columns, Mattavaranis, Rangashirsa etc.

Brahmanas are fed at every step. In the Pusya constellation, a white thread, strong enough to measure the building, should be laid round the theatre. If the thread is broken into two pieces, the death of the proprietor is indicated; if it is broken into three, a political disorder will occur in the land, and if it is broken into four, it is believed that the master of the dramatic art will perish. To avoid these, measurement of the theatre should be done on an auspicious day.

Deformed and ugly persons should not be employed in any work concerning the theatre-house. Even monks and mendicants should not be allowed to approach the building.

In the Rohini or Shravana constellation the pillars should be laid and the theatre director must fast for three days. In charity, jewels, cows and clothes be distributed.

Once the theatre-house in cnstructed, cows are supposed to live there for a week and Brahmans recite mantras. The director is to be initiated and after a three-day fast should salute with folded hands prominent gods, divine beings, Rajarsis, Munis and dramatic obstacles and success.

When Rangashirsa is constructed, jewels and precious stones are laid underneath it by expert builders. On the eastern side of the Rangashirsa diamond is to be kept; lapis lazuli on the south; emerald on the west, coral in the north and gold in the centre.

Similarly while erecting the Mattavaranis, garlands, clothes and perfumes be given away in charity. Offerings linked by

Bhutas should be given to the different castes (varnas) Milk should be offered under the pillars of the Mattavaranis. Food stuff - rice mixed with pulses be given to Brahmanas.

Even the Sanskrit play production is full of religious rituals and ceremonies. All the presiding deities of the theatre are worshipped with offerings (Bali) and sacrifices, different deities are invoked with different mantras according to the *Natyashastra*.

On the day of the performance, all the presiding deities of theatre and the flag-staff (Jarjara) of Indra are worshipped.

Even the preliminaries of play has a fundamental religious basis.

Offerings, sacrifices, mantras, herbs, recitation and food (Bhaksya) should be offered on the Natyamandapa. The show should not begin before the offerings are made. If this rule is not followed, the knowledge of the performers become futile and he goes to the nether world. So the stage manager should make the offerings with all ardour. If no worship is offered the dancer or financier, whoever he may be is degraded. According to theatrical doctrines, he who make offerings gets the desired object and goes to heaven.

**Rangashirṣa**

Denotes the surface of a stage; mentioned in Bharata's *Natyashastra* (2.34).

Bharata's stage is, divided into three compartments.

(I) The Nepathya Griha

(II) The Rangashirsa

(III) The Rangapitha

There are two doors from the Nepathyagriha to the stage. One is used only as entry to the Rangashirsa for character of high ones like the Hero or the Heroine.

**[see 'Ranga' and 'Rangapitha']**

**Rasa**

The term is used to refer to 'tasting', 'enjoying' or 'self-experiencing'; an aesthetic experience, an 'aesthetic pleasure' etc.

It has rightly been stated tht the concept of Rasa and Bhāva is so prodigious that it cannot be explained in general terms. Most of the scholars uses the term 'Sentiment' for Rasa. Oflate, the word 'Rapture' is being used.

Chapter VI and VIII of *Natyashastra* give in detail the Rasas (Flavours or Sentiments) and Bhavas (Emotions or Psychological states) which are the essence of drama.

The desirable nine 'Flavours' of a work of art are erotic, heroic, furious, piteous, comic, fearful, repulsive, marvellous and peaceful and collectively called Rasas (singular 'Rasa').

There are three additional essences called 'Uparasas' namely:-

(I) Vātsalya (Parent's love for the child)

(II) Bhakti (Devotions); and

(III) Gāna Rasa (Musical Aesthetics)

The deities of Rasas, according to Bharata's *Natyashastra* are:-

(1) Vishnu - The God of Love

(2) Pramatha - The God of Humour

(3) Rudra - The God of Wrath

(4) Yama - The God of Pathos

(5) Mahākāla - The God of Abhorrence

(6) Kāla - The God of Fear

(7) Mahendra - The God of Chivalry

(8) Brahma - The God of Wonder.

Presenthy, Lord Bnddha is hailed is the God of Peace.

Shringara

Raudra

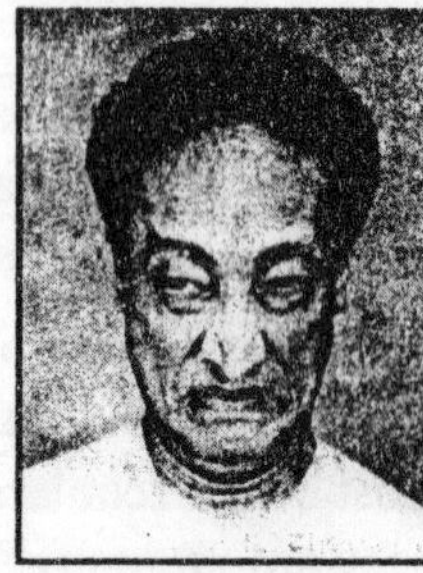

Vibhatsa

Hasya

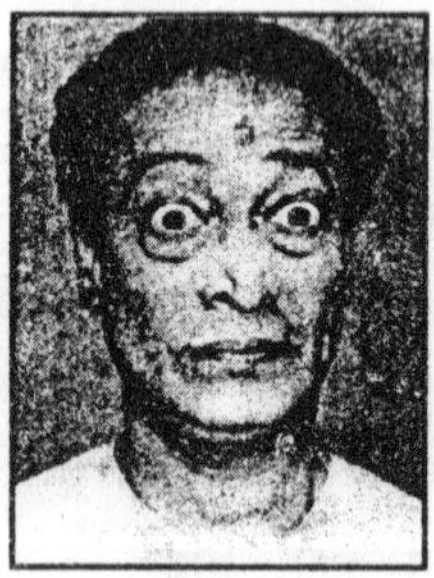

Vira

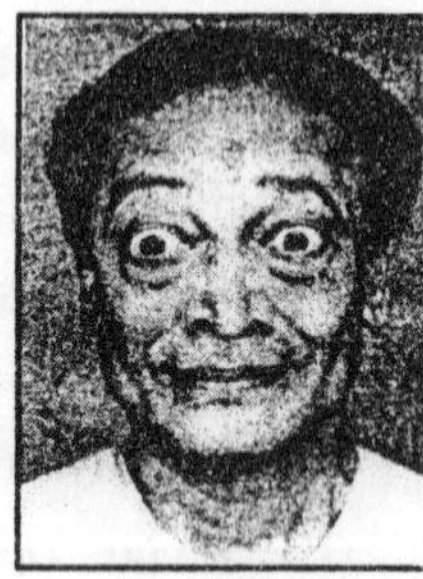

Adbhuta

Karuna

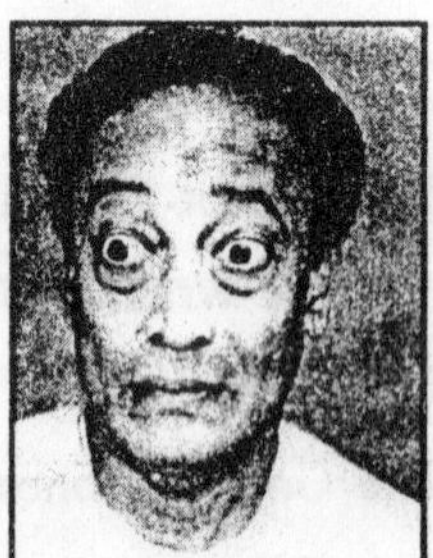

Bhayanaka

Shanta

**Navarasas**

A rasa is a result of Sthayi Bhava (permanent state) that produces a pleasurable sensation through the operationof transitory (Vyabhichari) states. The rasa is a response to bhava.

Bhava denotes an emotion and its external expression. If the audience absorbs the bhava it produces rasa or an enjoyment of the bhava.

Sanskrit dramatic treatises have agreed upon this point that the main purpose in playwrighting as well as its performance is not merely any subtle delineation of characters or the elaborate construction of intersting situtions in a plot: nor is it any ill-conceated attempt at moral admonition; the chief aim of the Sanskrit drama has been, since the very beginning, to entertain and please the audience by evoking emotional response to the gradual build-up of one principal emotion, supported, diversified and enriched by other subsidiary feelings.

Bharata is the originator of the Rasa theory of poetry, particularly the drama. According to him, Rasa is a vital element in this artform-indeed it has no other aim than the development of a sentiment. So he first dealt with this aspect before discussing other elements of the drama. He propounded a very wellknown formula of the Rasa which states Rasa develops from an amalgamation of Vibhāva, Anubhāva and Vyabhicari.

Bharata in his *Natyashastra* has stated that just as the mixing together of different ingredients of spices and blending them together would yield a drink with a flavour that is altogether different from those of the various ingredients which go to make it up, in the same manner, a propr amalgam of Vibhavas (Supporting and stimulating determinants); Anubhāvas (consequent feelings and reactions), and Vyabhicharibhavas (Transitory feelings or states) would result in the development of 'Sthayibhavas' (permanent state) and fitting them into their corresponding sentiment (Rasa).

Following this very formula, later authors have conceived many theories about the nature and development of Rasa in course of centuries.

However, Bharata did not dealt meticulously as to how a sentiment is developed. But Abhinavagupta in his commentary has elucidates this aspect in his commentary. The Vibhāvas, Anubhāvas and Vyabhicaribhavas are indispensable for the development of a permanent mood into its fullness as 'Rasa'.

Rasa is relished or enjoyed, as stated above according to *Natyashastra* "Just as people eating food prepared with various spices and ingredients feel delighted, in the same way connosseuers (Sumanasas) enjoy the Rasa (in a drama) which is manifested through acting calculated to reveal feelings. As the permanent feelings are enjoyed by the cultured members of the audience, in their fully developed form, they are called Natyarasas.

Rasa is an experience of joy, pure and serene However, a school helds the view that Rasa is ot merely an experience of joy or pleasure.It is an experience of pain or sorrow as well. Authors of the *Nāṭya Darpaṇa*, therefore, differ with Bharata and Hemachandra. They opine that Rasa has the power to produce the feelings of both pleasure and pain and divide Rasa into two classes, namely, Sukhatmaka and Dukhatmaka. They putforth that people got to witnes the Dukhatmaka dramas, owing to the skill of the playwright or the actor. Actor, too, enjoy the different sentiments in their own mind, which they attempt to evoke in the minds of the spectators, just as a prostitute or a singer who while trying to please others may, at times, herself get great pleasure. Nevertheless the authors of *Natya Darpana* did not find any strong support among the later authorities.

**Positive Aspects of the Rasas**

Positive (leads to)

| | | |
|---|---|---|
| Shringara | - | Hasya |
| Raudra | - | Karuna |
| Vira | - | Adbhuta |
| Vibhatsa | - | Bhayanaka |

**Opposite Aspects of the Rasas**

Adverse

| | | |
|---|---|---|
| Shringara | - | Vībhatsa |
| Vira | - | Bhayanaka |
| Raudra | - | Adbhuta |
| Hasya | - | Karuna |

Rasa refers to 'Artistic enjoyment' and according to Sanskrit Dramatic Theory, Netā (Hero), Vastu (Story) and Rasa (Sentiment or Artistic enjoyment) constitute the three essential ingredients of a dramatic composition. Furthermore according to the difference in these respects the ten varities (Daśarūpakas) are to be recognised.

In one of the verses in Chapte VI of *Natyashastra*, Bharata has furnished eleven elements of Drama which can be collectively called the 'Digest of Natyashatra. These significant dramatic components are :-

Rasa (Sentiment)

Bhava (Emotion)

Abhinaya (Acting)

Dharmi (Modes of representation)

Vritti (Styles of expression)

Pravritti (Local usages)

Siddhi (Success of production)

Svara (Note)

Atodya (Musical instruments)

Gana (Song)

Ranga (Theatre)

The 'Rasa' is thus the quintessence of Sanskrit drama.

**Rāsaka**

This is a minor type of drama (Uparupaka), a one-act in which five characters appear. The *Avaloka* of *Daśarupa* mentions that Rāsaka is a kind of Nritya, with a piece consisting of singing and dancing.

**Rasika**

A man of taste, appreciator of excellence, capable of tasting the rasa in a work of art is called 'Rasika'.

**Rasodbhavana**

This means 'the creation of sentiment'. Ancient Rhetoricians held that a dramatist should set before him the creation of sentiment as his chief object. That is why all classical Sanskrit dramas make all efforts in on the successful portrayal of sentiments, (the soul of the drama) and does not insist on quick movement of action.

**Rati**

It denotes 'Pleasure', Joy etc.

The Permanent state of 'Pleasure' (Rati), which in its nature is always full of delight, is produced by the effect of a pleasant season, garlands, unguents, ornaments, fine eatables, a rich residence and absence of detestable things.

Rati, the first sthayi bhava is conveyed in acting by a slight smile, delicacy of face, melodious speech, delicate action of the brows, oblique look and the like.

**Raudra Rasa**

Raudra means 'Wrath, Furious, Violent', etc.

Raudra rasa or the Terrible sentiment depicts the condition of an angry person and its employment quickens the dramatic action such as individual fight, war, slaughter etc, therefore, involves conflict.

Wrath is projected by specific actions such as release of weapons, mutilating the head, the body and the arms.

The Vibhāvas for Raudra rasa, the terrible are insult, envy, deliberate offence, injuries, false speech etc.

The Vyabhicharibhavas (the Transient emotins) centributing to this sentiment are Haughtiness or cruelty (Ugrata), Indignation (Amarṣa), Pride etc.

The Sthayi bhava or the permannet state for this rasa is anger. *Dasarupaka* gives us two reasons for the provocation of anger. A man may get angry because of jealousy or due to animosity.

*Natyashastra* states that the presentation of this sentiment requires action full or anger and it has fighting for its cause. It deals with arrogant men principally and takes the shape of cruel deeds.

**Varna** : Rakta (Red)

**Mukharaga** : Rakta (Red)

**Hasta** : Kartārīmukha

**Svaras** : Shadja, Rishaba

**Raga :** In this rapture of 'Fury', the Raga excel are :-

**Athāna** (for pure anger)

**Ārabhi** (for anger with malice)

**Vasantha** (for anger with wicked triumph)

**Surati** (For derision)

**Kāmavardhiree** (for contempt)

**Chalanāta** (for hatred)

**Kalyāni** (for jealousy)

**Presiding Deity** : Rudra

**Rechaka (Recaka)**

Circular movements of limbs like the neck, hand, waist, and feet in a dance is called 'Rechaka'.

Bharata mentions four 'Rechakas', those of the foot (Pada), Waist (Kati), Hand (Hasta) and Neck (Griva). Here the particular limb is moved separately and not in association with other limbs.

**Ri (Ṛṣabha)**

This denotes the second scale degree.

[See 'Ṛsabha']

**Ritvik**

It refes to a priest who is an expert in conducting rituals and sacrifices. He is an important associate of a royal Hero and according to *Bhavaprakahana* he belong to Dharma-sachiva type of associates.

**Romancha**

This denotes "Thrill" (Third Sattvika Bhava/ Emotional state) which according to *Natyashastra*, should be enacted by quivers raising the hair of the body, causing goose - flesh and touching the body.

**Ṛṣabha**

This is one of the seven Svaras (Notes) and according to *Ragavibodha, Sangitaparijata, Sangitamakarandah* etc, the sounds of music are first perceived as relative pitches or intervals and then from the twenty two Shrutis (Main Intervals) come the seven Svaras, namely Ṣaḍja, Ṛṣabha, Gāndhāra, Madhyama, Pañcama, Dhaivata and Niṣāda.

It is interesting to mention here that the traditional authorities on music refer each Svara or Note to the sound of some animal. The Ṛṣabha is the sound of Chātaka bird.

**Rudra**

He is the 'Storm-god (chief of the Maruts): In Brahmana, he is regarded as a form of Agni, but later identified with Shiva.

Euphemistic name of Rudra, in classical (post-vedic) Sanskrit transferred to one of the members of the Hindu trinity, Shiva.

According to Bharata's *Natyashastra* (6,44), Rudra is the God of Wrath (Raudra rasa).

He is one of the presiding deities of theatre who should be worshipped with offerings and sacrifices, tells Bharata's treatise.

**Rupa**

It means 'to represent on the stage, gesticulate.

**Rūpaka (Metaphor)**

In accordance with *Natyashastra*, Rupaka is one of the four 'Alankaras (Figures of Speech) available to a playwright. Rūpaka refers to 'Metaphor' and this second variety is illustrated by Bharata in the following words.

Vapistriyo (Lake - women) with their lotus - faces,

*Kumud* smiles, open and beautiful

and swans cackling around,

*Nilotpala* - eyes seem to be calling one another (NS, XVII, 57).

**Rupakas**

It is Dhananjaya who used the word 'Rupaka' of Bharata as a synonym for Natya. Drama is Rupaka because it is a visual presentation; and there is also a metaphorical identification involved here, as when we call a face the moon, in order to imply its loveliness. In drama, there is a double identification or saperimposition: A writer creates a character of Rama and we take it to be real Rama; this is one superimposition. When an actor plays that part in a stage performance we accept that actor as the real Rama, atleast for the time being; this is another superimposition. It is due to this supermposition (Arōpa) that a drama is called 'Rupaka' and the principle behind this identification is Anukarana which leads to the belief of identity. Even *Rasarnavasudhakara* of Singha Bhupala and *Sahityadarpana* of Sarṅgadeva accept this idea.

**[see also Uparupakas]**

**Rūpānusārini**

The *Natyashastra admits* of three modes of representation of dramatis personae. In Sanskrit drama, the roles were of three different qualities, namely, Anurupa, Virupa and Rupanusarini.In Rupanusarini, a man plays the part of a woman. A male character maybe portrayed by a female and vice-versa according to the desire of the managcr. But when a man's role is given to a woman, it should be done with great care. In Mahavasya, we can trace the word 'Bhrukuṁsa' which referred to a male imperonating a female. For example, in Malatimadhava, the Sutradhara and Pariparshvika assume the roles of Kāmandaki and her pupil Avalokita respectively.

**Rūpayati**

Represents on the stage, enacts on the stage, a stage direction.

# S

**Sa (Ṣaḍja)**

This is the first scale degree.

**[see 'Ṣaḍja']**

**Sabhapati**

Sabha means 'an assembly' and Sabhapati is the chief patron of the assembly and in this context, of the dramatic performance.

In is stated in the traditional dramatic treatises that in Nandi (Benedictory) verse show be recited every day the drama is enacted and be in honour of gods, Sabhapati and other dignitories.

**Ṣadaṅganatya**

This refer to the six limbs of Nātya may probably be gathered from Bharata's statement of the Digest of Natya (*Natyashastra*, VI, 10). They appear to be Rasa-bhava, three fold Abhinaya, and instrumental and vocal music. More precisly, Rasa-bhāva, Abhinaya; Dharmi (mode of Presentation, including Vritti and Pravritti); vocal and instrumental music (Ātodya, Gāna); theatre (Ranga); stage-siuccess (Siddhi) maybe taken as the six limbs.

**Ṣāḍava Raga**

The Rāgas of Indian classical music aré conventionally categorized into three classes (jatis). These are Saṁpurna (of seven Shrutis). Sāḍava (of six Shrutis) and Auḍava (of five Shrutis). Ṣāḍava Rāga is obtained by removing any one of the seven Shrutis, excepting Ṣadja (S), because S is not only a constant Shruti but is the one Shruti which can not be absent in any Rāga. S is regarded as the vital Shruti and Svara in relation to which the remaining Shrutis and Svaras are identified.

**Ṣaḍdāruka**

Denotes a wooden partition wall separating the green-room from the stage; mentioned in *Natyashastra* (2.68).

**Sādhana**

Means the discipline employed in learning an art and Natyasādhana refers to the acts and efforts of a person committed to achieve excellence in the field of dramatic art.

**Sādhāraṇa**

This denotes an altered note in a Scale or Rāga

**Sadharana Nayika see 'Apsara's, 'Ganika' and 'Nayika'**

**Sādho**

It means 'Blessed one' Bharata has prescribed a set of words for calling the different characters according to their position for example, an ascetic was addressed as 'Sādho'.

This is a mode of address in a Sanskrit drama.

**Sādhu**

An exclamation of appreciation to a (dramatic) performance meaning 'welldone'.

**Ṣadja**

This is one of the seven svaras (Notes) and according to *Ragavibodha, Sangitaparijata, Sangitamakarandah* etc, the sounds of music are first perceived as relative pitches or intervals and then from the twentytwo Shrutis (Main Intervals)come the seven svaras, namely Ṣaḍja, Ṛṣabha, Gāndhāra, Madhyama, Pañcama, Dhaivata and Niṣāda.

It is interesting to mention here that traditional authorities on music refer each Svara of Note to the sound some animal. The sound produced by the peacock is at its highest pitch called 'Saḍja'.

**Sadshri (Simile of Uniqueness) see Alankaras and Upama**

**Sahaṛdaya**

One who has the similar space in the heart for the art; a rasika, a responsive spectator.

**Sailusha**

In the *Purushamedha Prakayana* of the Taittiriya Brahmaṇa (3rd Ashtaka and 4th Prashna), names of professional artists and musicians are given whose services were required in the sacrificial hall.

Sailusha denoted a professional dance master, Nartana jivikaḥ.

**Sakata**

This dance gesture is employed to indicate the demons in Indian dance.

**Sakha**

It means 'a companion'. In Sanskrit drama, it usually refers to the companions of hero. For example we have Vidusaka (the jester) as a companion of the Royal hero. Or a Pithamarda, an efficient helpmate of the hero.

**[see 'Vidusaka' Pithamarda', 'Dharmasachiva' 'Arthasachiva', 'Kamasachiva', etc.]**

**Sakhi**

This refers to the 'companions and friends' of the Heroine

(associates), who have an affection and attachment to the Heroine (as stated by Dhananjaya in his *Daśarupaka*).

**[see 'Nayika Sahayikas]**

**Samādhi see Gunas**

**Sāmagayaka**

The singer of sacred Sāmans or Samagāyan are called Samagayaka.

**Samāja**

A gathering of people who assemble for entertainment.

**Samanakha**

Prescribed by Bharata in his *Natyasastra*, Samanakha is the fifth and one of the 108 Karanas or cosmic Shiva, Bharata Poses. Here standing in Samapada, both the hands are let down on both sides and body must be in normal posture.

**Samanya Abhinaya see Sattvika Abhinaya**

**Samanya Nayika see Nayika**

**Sama Sutra**

Sama Sutra is a treatise of seven chapters denoting the method of reciting the hymns of the Vedas. As stated, particularly of Sama Veda.

**Sāman**

This refers to a Sāmavedic chant or hymn.

**Samatā see Gunas**

**Samatala Ranga shirsa**

The surface of the Rangapitha, ie, Rangashirsa of the square theatre should be Samatala, prescribes *Natyashastra* in the stanza (2. 100). It means in the square shaped theatre, the surface should be level. The plays performed in this type of stage are not having so many actors acting on the stage at the same time so that some actors have to stand behind other actors. Therefoıe, the stage need not be sloping like a Rectangular - shaped Theatre, but is specified to be level.

**Samavakara**

Samavakara is a three acts drama that depicts three kinds of deception, the three kinds of excitements or the three kinds of love. The first act should continue till 12 nadikas (a nadika being equivalent to 24 minutes); the second should last for four and the third, for two.

According to dramatic rules, it may have as many as twelve characters.

This is one of the main recognised types of drama and is named so because various themes are scattered about [Samavakīryante] in it. The contents of the play are taken from wellknown legends of gods and demons.

In brief, this is a Rupaka, a major kind of Sanskrit drama, found in all region of India that dealt exclusively with the activities of the gods and divine persons; demons, etc. The dominant sentiment is heroic (Vira); having three acts. The Pancharatra of Bhasa is a Samavakara variety.

**Samabhoga Shringara see Shringara rasa**

**Samdamsa**

This hand gesture in Indian dance has varied uses depending upon the sentiments and mood. The plucking of flowers, worship offerings etc.

**Samdhima see Pusta**

**Samdhis**

In a dramatic composition, plot is a presequisite. The plot or the theme is a succession of happenings or events which one or more characters experience. Plot must have a begining, ie, the context or a situation from which the incidents of a drama can sprout out. The plot will develop with some hope of the realisation ofthe ultimate end in view. But if the action which is begun run through difficulties in its progress, it becomes more dramatic, reaches a crisis and if only then finally resolve into its desired fulfilment, ie, the fulfilment of the theme hard won, and therefore such drama better appreciated. Our ancient Sanskrit theorists have accepted these stages and putforth a theory. Sanskrit dramatic theory holds that the plot of a drama is comprised of five major divisions which it named 'Saṁdhis' (Juncutres). These junctures represent the links in the entire chain of the dramatic theme, exhibiting the successive stages of its development.

It is also to be noted that they are themselves made by the combination of the different essential elements of the theme called *Arthaprakriti* and the different stages of development of the plot or in otherwords, the different stages in the progress of the theme towards its fulfilments, called *Avastha*. According to Bharata, a dramatic plot is divided into five junctures (1) Mukha (2) Pratimukha (3) Garbha (4) Avamarsha (5) Nirvahana. Each junctures or Samdhis is an admixture of five Arthaprakriti and five Avastha.

Artha - prakritis are:-

(1) Bija (The germ)

(2) Bindu (The sign of continuity)

(3) Patākā (The episode)

(4) Prakarī (The incident)

(5) Kārya (The purpose to be achieved)

Similarly represents five Avastha viz.

(1) Arambha (The beginning)

(2) Yatra (The effort)

(3) Praptyasha (The prospect of success)

(4) Niyatapti (Certainty of success)

(5) Phalagama (Attainment of the result)

With Mukha commences the plot or theme. Arambha is the stage, and the incident comprises of Bija (where the process of germination takes place) and thc first signs of conflict are felt. In Pratimukha efforts (Yatna) are required as Bija is confronted with real impediments and conflicts begins to rise.In Garbha, the progress of conflict is rapid. It reaches its climax either in the Garbha or in the begining of the Avamarsha and then the conflict begins to drop, only to disappear in the Nirvahana as the drama ends happily in Sanskrit drama.

The movement of the dramatic action would form an arch rather than a straight line. Dramatic action represented through these Samdhis presents a complete whole, ie, it has a beginning, a middle and an end.

**Samghotana**

This is the seventh constituent parts of Púrvaranga (preliminaries of a play), taken up behind the curtain.

Samghotana meant for rehearsing the use of different hand poses for indicating the time - beat. Before this parighattana or the tuning of the stringed instruments (tantri) is carried out.

**Sāmika**

The Rigvedic hymn passed through three stages first was Archika, when only Udātta or raised note was known, followed by Gātha or Gātika period of vedic singing, based on Udātta and Anudātta notes. In course of time, an intertone known as 'Svarita' between Udātta and Anudātta was established. A balancing note between the two, it is a an admixture of the notes Udātta and Anudātta and its first half is Udātta. This phase of Vedic music is called 'Sāmika' period.

**[see Svaras (Vedic)]**

**Saṃkṣobha (Concealment) see Vagyaḅhinaya**

**Saṁlāpaka**

This is a minor type of drama (Uparupaka) containing one, three or four acts, states the *Sahitya Darpana*.

**Sampakveṣṭākaḥ**

This is one of the five Mārga Tāla patterns, with a proportional structure of 3: 2: 2: 2: 3.

**Saṁpurṇa Raga**

The Ragas of Indian classical music are conventionally categorized into three classes or (Jatis). These are Saṁpūrṇa, Ṣāḍava and Auḍava. Saṁpurna is of seven Shrutis - Sadja, Ṛṣ abha, Gāndhāra, Madyama, Panchama, Dhaivata and Niṣāda. Among this seven Shrutis called Saptaka, Ṛṣabha, Gāndhāra, Madhyama, Dhaivata and Niṣāda have their *Komal* (soft or lower) and *tivra* (sharp or upper) variations while Ṣaḍja and Panchama are sthira (non - variable). Very rarely do komal and tivra svaras present themselves side by side in Indian Rāgas. A rare occurence is Rāga lalit, in which both komal and tivra Madhyama come into play.

**Samputa Hasta**

This is a double hand gesture in which all the fingers bent forward and the palms kept apart in *chakra*.

It denotes "covering of things as well as a container."

**Samshaya (Hesitation) see Vagyabhinaya**

**Samunnata Rangashirsa**

The surface of the Rangapitha, ie, Rangashirsa of the Rectangular theatre should be Samunnata, prescribes *Natyashastra* in the stanza (2.100). The word 'Samunnata' denotes rising, ascending. Therefore, it seems that the Rangashirsa of Rectangular theatre should be constructed such that it is rising, ascending, from the audience - hall towards the green- room. A critic observes that in Rectangulr theatre, the number of dramatic personae is very large (For e.g. in 'Dima'; it may have sixteen numbers of Heroes. Usually, the players stand in one row and not behind each other, as otherwise, the actor standing behind another actor cannot be seen from the Audience - Hall. But in case there number is large, some of the players have to stand behind others. In such cases, if the floor of the stage is rising then players standing behind other players could also be seen from the Audience - Hall Therefore, the stage of the Rectangular should be ascending towards the Green-Room.

**Saṁvadi**

It means 'consonant'. Bharata's *Natyashastra* divides Svaras (Notes) into four varities, namely, Vādī (Sonant), Samvādī (Consonant), Anuvādī (Assonant) and Vivādī (Dissonant), according to the number of Shrutis (Intervals) between them and eversince this has remained the accepted ramification.

It is said that Samvadi is no less significant than the Vādi and is more important than the other notes. Brihaddeshi commentary mentions that the nature of Saṁvādī is to reinforce the Vādī by which the expressiveness of the mode is engendered. The Samvadi is almost always a fifth or fourth above the Vadi. This corresponds with an interval of twelve or eight Shrutis. Samvadi is like the minister while Vadi is the king of notes. The speaking note is Vadi and the note which converses with it is 'Samvādi'.

**Samyuta Hastas**

This refers to Double Hand Gestures. According to *Abhinaya Darpanam* there are twenty three kinds of *Samyuta Hasta : 1. Anjali 2. Kapota 3. Karkata 4. Svastika 5. Dolā 6. Pushpaputa 7. Utsanga 8. Shivalinga 9. Katakavardhana 10. Kartarisvastika 11. Shakata 12. Shanka 13. Chakra 14. Samputa 15. Pasha 16. Kilaka 17. Matsya 18. Kurma 19. Varaha 20. Garuda 21. Nagabandha 22. Khatva 23. Bherunda.*

**Samyuta Hasta: (Nagabandha)**

Apart from twenty three varities of 'Samyutahasta' given by *Abhinaya Darpanam,* the *Natyashastra* of Bharatamuni mentions few more gestures which are not mentioned by Nandikeshvara in the his treatise. They are :- *Makara, Gajadanta Avahittha, Vardhamana.*

**[see also Hasta mudras]**

**Sañcārī**

This is one of the four kinds of Varṇa (melodic movement). Four varieties are :- Sthayi (level), repetition of the same sound : Ārohi (ascent); Avarohī (descent); and Sañcārī (wandering or ascent and descent combined).

**Sancharibhavas see Vyabhicharibhavas**

**Sandamsha Hasta**

Closing and opening in a vibrating motion in the *Padmakosha* is Sandamsha Hasta. Used to denote "belly, sacrifice to please deities, wound, a worm, terror, worship, and the number five."

**Sangita**

Means 'Music'. It may denotes many things, such as Chorus, a song sung by many voices;

Singing accompanied by instrumental music and dancing; triple symphony;

A concert; The art of singing with music and dancing; dramatic performance with song, music and dancing etc.

In early Indian thought, Sangita was regarded as a composite art consisting of Melos (Gīta), syllabic accompaniment (Vādya), and limb movement (Nritta or Nartana).

The words Sangita and Gita are not synonyms, Kallinātha's commentary on *Sangitaratnakara* describes Sangita as Tauryatrika, that is, the union of song, dance and instrumental music, triple symphony, while Gita (Vocal music) deals with one aspect and is a combination of svaras (tones of the musical scale or gamut).

Gītaṁ vādyaṁ tathā nṛtyaṁ yatastāle pratiṣṭhitaṁ - *Sangitaratnakara* of Sharangadeva states that Sangita comprises Gīta (vocal music), Vādya (Instrumental music) and Nartana (dancing) and depends upon rhythm.

So far as the genesis of Indian music is concerned, myth tells us that Brahma, the Eternal supreme power, the creator of this universe is its originator. He taught this heavenly art to Shiva, the God of eternal bliss who delivered it to Saraswati - the Goddess of knowledge and wisdom. She taught this art to the heavenly musicians and dancers, namely Gandharvas and Apsaras and lastly the Kinnaras - centaur - like performers on musical instruments. These divinities taught this art to the great hermits like Narada, Hanuman, Bharata and others, who passed it on to the human beings on the earth.

Anil Baran Ganguly offers an interesting legend from the Brahma Purāṇa about how music was created out of chaos. The story goes like this. When Lord Śiva restored His wife Satī to life and took her with Him to Kailāsa, Nārada communicated this news to Nārāyaṇa, Brahmā and other gods. They all expressed a keen desire to meet the couple and also to stage some entertainment in their honour and to greet and welcome them.

Accordingly, Śiva, Satī and the other gods were invited to Vaikuṇṭha Purī, the abode of Nārāyaṇa. Nārada used to pride himself on his prowess as a great music artiste, and he offered to sing before this distinguished assembly of gods and goddesses.

With the kind permission of Lord Viṣṇu Nārada started singing. Nārada had an impression that nobody could sing like him in the Tribhuvana (*i.e.* the three worlds). For the vocal recital of good music a melodious voice is the most essential factor and thorough knowledge of the modes of singing can only make the vocal recital of the artiste perfect. Correct singing of notes indicates the specific objects and these are visualised by the listeners concerned. Though Nārada prided himself very much for his mastery of the art of music, he failed miserably to make a correct and perfect representation of the musical notes. It is said that because of this failure of Nārada to maintain the correct symmetry of musical notes, a great disaster took place; and the disaster was that the Rāgas and Rāgiṇīs had their arms and feet, faces and heads completely chopped off. Those days a musical Rāga or Rāgiṇī was believed to be animate like human beings. Each Rāga and Rāgiṇī had the body and the face, arms and feet and each was glowing with beauty and lustre. Correct recital of musical notes was absolutely essential for maintaining their normal figures and forms and any incorrect recital of musical notes would result in the multilation of their figures. In the vocal recital of Nārada the musical notes were not sung correctly and, therefore, Rāgas and Rāgiṇīs became grotesquely disfigured. For restoring the former normal figures of these mutilated creatures the assembly of gods and goddesses decided that some master singer should be invited for demonstrating a correct vocal recital of those musical notes. Now who could be there in the Tribhuvana except Lord Śiva to render the musical notes perfectly. He was the best musician, unrivalled in the art. All the gods and goddesses present prayed unto Lord Śiva for his agreeing to give a vocal recital of celestial music. Śiva agreed, but he asked, "If I have to sing, where is the person who could rightly appreciate my music." Eventually Lord Viṣ ṇu was invoked to become a listener to Lord Śiva's music. Lord Śiva started singing, he rose to the highest pitch of his celestial music and lo, the figurines of Rāgas, Rāgiṇīs regained their old forms and their original lustre. And here Lord Viṣṇu was so intensely engrossed in the celestial music of Lord Śiva that it is said that Viṣṇu started to melt into water. Brahmā came forward and swiftly held the water thus melted into his water jug. The ancient Hindu belief is that this water collected in the water jug of Brahmā later formed the river Gangā, flowing from the feet of Lord Viṣṇu.

Thus, we find how a Rāga could be responsible for bringing good as well as evil results to listeners. A Rāga when properly presented would produce good results and when done imperfectly would spell disaster. There was in that sense an excellent objective criterion of judging music in ancient India. That helped create a healthy tradition and thereby encouraged the development of worthy disciples who mastered, preserved and passed on this precious heritage to succeeding generations, of which India could well be proud."

In later Indian thought and practice, the sense of Sangita narroved to the point where it can more accurately serve as the equivalent of music, ie, the closest equivalent to the Western concept.

**Divisions of Music**

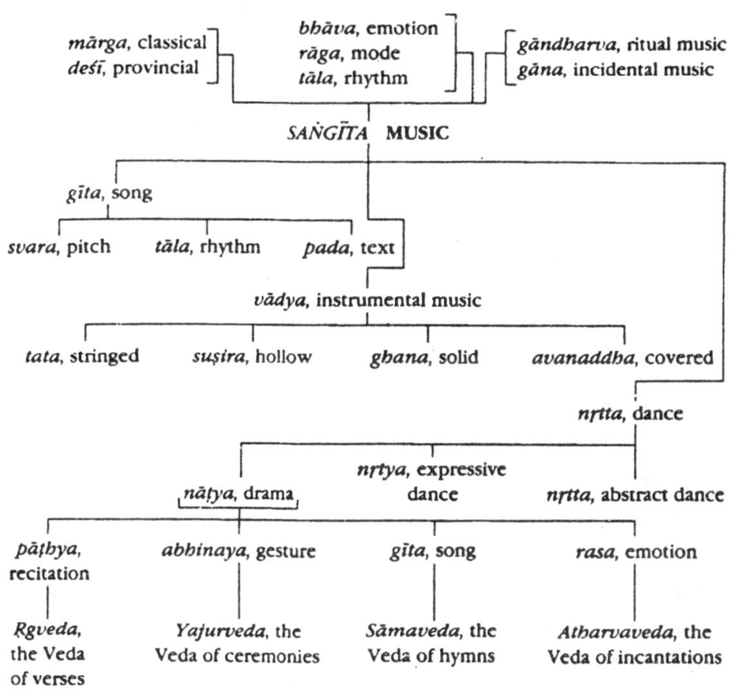

According to ancient musical treatise, there are two main distinctions in the theory and practice of music. There are Marga Sangita, ie, the high style practised by the celestial musician. Presently, music that accord to the ancient path, ie, classical and other Desi Sangita, the Terrestrial or all earthly music.

Sangita, says Bharata, forms the bed (Śayya), that is the bed rock, of drama (32. 436) Chapter XXVIII to XXXIII of *Natyashastra cover* the theory and practice of Music. Infact, these six chapters collectively form an independent exhaustive treatise itself on the science and art of Music, perhaps unique to have been embodied in a book on dramaturgy. Bharata divide music into two groups. Vocal (Gāna) and Instrumental (Atodya).

**[see 'Dhruva songs', Deshi Sangita, Marga Sangita, Vadya, Nirgita - Vadya, Svara, Jatis, Tala, Laya, Raga etc.]**

**Sangitank**

Concert, symphony

A public entertainment comprising of songs attended with music and dancing.

**Sangit - arthah**

Refers to the subject of a musical performance;

The materials or necessary apparatus for a musical concert.

**Sangita-shala**

Denotes a concert - hall.

**Sangitih**

Means a concert, harmony etc.

**Sanjiba**

It cannotes 'Living Creatures' According to Bharata's theory, Aharyabhinaya, is one of the four varities of acting that covers painting, make-up, costume, ornament, property required by the characters and is, therefore, produced through Nepathya which is of four types, viz, Pusta, Alankara, Angarachana and Sanjiva.

Sanjiva, according to *Natyashastra* (XXI, 151) is the entry of animals, bipeds, quadrupeds and those without feet, on the stage. These animals should carry (or even be in the form of different kinds of battle-weapons (XXI, 154).

**Sankhya Hasta**

This means Hastas for number. They are :-

| | | |
|---|---|---|
| *Prathama* - one | ....... | *Suchi.* |
| *Dvitiya* - two | ....... | *Ardhapataka.* |
| *Tritiya* - three | ....... | *Trishoola.* |
| *Chatura* - four | ....... | *Pataka* with four fingers separated except thumb. |
| *Pancha* - five | ....... | *Mukula.* |
| *Shashta* - six | ....... | *Hamsapaksha* after showing *mukula.* |
| *Sapta* - seven | ....... | *Katakamukha* after showing *mukula.* |
| *Ashtha* - eight | ....... | *Hamsasya* after showing *mukula.* |
| *Nava* - nine | ....... | *Sandamsha and pataka* with four fingers separated. |
| *Dasa* - ten | ....... | *Sandamsha* twice. |

**Sankika**

This refers to 'Shyness' while singing (one of the fourteen Gāyaka Dōshas or defects).

**Sannipāta**

This refers to one of the four audible Tāla gestures (hands clap together)

**Sannivesha**

This denotes an open space near a town where people assemble for amusement, a theatre; mentioned in Bharata's *Natyashastra* (2-7).

**Saptakash, Saptapatala Hastas**

This denotes Hastas for Seven Upper Worlds and Seven Lower Worlds. Seven Upper Worlds are :-

Bhu

Bhuvara

Svarga

Gnana

Tapa

Satya

Mahara and;

Seven Lower worlds are :-

Atala

Vitala

Sutala

Talatala

Mahatala

Rasatala

Patala

*Pataka* twisted upwards for *saptakash* and twisted downwards for *saptapatala*.

**Sapta - Tantri Veena**

This is a harp with 7 strings of ancient times. It was plucked with the fingers (stringed instrument / Tata Vadya).

**Saptaka**

This denotes "the set of seven", ie, the degrees of the heptatonic scale.

It is the *Sāmavidhāna Brāhmaṇa* which first stated that the seven shrutis form a Suptaka and were in the order of P D N S R G M and there Saptaka were not in the order with which we are familiar today, ie, in the order S R G M P D N.

A set of seven Shrutis is called 'Saptaka' (corresponding to the octave in Western music, in which, however, the first note of the Indian scale becomes the eighth note). In a Raga, the largest number of Shrutis is Seven and the smallest is five. Some believed that there was a Chatuṣ shruti jati or at least a few Ragas of that class. The latter jati might originated from the style of singing the Sāmans of the Sāmaveda.

**Sa-rasa Vastu**

That portion of the plot which is capable of evoking *rasa* and which can be represented through extended bhāvābhinaya.

**Saraswati**

In *Natyashastra* we find that there are various Indian deities deputed to protect different dramatis personae where they are performing on the stage. A vere says: Let Indra protect the actor playing the role of hero, Saraswati assume the role of heroine, Onkara the Vidusaka and Siva the rest of the characters.

She is one of the presiding deities of theatre and according to *Natyashastra*, she should be worshipped with offerings and sacrifices.

**Sargam**

This is the seven sol-fa syllables as an oral or written notation.

**Sarpashirsa Hasta**

This is a single hand gesture in which the tips of the fingers are bent forward in *Pataka*.

The gesture denotes "sandal paste, a snake, the middle tone, sprinkling, nourishing, water oblation to Gods, shape of an elephant's head and slapping of arms like wrestlers."

**Sarupya (Identity) see Vagyabhinaya**

**Sarvashravya see Prakasha**

**Satatantu Viṇa see Vāṇa**

**Ṣaṭpitāputrakaḥ**

This is the most popular of the five Mārga Tāla patterns, with a proportional structure of 3: 1: 2: 2: 1: 3.

**Saṭṭaka**

This is a minor type of drama and is basically a Natika written in Prakrit omitting Viskambhaka or Praveshaka. Like the Trotaka, it also employs a specified kind of dance. In Sattaka, the acts are called Javanikantaras and not the ankas.

**Sattva**

Inward concentration of pure mind, essential pure quality of a being.

**[see 'Sāttvika Bhāvas]**

**Sattvati Vritti see Vritti**

**Satvika**

It means 'Godly, one of the three main types of characters in Indian theatre; other being 'Rajasika' (Worldly) and 'Tamasika' (evil-minded).

**Sāttvikabhinaya**

One of the four kind of abhinaya expressed through the upsurge of genuine involuntary emotions, resulting in change of voice, change of colour etc.

Chapter XXIV explain in detail the Sattvikabhinaya, ie, acting through involuntary responses, such as tears, trembling, horripilation and similar other manifestations of the Sattvika - bhavas.

**Sāttvikabhāvas**

There are Sāttvikabhāvas or involuntary states in the development of the Rasa which are eight in number :

(1) Stambha (Paralysis)

(2) Pralaya (Fainting)

(3) Romancha (Horripilation)

(4) Sveda (Perspiration)

(5) Ashru (Tears)

(6) Vaivarnya (Change of Colour)

(7) Vepathu (Trembling)

(8) Vaisvarya (Change of voice or Svarabheda (Breaking of voice)

**Saukumarya see Gunas**

**Sauṣṭhava**

The basic posture of a superior character.

**Shabari**

This is one of the sub dialects of Prakrita used in the Sanskrit plays. Shabari was prescribed for those who lived in places where elephants, horses, goats, sheep, camels or cows were kept.

**Shabda-cyuta see Dosas**

**Shailūṣa**

This means 'a musician - actor'. He may be a public dancer; Leader of the band etc.

**Shakara**

This is one of the prominent characters from the Royal Harem and became popular from Śakāra as portrayed in Sudraka's drama 'Mrcchakatika'.

According to *Natyashastra*, Shakaras are forest tribe of low caste and it also refers to Shakāra-bhasa, the particular dialect they speak; Abhinava states that the dialect is full of Ś-sounds.

*Dhanikà* on *Daśarupaka* mentions him as a kings brother-in-law and of a low caste. *Sahitya darpana* describes him as the brother of a King's concubine. *Natyadarpana* states that Shakara is a low character because he is born low (a bastard). The character is concerned in the context of a king and of laughter. It also states that any brother - in - law of a king is not be called Shakāra but only the one who is low cate and who stimulates laughter by his perversities.

*Bhavaprakashana* observes that Shakāras are a mountain - tribe who live with their women in hilly bowers and have red eyes, black hair, protruding teeth, fat or pot - bellied. They wear garments of cotton patches and speak the Shakara dialect. Shakaras are recognised as an unique characters figuring in Sanskrit drama and fall under the category of 'Artha-sachiva', if we classify the Associates of the Hero in the three context of Dharma, Artha and Kāma, in which matters they counsel and assist a Royal Hero.

Sudraka ḩas depicted Shakara as a comic Villain whose action are shocking, but his perverted and non-sensical talk would make one roar with laughter. To a large extent, *Bhavaprakashana's* description of this character matches Sudraka's characterization of Shakara in Mṛcchakatika.

Accordingto *Bhavaprakashana* Shakara is regarded as outcaste by religious law and be considered as 'outside characters', not belonging to the inner circle or the domestic fold of the Hero and the Heroine. He is fond of wearing guady clothes and ornaments. He speaks the Prakriti language and his behaviour is vulgar. His temperament is fickle; he is easily provoked to anger and is pleased also quickly by the slightest reason. His speech is particular : it contradicts the authority and verity of Vedas and Puranas; it is a perversion of the country or the place, family (connection), logic and established truths, people and their customs or practises; it serves no purpose or is an utter nonsense.

Shakara is the borther of a king's concubine, a character in Sanskrit dramas characterised by his folly, frivolity and vanity.

**[see also 'Adhama']**

**Shakara-bhasa**

Abhinava states that the dialect is full of Ś-sounds. According to *Natyashastra*, the Shakaras who are a forest tribe of low caste speaks this particular dialect and they serve in the Royal Harem.

**Shakari**

This is one of the vibhasas or sub-dialects of Prakrita used in the Sanskrit plays and is assigned to the Shakara and the Shakas and other groups of the same nature. This sub-dialect was used by Sudraka in his famous play 'Mrcchakatika'.

**Shakata Hasta**

This is a double hand gesture in which the two hands in *bhramara* (but without joining the thumb and the middle finger) are placed one above the other near the wrist. This gesture is used to denote. "demon (*rakshasa*)."

**Shakha**

'Shariraji' refers to the expressions through the limbs of the body which is sub-classified as Anga (Major limbs), Pratyanga (minor limbs) and Shakha, *ie, the branch limbs of the body. They are as follows:-* The movements of the heel is called '*Parshnibheda'; movements of the ankle is 'Gulpha bheda¿*, movements of the sole '*Tal bheda*'; movements of the toes '*Padanguli bheda'*, movements of the finger '*Karan gulibheda'*.

**Shamyā**

This is one of the four audible Tāla gestures (right hand slaps down).

**Shaṅkā**

It means 'Apprehension, Doubt, Hesitation' etc.

Shanka is the third Mutable State / Vyabhichari Bhava. "Apprehension' should be shown by repeated looks, hesitation, dryness of mouth, licking of the lips, change of facial complexion, loss of voice, trembling, dryness of lips and throat, etc.

**Shankha**

*Brha. Upanishad* mentions "Shankha as a wind instrument made of Conch shell. A shell or conch used for blowing as a wind instrument."

*Āpasthamba Shrauta Sutra* mentions Shankha as a musical instrument played in the time of Mahavrata ceremony.

Shankha is the manifestation of soundin nature and considered to be pious. It produces a deep and voluminous sound.

In India Shankha or Conchshell is known throughout the subcontinent Previously used in war as heraldic instrument and nowadays used in worship and dance. It has a prominent place in Pancha Vādya.

The *Natyashastra* helds music, an indispensable adjunct of Sanskrit drama. It informs about musical instruments like Mridanga, Paṇava, Dardura, Dundubhi, Muraja, Jhallarī, Paṭ aha, Vaṁsha, Shaṅkha and Ḍakkinī.

**Shankhadhma**

This means a 'Conch blower'. In the Purushamedha Prakayana of the *Taittiriya Brahmaṇa* (3rd Ashtaka and 4th Prashna), names of professional artists and musicians are mentioneld whose services were required in the sacrificial hall. Sankhadhma is one such musician.

**Shankha Hasta**

This is a double hand gesture in which the right hand in *shikhara* enclosing the left thumb with four fingers of the left hand touching the right hand and the right thumb touching the top of the left middle finger.

Used to denote "conch-shell etc."

**Shantarasa**

This sentiment is a later addition and can be developed in drama from its permanent state 'Nirveda' (Discouragement).

Nirveda occurs from frustration or conflict between expectation and achievement.

According to *Dasarupaka* Nirveda arises from 'Tatvajnāna' (Knowledge of him) and Āpad (Calamily).

According to *Natyashastra*, Nirveda is caused by poverty, illness, insult, anger (on somebody's part), separation from the loved one or resignation.

| | | |
|---|---|---|
| Sthayibhava | : | Shama (Tranquility) |
| Vibhava | : | Spiritual knowledge, pure heart, detachment etc. |
| Anubhava | : | Closed eyes, meditation, natural smiling face, etc. |
| Vyabhichari bhava | : | Nirveda, Smriti, Shrama, Shoucha, etc. |
| Satvikabhava | : | Stambha, Romancha etc. |
| Varna | : | Svachchha (Clean) |
| Mukharaga | : | Svabhavika (Natural) |
| Hasta | : | Sukhatunda - Hamsapaksha |
| Presiding deity | : | Buddha. |

**[see 'Rasa', 'Bhava', 'Nirveda' etc]**

**Shastra**

A religious or sacred treatise, any department of knowledge or science. Natyashastra denotes 'Dramatic treatise'.

**[see 'Natyaveda']**

**Shatha Nayaka**

*Bhavaprakashana* of Sharadatanaya classify the Nayaka (the Hero) in the context of love, implying the attitude and behaviour of the Hero in regards to the matters of love. His fourfold distinctions are :- Anukula, Daksina, Shatha and Dhrista type of Nayaka.

According to *Sahityadarpana,* the Shatha or Rogue is a Nayaka who has his love fixed on one women, makes a show of love to other women, and secrety acts contrary to the professed love in the case of a third woman. This type is usually to be found in Prahasana and Bhāna.

**[see 'Nayaka']**

**Shauraseni**

According to Bharata and *Nataka-Laksana - Ratnakosha,* the main Prakrita dialect to be used in dramas should be 'Shauraseni', both for prose and verse. It can be used by anybody in the play which is popular dialect of the Doab of the Yamuna and Ganga. Dramatic theories state it as the language of the Nayika (Heroine), her friends and attendants and generally of women of good families. Shauraseni is also spoken by ordinary people.

**Shesa**

One of the three great serpents who is supposed to preside in the knot of the flag-staff of Indra, the setting up of which is the most important of the sacred rites on the stage.

**Shikhara Hasta**

A single hand gesture in which the thumb should be stretched up in the *mushti*.

This is used to express amour, cupid (the god of love), bow, pillar, certainty, oblations to forefathers, lips, entering, tooth, questioning, the *shivalinga,* negative reply, recollection of memories, to tie something on the waist, the act of embrace, sounding a bell etc.

**Shilapaka**

This is a minor form of drama (Uparupaka) that has four acts in which all the vrittis are allowed and the comic sentiment is avoided. Descriptions of burning grounds (Śmaśāna) and similar things are found in it. Probably it was a kind of Pantomime, states *Sahitya darpana.*

**Shilpa**

An art (fine or mechanical), skill, craft. Songs, musical instruments and pure dance have been bracketed together under this heading from olden times in India.

**Shilpini**

*Dasarupaka* of Dhananjaya defines this female character in a Sanskrit drama as one who is an artist, like a girl skilled in painting, music, dance, etc (an associate of the Heroine).

**Shirobheda**

It means the movements of head in Indian dance idiom.

Nine types of movements of the head are Sama, Udvahita, Adhomukha, Alolito, Dhuta, Kampita, Paravritta, Utkshipta and Parivahita. The *Natyashastra* provides some more head movements which are not mentioned in *Abhinaya darpana.* These are Akampita, Vidhuta, Ādhuta, Avadhuta, Anchita, Nihanchita.

(1) **Sama:** It means to keep the head straight without any movement. It is employed in the beginning of a dance, prayer or in pride, anger (in love), etc, motionless, in activity, stunned.

(2) **Udvahita:** According to *Abhinaya Darpana*, one has to move the face upwards and keep the head in that position. Used to denote a flag, the moon, the sky, a mountain, movements in the sky, objects at a height.

(3) **Adhomukha:** One has to move the face downwards and keep the head in that position. Used for coyness,

grief, salutation, evil thoughts, fainting, things placed below (or on the floor) and submerging in the water.

(4) **Alolita:** Here one has to move the head in a circular way. It is used to denote sleepiness, possessed by an evil spirit, intoxication, a wild and uncontrolled laughter, unconsciousness.

(5) **Dhuta:** This is one of the nine types of head movements. Here one has to move the head from left to right and vice -versa. This is employed to exhibit the denial of something, refusing, looking at both sides, astonishment, sadness, unwillingness, cold, fever, fear, after - effect of consuming liquor, fighting, striving, forbidding, glancing at own limbs, calling over one's shoulders.

(6) **Kampita:** Here one has to move the head up and down to portray anger, questioning, counting, acceptance, threatening, agreeing or asking to be seated.

(7) **Paravritta:** Here one has to turn the head to either side and look over the shoulder. Used for "ordering that should be done, anger, shame, not bothered, insulting, ignoring and a quiver.

(8) **Utkshipta:** One has to turn the head to one side slightly and looking up. Used for 'showing the way to some one, the act of acceptance or looking after.

(9) **Parivahita:** One has to move the head from one side to the other alternately (without turning the face). Used to depict 'desire, separation, chanting prayers, satisfaction, approval and consideration etc.

(10) **Akampita:** Though *Abhinaya darpanam* do not mention this, this is a head movement prescribed in *Natyashastra* where the head is moved slowly upwards and then downwards. Used to depict 'Chanting, preaching, agreeing natural talking, calling some one etc.

(11) **Vidhuta:** This head movement is only prescribed in *Natyashastra* and not discussed in the *Abhinaya darpanam*. Here the head is moved sideways, quickly to denote attack of cold / heat, terror, high fever, panic striken after drinking liquor etc.

(12) **Adhuta:** This head movement is not mentioned in *Abhinaya darpanam*. But Bharata's *Natyashastra* describes this in which the head is moved by slanting it up wards and moved to denote 'pride, admiration or condemnation, self respect, looking sideways and abov.

(13) **Avadhuta:** In this gesture, the head is moved by slanting it downwards. In dance, it indicates 'asking someone to come, conversation and making a sign while drawing or sketching, exhausion, sleeping in the sitting position.

(14) **Anchita:** This is not mentioned in *Abhinayadarpanam,* but this head movement has been described by Bharata. Here the ead is bent an either side to show 'fainting, intoxication, uneasiness, mourning etc.

(15) **Nihanchita:** This head movemen is not discussed in the *Abhinaya darpanam,* but *Natyashastra* states that in this the shoulders are to be raised up and head be bent downwards to show 'indifference, cynicism, pretension of ignorance, anger etc.

**Shisya (Vidusaka)** **see Vidusaka**

**Shiva**

One of the distinguished features of Sanskrit drama is that the play begins with an invocation, usually to god Siva who is the presiding deityof dance and drama. In *Natyashastra* we find that there are various Indian deities deputed to protect different dramatis personae where they are performing on the stage. A verse says :

Let Indra protect the actor playing the role of hero, Saraswati assume the role of heroine, Onkara the Vidusaka (Jester) and Siva rest of the characters.

He is the Destroyer, the third deity of the sacred Hindu Trinity, a supreme god. Shiva as Lord of Dancers called 'Nataraja'.He is one of the most prominent presiding deities of the theatre and *Natyashastra* has mentioned that he should be worshipped with offerings and sacrifices.

**[see also 'Tandava' 'Lasya' 'Nataraja', Nritta, Nritya etc.]**

**Shivalinga Hasta**

This is a double gesture in which the left hand in *ardhachandra* with the palm facing upward and the right hand in *shikhara* placed on the left palm. Used to denote : "Shivalinga."

Lord Shiva is represented symbolically by this gesture in Indian dance form.

**Shlesha see Gunas**

**Shloka**

It dinotes the verse farms affearing in Sanskrit plays.

**Shobha (Brilliance) see Vagyabhinaya**

**Shoka**

It cannotes 'Grief, Sorrow, Sadness' etc. Shoka means "Grief" the Permannet State/ Sthayi bhava is produced by means of separation from the beloved, loss of wealth, sadness at demise or captivity of dear ones and the like. Grief or Shoka is third Sthayi bhava. "Grief" is expressed in acting by silent weeping, crying, deep breathing, stagnancy, insanity, delusion, death and the like.

**Shrama**

It denotes 'Fatigue, Weariness, Exhausion. Shrama is the sixth Mutable State Vyabhichari Bhava which should be enacted by pressing and massaging the body, deep breathing, yawning, slow walk, distorted eyes and face and making faint, indistinct sounds.

**Shravya see Aksepiki**

**Shresthins**

This denotes 'Masters of Guilds' the dramatis personae in Sanskrit plays who speak Ardhamagadhi, a principal Prakrit dialect.

**Shrigadita**

This is a kind of minor drama (Uparupaka) having one-act. The name 'Śringadita' derieves from the word 'Śri' often comes up and because the goddess Śri appears singing and reciting in it. The Avaloka on the *Daśarupa* mentions that Shrigadita is a form of Mimic dance.

**Shringara Rasa**

The word 'Shringara' refers to Love, Erotic, Amorous, Romance etc.

Shringara rasa is of two types : Sambhoga and Vipralambha. However, *Dasarupaka* adds a third called 'Ayoga' to these two main categories.

*Dasarupaka* defines Ayoga Shringara as those erotic sentiment where lovers have not met eachother at all. *Dasarupaka* gives us ten stages through which the Ayoga passes. They are

(1) Longing (Abhilasa)

(2) Anxiety (Chinta)

(3) Recollection (Smriti)

(4) Enumeration of merits (Gunakatha)

(5) Lamentation (Pralāpa)

(6) Madness (Unmāda)

(7) Feverishness (Sanjvara)

(8) Distress (Udvega)

(9) Stupor (Jaḍata)

(10) Death (Marana)

*Natyashastra* gives these states as the ten Kamavasthas and may, therefore, be experienced in Vipralambha (Separation).

The Sambhoga Shringara is the love-in-union. A critic rightly points out that Dramatists delight in delineating the growing love between two lovers who have to fight, inch by inch, in attaining their goal. The common pattern of themes in love-plays is based on the struggle of the lovers against all odds, obstructions and impediments, and resulting in their union at the end of their travail.

Vipralambha Shringara is the separation of two persons between whom intimacy has sprangup. *Daśarupaka* designates it as Viprayoga. The separation, according to it, can arise either from Resentment (Māna) or from absence (Pravāsa). The Resentment can results from fondness or jealosy and according to late works, it has few more sub-divisions, Māna, Pravāsa, Sāpa etc.

Though the separatin of lovers can have thousand causes. But in general, it occurs due to the absence of one of the two parties or because of some misunderstanding circumstances. The love - in - separation is beautifully depicted in Abhijnana Shakuntalam where the King is so mentally agitated.

According to *Natyashastra* and later treatises on dramaturgy, Shringara Rasa demands that the setting should be gorgeous with women, lovers, scenes in parks and ponds etc should be undertaken. Anubhavas are the effect of the ambiance on the characters.

The Vyabhicharibhavas or the transitory states like Vyādhi (illness), Stambha (paralysis), Nidra (Sleep), Nirveda (Despondency), Chinta (Worry) etc. should be incorporated in the development of Shringara Rasa.

Shringara or the erotic sentiment gets developed when Rati (Love), the permanent sentiment (Sthayibhava) is excited between a man and a woman.

Love is represented in acting by means of cheerful eyes and the face, smiles and sweet words, patience and delight, and graceful movement of limbs.

| | | |
|---|---|---|
| Varna | : | Shyama (Green) |
| Mukharaga | : | Prasanna (Pleased) |
| Hasta | : | Alapadma |
| Svaras | : | Madhyama, Panchama |

Raga

For *Samyhuktha Shringara,* ie, love in proximity, the suitable Raga is '*Khamaas*'.

In *Vipralambha Shringara,* ie, love in separation, '*Mukhāri*' Raga is employed.

In *Nashta Shringara,* ie, love in expectation, the suitable Raga will be '*Kānada*'.

For *Abhisāra Shringara,* ie, love in pursuit, '*Thodi*', Raga is used.

In *Samara Shringara,* ie, love in quarrel, the proper Raga will be '*Ārabhi*'.

For *Milana Shringara,* ie, love in meeting, one may employ '*Mohana*' Raga.

In the last of the eight varities which is '*Punarmilana Shringara*', ie, love in re-union, the suitable raga will be '*Anandabhairavi*'.

*Presiding Deity* : Vishnu.

**Shrinkhala**

In Indian dance, it represent Chain formation-the partners form a chain by holding each other's hands and dance.

**Shruti**

In general denotes 'Intonation'. But especially it refers to the twenty-two divisions of the octave. 'Dhvani' means sound and the sound of music is called 'Nādā'. According to Indian theory, the sounds of music are first perceived as relative pitches or intervals and then from the 22 main intervals 'Shrutis' come the seven notes 'Svaras', namely, Ṣaḍja, Ṛṣabha, Gāndhāra, Madhyama, Pañcama, Dhaivata and Niṣāda.

*Sangita ratnakara* of Sharangadeva states "Sound is first heard as an interval, a Shruti, but the resonance that immediately follows, conveying of itself (without an external aidan expression to the mind of the hearer, is called a "Svara", musical note. According to Bharata, Svaras (notes) are divided into four variety such as Vādi (Sonant), Saṁvādī (Consonant), Anuvādī (Assonant), and Vivādī (Dissonant), according to the number of Shrutis between them and this has remained the accepted divisions ever since.

Shruti is a unit of measurement of the relation of Notes in an octave. As a comparison, there are the semitones in western music, twelve of them to an octave. Similarly Indian music 'divides' a *saptaka* (*Sa to* $s^{a}$) into twenty-two intervals which are 'Shrutis', not necessarily equal in size, infact they are not). Shruti intervals between consecutive notes in a standard scale are given in the following illustration and if all of them are counted they be we will have 22.

| Hindustani | Karnataka | Sol-fa | Scale of C | Tone | Ratio | Sruti | Symbol |
|---|---|---|---|---|---|---|---|
| *Shadja* | *Shadjam* | *Doh* | C | | 9/8 | 4 | *Sa* |
| Komal rishabh | Suddha rishabham | | C#, Db | Major | | | ri<br>Ri |
| *Suddharishabh* | *Chatussruti rishabham (Suddha gandharam* | Re | D | | | | |
| *Komal gandhar* | *Sadharana gandharam (Shatsruti rishabham)* | | D#Eb | Minor | 10/9 | 3 | ga |
| *Suddha gandhar* | *Antara gandharam* | Mi | E | | | | |
| *Suddha mand-hyam* | *Suddha madhyamam* | Fa | | Semi | 16/15 | 2 | *Ga*<br>*Ma* |
| *Teevra Madhyam* | *Prati madhyamam* | | Maj F# | | 9/8 | 4 | *ma* |

| | | | | | | | |
|---|---|---|---|---|---|---|---|
| *Pancham* | *Panchamam* | Sol | G | | | 4 | *Pa* |
| *Komal dhaivat* | *Suddha dhaivatam* | | G#, Ab | | | | |
| *Suddha dhaivat* | *Chatussruti dhaivatam (Suddha nishadam)* | | La | A | Maj | 9/8 | *dha* 4 |
| *Dha* | | | | | | | |
| *Komal nishad* | *Kaisikhi nishadam (Shatsruti dhaivatam)* | | A#,Bb, | | | | *ni* |
| *Suddha nishad* | *Kakali nishadam* | Ti | B | Min | 10/9 | 3 | *Ni* |
| | | | | Semi | 16/15 | 2 | |
| *(Tara shadja)* | *(Tara shadjam)* | Doh | Cl | | | | *Sa'* |

If all the *shrutis* are added from Sa to Sa they will total up to 22, And if all the ratios are multiplied by one another they will give a product of 2. This is the measure of an octave or a *Sthayi*.

## Shukatunda Hasta

A single hand gesture in which the ring finger should also be bent in the *Arala*. This gesture is used to express shooting of an arrow, a spear, remembering one's abode, uttering mystic things, violent mood etc.

**[see also 'Jati']**

## Shuskavakrișța

This is one of the twenty constituent parts of Purvaranga. (Preliminaries of a play) performed on the stage. Shukavakrista follows after the Tandava dance is over, ie, Vardhamāna. The item is an introduction in which the Sutradhara recites some verses in a sonorous voice.

## Siddhi

Siddhi is the rule of success in dramatics.

Chapter XXVII of *Natyashastra* contains a detailed criticism of dramatic performances and explains the criteria of success (Siddhi) in the production of plays. It also enlists the various obstacles and blemishes that may mar a dramatic presentation. Interestingly it also informs us about the qualifications expected of ideal spectators.

In one of the verses in Chapter VI of *Natyashastra*, Bharata has furnished eleven elements of Drama which canbe collectively called the 'Digest of Natyashastra. These significant dramatic components are:-

Rasa (Sentiment)

Bhava (Emotion)

Abhinaya (Acting)

Dharmi (Modes of representation)

Vritti (Styles of expression)

Pravritti (Local usages)

Siddhi (Success of production)

Svara (Note)

Atodya (Musical instruments)

Gana (Song)

Ranga (Theatre)

Siddhi is, therefore, an important aspect of Sanskrit drama.

Siddhi denotes 'Success' and the *Natyashastra* states that there are certain factors that indicate the success of the presentation of Sanskrit dramas. It categorize Siddhi into two varities - Manushi, ie, human and Daiviki ie, divine depending on speech, temperament and gestures and rrelating to various emotions and sentiments. Manushi siddhi has ten features while Daiviki has two; and these features comprise mainly of varied temperaments expressed vocally (Vanmayi) and Physically (Shariri) the Vanmayi Siddhi, ie vocal success is of eight types : Smita (Smile), Ardhahāsya (Ordinary laughter), Atihasya (Excessive laughter), Sādhukara (well done), Ahokara (How wonderful), Kasta (How pathetic), Pravriddhanada (Tumultuous applause) and Avakrusta (Swelling uproar).

Shariri Siddhi or Physical success is obtained when the hair of spectators stand on ends resulting from excessive delight or when they begin to crack their fingers. This Siddhi is of two types. The first type follows dialogues exciting wonder or enthusiasm and the second, scenes of quarrels and excitement when spectators become one with the Nata (Actor). If the conduct of the spectators becomes one with the conduct of the actors representing different emotions and sentiments the play could be called a really good play.

The Daiviki Siddhi or the Divine success is achieved when an actor identifies himself with a character whom he is impersonating and when there are no obstacles, no noise, no unusual occurance in the course of the enactment and the Hall is packed.

*Natyashastra* informs that in ancient India during a drama competition, the Siddhis (successes) and Ghātas (obstacles) of a play were carefully noted before a natyamandali was declared victorious. The merit and demerits were recorded by Siddhilekhakas who were experts in recording in discriminating the success and failures and they were not all of the same age, but all acquired wide and varied experiences. On their recommendations (who carefully witnessed the performances of every actor of every company) that the question of offering the Patāka (Banner), a kind of trouphy to a Natakamandali was decided. In case of disagreement, the opinion of the Prāshnikas (critics) were considered who acted as the arbitrators (Pañca).

And now if two Natakamandalis were found to be equal in merit, the final judgement was made by the king. If the king also fails to take any decision, both the groups were awared Patakas (Banners).

**Siddhi (Persuation) see Vagyabhinaya**

**Siddhilekhakas**

It means recorders of successes and obstacles of dramatic performances by various theatrical troupes or natakamandalis.

**[see under "Siddhis"]**

**Sikhara**

This indicates holding of reins, sound by a bell embrace etc in dance.

**Simhamukha Hasta**

This is a single hand gesture in which the middle and the ring finger are bent forward to touch the thumb in *pataka*. This is used to express "sacrificial free (*homa*), elephant, waving *kusha* grass, a lotus garland, a lion's face, preparations of medicine and research."

**Sirasīgata**

This denotes 'excessive shrillness of the voice', one of the fourteen Gāyaka Dōshas or Defects.

**Skandha bheda**

This refers to the movements of the shoulders and are of five varities :-

(1) **Ekochcha** (one shoulder raised up): This is used to express 'striking with fist or a sword'.

(2) **Karnalagna** (raised up to the ear): Used to denote 'weather, embracing the beloved ones'.

(3) **Uchchharita** (streched upwards): Thisis employed to express 'joy, pride, and bravery.

(4) **Srishta** (dropped down and moving around): Used for 'tiredness, shame, sadness, guiltness.

(5) **Lolita** (swinging): Used to denote 'playing drums'.

**Smriti**

It denotes 'Recollection, Remembrance, Memory' etc.

Smriti or "Recollection", is the Eleventh Mutable State/ Vyabhichari Bhava and according to Bharata, Smriti should be represented in acting by shaking the head, looking down and raising the eye brows, etc.

**Sphota**

Sudden expansion of mind as a result of distinctly clear understanding of the inner idea of a work of art.

**Stage-objects see Aharyabhinaya, Pusta**

**Stage Productions see (Aviddha style, Sukumara style, Pravritti, Vritti etc.)**

**Stambha**

It denotes the 'column' or the 'Pillar' of the theatre-house.

**[see under 'Ranga']**

**Stambha (Bhava)**

This means 'Stunning', Steady, Inertia, Paralysis etc. First Sāttvika Bhava/Emotional State, which according to Bharata should be represented in acting by being still, motionless and without senses and by stiffening the body.

**Sthāna**

Standing posture, a stance in 'Angika abhinaya'.

**Sthāna (Music)**

Means 'register', ie, high, medium low, a term used in music.

According to *Naradi Siksha,* a handbook on the Śama Veda states three main Sthanas or voice positions, namely, stomach, throat and the head.

This is one of the attributes of musical rendering (Pathyaguna) Sthana or three voice locations are :- Ura (chest), Kantha (throat) and Shira (head).

**Sthanaka see Khanda**

**Sthanaka Bheda**

Sthanakas means '*positions of the feet in standing posture*' and Sthanaka Bheda falls under the head '*Cheshtakrita*' (comprises the movement of the entire body) and the Cheshtakrita comes, under '*Angikabhinaya*'.

According to *Abhinayadarpanam,* Sthanaka Bheda are of six kinds as follows :-

(1) **Samapada:** Standing on both the feet together. It is used in offering flowers, depicting the image of God.

(2) **Ekapada:** Standing on one leg while the other leg is placed on the knee of the first. It is used in depicting motionlessness and concentration in *Tapasya,* meditation in standing position.

(3) **Nagabandha:** The legs are intertwined so too the hands. It is used to show the serpentine coiling around.

(4) **Aindra:** Same position of *Ekapada* except that the second leg does not touch the knee of the other leg. It is used for depicting Indra and kings.

(5) **Garuda:** From Aleedha Mandala one knee is placed on the ground, the arms stretched out like the wings of a bird. It is employed to portray '*Garuda*'.

(6) **Brahma:** Sitting in *Padmasana,* both the feet are placed upon the opposite thighs. It is used in depicting '*Brahma*' and meditation.

In Sthanaka Bheda, *Abhinaya - darpanam* has not mentioned two more varities namely, *Vaishanava* and *Vaishakha* which are mentioned in *Natyashastra* of Bharata.

(7) **Vaishnava**: Here one foot is kept straight and the other is placed two and a half spans apart obliquely and toes pointed sideways with raised chest and slightly bent shanks, a posture typical of Lord Vishnu.

This position is used in throwing a disc, holding a bow, ailing person, donating, movement of the limbs and anger. The reverse of this position is used in showing 'frustration or anger in love, rebuke, loneliness, doubt, envy, anxiety, intellect, recollection, miserliness, waveringness, vain and in Shringara, Adbhuta, Bibhatsa and Vira Rasas.

(8) **Vaishakha:** The feet are obliquely placed three and half spans apart and Lord *Kartikeya* is the presiding deity. This posture is employed to show 'horse-riding, an exit from the battle field, large birds, shooting an arrow, and exercising the limbs.

**Sthānavivarjitam**

This means singing in all the three sthānas that which is to be sung in one particular (svara) sthāna - a jumble of all musical sounds. One of the fourteen defects in singing.

**Sthapaka**

He is a third official in the production of a Sanskrit drama. First comes Sutradhara who is assisted by a deputy or right-hand man, the Pariparsvika and a third official, the Sthapaka. The duties of the Sthapaka was centred on the actual construction and management of the stage in classical times.

According to tradition, after carrying out the different items of the Purvaranga, Sutradhara should effect his exist and Sthapaka (Introducer) should make his entry and entertain the audience with dainty pieces of songs, mention the name of the playwright of the ensuing production and carryout the formal prologue. This being done, Sthapaka retires from the stage. This was the practice in the earlier times. But in later period, the duties of the Sutradhara and Sthapaka were combined and merged in the Sutradhara himself, perhaps for practical reasons of economy and the rationalised use of the personnel available.

**Sthapana see Sthapaka**

**Sthapita**

Sthapita are those women in Sanskrit dramas who by their youth and beauty have won the kings heart and are maintained by the king; they would always dress to perfection; though capable of harshness, jealousy and cruelty, they are adept in judging the whims of their royal master, ready to please him, and are extremely clever in the art of love.

**Sthayi**

It denotes 'Level', the repetition of the same sound. One of the four kinds of Varna (melodic movement). Others are Arohi (ascent), Avarohī (descent) and Sañcarī (wandering or ascent and descent combined).

**Sthāyibhāvas**

It denotes permanent mood or feeling - which, when energised and stimulated by appropriate *Vibhāvas* (supporting or stimulating determinants), *Anubhāvas* (consequent feelings and reactions) and *Vyabhicari-bhavas* (Transitory feelings or states), attains to its fullest development, and is then designed as its, corresponding 'Rasa'.

According to Bharata, there are eight Rasas and have eight corresponding permanent states :-

| **Sthayibhavas** | **Rasa** |
|---|---|
| Rati (Love) | Sringara (The erotic sentiment) |
| Hāsa (Laughter) | Hasya (The comic sentiment) |
| Śoka (Grief) | Karuna (The Pathetic sentiment) |
| Ulhāsa (Energy) | Vīra (The Heroic sentiment) |
| Jugupsā (Disgust) | Bībhatsa (The Disgusting sentiment) |
| Krodha (Anger) | Raudra (The Terrible sentiment) |
| Vismaya (Astonishment) | Adbhuta (The Marvellous sentiment) |
| Bhaya (Fear) | Bhayānaka (The Fearful sentiment) |

Besides this generally noticed 'Sthayibhāvas', there is the *Nirveda* developing into its corresponding Śanta Rasa.

In the *Natyasastra*, the section covering Śānta Rasa is believed to be a later addition to the treatise.

Natyashastra thus recognises eight Sthayi bhavas and another Shanta or (Content or Peace), as said, was recognised later. Adya Rangacharya briefly, but more clearly discusses Sthayibhavas as:-

1. Rati or Love:

   (a) *Vibhāva:* stimulus would be season, flower, ornaments or anything beautiful or desirable.

(b) *Anubhāva:* or involuntary reaction; looking sideways, coy glance, sweet words, etc.

(c) *Vyabhicārībhāva:* lassitude, suspicion, jealousy, etc.

2. Hāsya or Humour:

(a) *Vibhāva:* peculiarity of dress or speech, etc.

(b) *Anubhāva:* spouting, mimicking, etc.

(c) *Vyabhicāribhāva:* smile, snicker, laughter, guffow, etc.

3. Karuṇā or compassion:

(a) *Vibhāva:* loss, death, calamity, etc.

(b) *Anubhāva:* tears, fainting, lamentations, etc.

(c) *Vyabhicārībhāva:* sorrow, trembling, fear, etc.

4. Rudra or horror:

(a) *Vibhāva:* anger, violence, treachery, etc.

(b) *Anubhāva:* red eyes, rubbing hands, biting lips, etc.

(c) *Vyabhicāribhāva:* sweating, excitement, impatience, etc.

5. Vira or heroic:

(a) *Vibhāva:* determination, strength, bravery, etc.

(b) *Anubhāva:* courage, generosity, etc.

(c) *Vyabhicārībhāva:* decision, arrogance, etc.

6. Bhayānaka or fear:

(a) *Vibhava:* frightful things, lonely sights, etc.

(b) *Anubhāva:* trembling, pallor, loosing voice, etc.

(c) *Vyabhicāribhāva:* fainting, hurrying, standing rooted, etc.

7. Bibhatsa or awesome:

(a) *Vibhāva:* bad news,loud lamentations, etc.

(b) *Anubhāva:* repulsion, spitting, turning up nose, etc.

(c) *Vyabhicāribhāva:* fainting, illness, death, etc.

8. *Adbhuta* or wonder:
   (a) *Vibhāva:* seeing unusual things; achieving the desired, magic, etc.
   (b) *Anubhāva*: wide or staring eyes, thrill, excalamations, etc.
   (c) *Vyabhicārībhāva:* standing stunned, over-joy, etc.
9. Shanta (or content or peace)
   (a) *Vibhāva:* knowledge or truth, detachment or purity of intent etc (content being final bliss or mokṣa)
   (b) *Anubhāva*: self-control, meditation, universal sympathy, etc.
   (c) *Vyabhicārībhāva:* purity, firmness, thrill etc.

**Stobha**

An interpolated nonsense syllable in Sāmavedic chant is called 'Stobha'.

**Sūcā**

Expression of a meaning of the spoken word by delineating the Sāttvika or subtle body vibrations (spandana).

**Suchi Hasta**

This is a single hand gesture in which the index finger is stretched straight to point upward in the *katakamukha*.

Suchi is used to express "number one, the supreme soul (*Parabrahma),* one hundred, the sun, a place, the world, pointing 'this' and 'that' in the sense of solitude (loneliness), threatening, growing thin, a rod, body, wonder, a strand of hair, an unmbrella, capability, hands, drum-beating, potter's wheel, circumference, a chariot wheel, contemplation and dusk time."

**Sukatunda**

Used in dance this signifies "*Not I*" "*Not You*" "*Not to be Done*" etc.

**Sukha see Vilāsa**

**Sukhatmaka Nataka see Rasa**

**Sukumāra Prayoga / Style / Performances**

A delicate production with music, dances, female artistes and erotic rasa.

*Natyashastra* recognises two kinds of productions keeping in mind plot and the characters etc. For example the director has to examine whether the drama depicts ordinary men and women or divine characters, demons with their super-human elements and actions; whether to delineate everyday life of pain and pleasure, or of wickedness, cruely, deceit, etc, and so on. Sukumara means 'Delicate' Sukumara style is one which is to be adopted in Nataka, Prakarana, Bhana, Vithi, Anka and Natika and the vrittis would be Bharati and Kaishiki, dialogues, emotional acting, dancing and singing etc.

In Natya, as said, two kinds of performance are followed to present emotions and sentiments. They are Sukumara and Aviddha.

Though *Natyashastra* expressly admits 'Rupanusarini' as a mode of representation of a female role by a male actor. But at the same time, it stresses that since women are delicate (Sukumara) and hence they should be represented by women alone Natya should be performed by women well versed in the dramaturgic shastra Natyacharyas should instruct women in terms of the Natyashastra for theatrical representation was a delicate (Sukumara) subject. Roles in Shringara rasa (Erotic sentiment) should be done by women alone for they have delicate gestures and well-formed limbs.

**Supta**

It denotes 'Dream, Napping, Numbed' etc.

Stupa or 'Dream' is the twenty third Mutable State/ Vyabhichari Bhava, which according to Bharata, should be projected on the stage by deep breaths, dullness, closed eyes, senselessness and talking in sleep.

**Suṣira**

Regular musical instruments, according to Bharata are of four varities, viz Tala (stringed), Avanaddha (covered), Ghana (Solid) and Suṣira (Hollow) Suṣira or the 'hollow' are the flutes.

Presently we have Aerophones or wind Instruments like flute, Bansuri, Clarionet, Saxophone, Nagaswaram, Shehnai, Harmonium, Mukhavina etc.

**Suṣira**

**Suta**

In the Purushamedha Prakayana of the *Taittiriya Brahmaṇa* (3rd Asḥtaka and 4th Prashna), names of professional artists and musicians are given whose services were required in the sacrificial hall. Suta referred to those professional musicians of mixed caste who earned their livelihood through music.

**Sutradhara**

In ancient India, a theatre troupe performing Sanskrit plays used to act under the leadership of a Sutradhara, whose job was to supervise the construction or adaptation of the theatre and the production of the play, as well as acting one of the main roles. He was assisted by a deputy or right hand man, the Pariparsvika and a third official, the Sthapaka. Broadly it refers to :-

(I) A stage manager, leader of the drama troupe, teacher and at times the main actor. He conducts the prologue and recites the Nāndi-śloka.

(II) A draftsman, holders of the string, son of Maya, a non-aryan architect of *asura-s*.

**[see 'Purvaranga' and 'Sthapaka']**

**Svad Hasta**

This refers to Hastas for tastes. They are :-

(1) **Kasua** - astringent ........ *Pataka/chatura.*

(2) **Madhura** - sweet ........ *Alapadma.*

(3) **Lavana** - Saltish ........ *Mukula.*

(4) **Katu** - pungent ........ Stretching all the fingers in quick succession from *mukula.*

(5) **Tikta** - better ........ In *simhamukha,* rub the thumb against the fingers.

(6) **Amla** - sour ........ *kangula* up or down.

**Svadhinapatika Nayika**

She is one of the eight varities of Heroine in love as given by *Natyashastra. Dasarupaka* defines her as "one whose husband is loyal to her." So she has no reason to be unhappy.

**Svagata**

This is 'Soliloquy or speaking aside of one's deliberation and feelings - a stage convention of speech. This is also known as 'Atmagata' and defines by Bharata as a speech which comes from the very heart of a character, prompted by the emotions described in the dramatic composition and finding a vent due to many reasons. Most of the dramatic theorists prefer it to be 'Ashravya', ie not supposed to be heard by other characters in a play if at all they happen to be present on the stage at that time.

Svagata is a kind of Natyokti, dramatic speech in the form of revelation of a character's mind, its thoughts and emotions that may even assume the form of a dramatic soliloquy.

**Svāmini**

Such female characters in Sanskrit plays are usually daughters of ministers, army-chiefs or other royal servants who may not possess high honour, but who have won the king's favour by their natural qualities, character and beauty.

This is also one of the modes of address in a Sanskrit drama in which King's wives are to addressed by their attendants as Svāmini (Madam), other terms are Devi (Lady) Bhattini (Mistress).

**Sva Nayika see Sviya Nayika**

**Svapnavakyam**

A speech during sleep; a stage convention of speech.

**Svara**

The sound that generates an expression is a Svara. Saraṅgadeva in his *Sangitaratnakara* states "Sound is first heard as an interval, a Shruti; but the resonance that immediately follows, conveying of itself (without an external aid) an expression to the mind of the hearer, is called a Svara, a musical note.

Bṛhaddeshi of Matangamuni informs that the word 'Svara' denotes that which shines of itself - from *rājṛ* (to shine) with the word *sva* (self) prefixed to it.

In ancient time, a scale of four notes known as 'Svaratantra' were in vogue. The ancient Aryans, like the ancient Greeks, had their music confined to four notes only. How these four notes became the seven is not known to us. An account of the seven notes or svaras of present-day Indian music was first mentioned in the Manduki Siksha of the Atharvaveda.

*Natyashastra* gives us four kinds of Svaras, according to the number of Shrutis between them and this has remained the accepted division ever since. Four svaras are:-

(i) Vādī (Sonant)

(ii) Saṁvādī (Consonant)

(iii) Anuvādī (Assonant)

(iv) Vivādī (Dissonant)

Puranas, Upapuranas and Maha-kavyas (300 BC to 100 BC) contain the names of seven notes.

The seven svaras or notes of modern classical Indian music is abbreviated to *Sa, Ri, Ga, Ma, Pa, Dha and Ni* correspond to the European major scale. The whole span is more minutely divided into 22 microtonal steps (shrutis) of less than a semi-tone. Thus even a specific flat or sharp note can be found in actual singing and playing in delicately shaded, aesthetically flavoured variations which calls for a fine ear and repeated hearing. The fineness of Indian music lies in the micro-distinctions in the pitches of the Svaras.

| | | |
|---|---|---|
| Shadja | (Sa) | → Vira, Raudra, Adbhuta |
| Rishaba | (Ri) | → Vira, Raudra, Adbhuta |
| Gandhara | (Ga) | → Karuna |
| Madhyama | (Ma) | → Hasya, Sringara |
| Panchama | (Pa) | → Hasya, Sringara |
| Dhaivata | (Dha) | → Bibhatsa, Bhayanaka |
| Nishada | (Ni) | → Karuna |

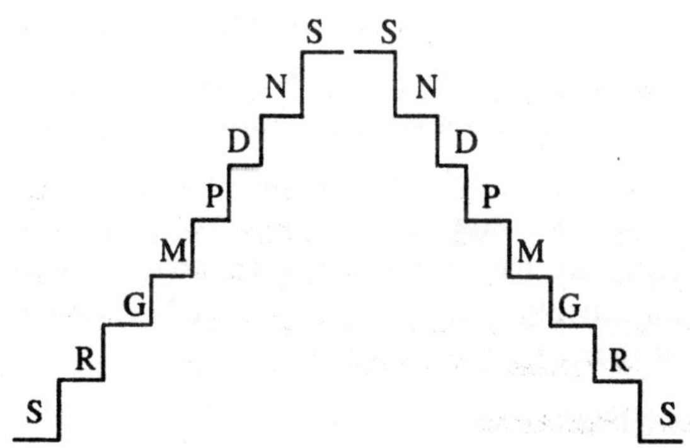


*Arohana* (ascending)

*Avarohana* (descending)

According to *Nārada Saṁhita* (2.53.54) "The note Sa (Ṣaḍajn the tonic) is said to be the soul, Ri (Ṛṣabha) is the head, Ca (Cāndhāra) is the arms, Ma (Madhyana) is the chest, Pa (Pañcama) the throat, Dha (Dhaivata) the hips, Ni (Niśadha) the fact". Each svara of the 'modal scale' (muvchhara) forms a different part of the figure of man.

**Svara (Notation)**

Symbols to indicate octaves and duration of *svaras* in musical notations.

, : A comma indicates the extension of the particular *svara's* duration by one unit (*akshara*). S,

; : A semicolon indicates *svara's* duration to be two units (*aksharas*). S;

- : a dash on the topof the *svaras* indicates, the doubling of the speed (*laya*) and a dash below the *svaras* indicate half the speed (*laya*) accordingly. SS SS

= : Two dashes would similarly indicate doubling the speed of the *madhyama kala*. SS SS

| : This single vertical line indicates the end of half of the stanza of a *avarta* (half cycle of the *tala*). S R G M |

|| : The two parallel vertical lines indicate the end of the *avarta*. (one cycle of the *tala*). P D N S ||

. : A dot on top of the *svara* indicates higher octave and similarly, a dot below a *svara* the lower octave. S S.

It refers to 'Note' and Bharata mentions about seven different notes of Svara. In one ofthe verses in chapter VI of *Natyashastra*, he has given eleven elements of drama which can be collectively called the *Digest of Natyashastra*. These significant dramatic components are :-

Rasa (Sentiment)

Bhava (Emotion)

Abhinaya (Acting)

Dharmi (Modes of representation)

Vritti (Styles of expression)

Pravritti (Local usages)

Siddhi (Success of production)

Svara (Note)

Atodya (Musical instruments)

Gana (Song)

Ranga (Theatre)

Svara is, therefore, an essential component in a dramatic representation.

Svara is the note of human voice and music.

It denotes 'the pitch of voice' (in general), but also denotes one of the seven scale degrus. Also refers to a Vadic accent. Regarding the musical scale or the seven Svara, Amarakosa explains that the cry of the peacock is Shadja (Sā); the lowing of the cow, Ṛshabha (Ri); the bleat of the goat, Gandharva (Ga); the call of the horn bull, Madhyama (Ma); the song of the cuckoo in spring, Panchama (Pa); the neighing of a horse, Dhaivata (Dha); and the trumpeting of elephant, Nishāda (Ni).

As music composition, the theatrical Dhruva songs have their two essential aspects of melody and rhythm. All the ancient music treatises from Bharata down to Sharangadeva in the earlier section of his chapters, are associated with dance and drama. In Bharata they were *Jatis*, in late writers, the Ragas. These melodic modes were analysed with reference to their emotional suitability. The intervals, notes and modes were all studied from the emotional viewpoint and schemes of harnessing different moulds for different dramatic situations were formulated. The emotional values of "*Svaras*" are given by Bharata thus:

(I) Ma and Pa To predominate in melodies used in love and comedy.

(II) Sa and Ri For the heroic, the wonderful and the terrible.

(III) Ga and Ni — For pathos.

(IV) Dha — In the loathsome and the fearful.

**Svara (Vedic)**

The *Nāradi Siksha* speaks about the origin of svaras, the nature of Vedic svaras and says svara is common to all vedas. The Vedic svaras fall under four groups, namely Archika (monotonous) Gāthika (with two notes) Sāmika (or 3 notes) Svarāntayram (or 4 notes). Due to variation or change in the pitch of the tone different svaras are found possible. The three main sthānas or voice positions are stomach, throat and the head.

Three primary Vedic Svaras or Ādisvaras of Rigveda are called 'Ārchika Svaras' by Narada in the *Nāradi Siksha*, for which Pāṇini has given the mātra values while Yāgñavalkya has attributed colour, deity, caste, Gotra and Chhandas.

| Adisvaras (Archika Svaras) | Colour | Deity | Caste | Gotra | Chhandas |
|---|---|---|---|---|---|
| Udātta | White | Agni | Brahmana | Bharadvaja | Gayatri |
| Anudātta | Red | Soma | Kshatriya | Gautama | Trishṭub |
| Svarita | Dark | Savita | Vaishya | Gargi | Jagati |

Besides three primary Vedic svaras, Narada and Panini provide a fourth note called 'Pracheya' an extension of Svarita in the real sense. When an Udātta is sung after svarita, the former becomes 'Pracheya'. In other words, the svara that comes after Svarita, which will naturally be an Udātta, is called Pracheya.

**Svara - Bhanga**

Svara-Bhanga or Svara-Bheda denotes "Choking of voice" sinking, change of voice etc. (Fourth Sattvika Bhava / Emotional State) which according to *Natyashastra* should be enacted by an actor by change of voice and chocking of voice. At many places Bharata has employed the term 'Svara-Bheda' for "Svaa-Bhanga, both bearing the same meaning.

**Svara - Bheda see Svara - Bhanga**

**Svara - Giti Upayas**

Svara also refers to one of the Gīti - upāyas under the Avantara Svaras, means 'singing the svaras instead of the sāhitya'.

**Svara - Tone see Ganam**

**Svarāntayram**

The *Naradi Siksha*, which provides a link between Vedic and Post-Vedic music, a handbook on the Sāmaveda recognises four Vedic svaras, namely Archika (monotonous), Gāthika with two notes, Sāmika or three notes and Svarāntayram or four notes.

**Svarita**

A circumflex accent in Vedic recitation is called 'Svarita'.

Other than Rig and Sama - Vedic verses, even the prose part of the Yajurveda are in Sanskrit with Vedic accents called as Udātya Anudātya and Svarita. These accents were the musical notes, used in Vedic chants.

**[see 'Sāmika']**

**Svastika Hasta**

This is a double hand gesturein which the two hands in *Pataka* cross each other near the wrist and are held slightly apart from each other. Used to denote "crocodile."

**Svasthikarechitha**

*Natyasastra* has given 108 Karanas or Cosmic Shiva Bharata poses. This is the seventh pose where both hands holding Svastika hasta are crossed each other, rotated upwards and over separated and placed on the hips.

**Svayam**

According to '*Dasarupaka*' of Dhananjaya, Duti, Svayam are female messengers; special girls enjoying trust and confidence of the Heroine; executing special missions for her or on her behalf in a Sanskrit play. (Associates of the Heroine).

**[see also 'Duti']**

**Sveda**

This means 'Sweat' (Second Sattvika Bhava/ Emotional State) which according to Bharata, should be represented in acting by using a fan in the hand, removing perspiration and showing an ardent desire for air.

**Sviya Nayika**

*Rasarnavasudhakara* states that 'Sviya Nayikas' are those women who are endowed with the qualities of excellent character and straight forwardness which knows no guile; such women stick to their lovers through thick and thin. A Sviya Nayika is herself of three types :-

(1) Mugdha (very young and inexperienced)

(2) Madhya (a little advanced in age and experience)

(3) Praudha/Pragalbhā (mature woman)

**[see 'Nayika', Mugdha, Madhya and Pragalbha]**

# T

**Tādātmya**

Complete self-identification of the spectator with the performer.

**Taksaka**

One of the three great serpents who is supposed to preside in the knot of the flag-staff of Indra (Jarjara) which is regarded as the most important of the sacred rites on the stage.

**Tāla**

Time measure; a musical instrument made of bell-metal; canon of proportion etc.

In music it refers to beating time; musical time; rhythm etc.

Primarily 'Tāla' connotes two things :-

(1) The Rhythmic / Metric system;

(2) One of the four audible Tāla gestures (left hand slaps down).

In early Sanskrit musical treatises 'Tāla' is both a general term for the entire system of Rhythm and a special term for one of the eight hand gestures, in which the left hand slaps down audibly upon the right palm or the left knee.

It denotes 'beat and laya, rhythm (equal time in dance or music), explains Amarakosha.

Apart from the Raga, another striking feature of Indian music is the system of musical time which is the basis of Indian rhythm. The rhythm patterns set to different and complex beats of 4, 6, 7, 9, 10, 12, 14 and 16 etc are called 'Talas'. These correspond to uniform measure of time. The poetic wording of a vocal rendering are composed within the framework of a given melodic theme and tala pattern. Thus the Raga embodies the very synthesis of melody, poetry and rhythm. Indian music has a very complicated Tala structure. A single cycle of rhythm or bar can be built out of units of different duration. The total duration for the cycle can be divided in various ways. When the cycles are repeated in the continuous singing or playing, the pattern of accenting may vary even if the total duration of two rhythm schemes is the same, and the cycle itself may be long. But one clear punctuation for the listening ear is available in the first beat (sam) which is the most emphatic of all the beats in the cycle.

The essential characteristic of Tala is its cycle or repetitive nature. That a set of rhythmic units are juxtaposed in a cycle and repeat themselves. Such cycle termed as 'Avarta'.

**[see under 'Avart']**

Tala denotes the time measures and Bharata in his *Natyashastra* (chapter 31) has given details of the time - measures governing the rhythms of the songs.

In the rhythmic side of the music in the context of drama, we see that Dhruva songs of Bharata were in specific tālas or time - measures, and in as great detail as in the case of melodies, the time - measures are analysed in the *Natyashastra* from the point of view of situation and feeling. Not only was the tempo of the Dhruva set so as to promote the Rasa, but even when there was no Dhruva song and the actor moved or bent himself down or did something, there was pure instrumental playing intended to underline the mood the different kinds of tempo, layas, of both the songs as well as of pure instrumental accomponiment can be seen. The gait and bearing, the very manner in which a character walks in, being most important for producing the first impression of the character and situation in the minds of the audience. Bharata devotes much attention to the fitting of suitable instrumental rhythmic accompaniment to the movements. For clandestine love, Kohala has give the Dhruva-tala called Subhadrā Nartanaka or Utphulla is the measure for scenes of terror and violence. Ullasana for the heroic, Jumbhalika for pathos, Khandadhara composed of several quick steps with a long one at the end to depict movement by chariot are some examples to illustrate the musical treatment of gait.

**Tala bheda**

This refers to the movements of the sole and are of five types:-

(1) **Patitagra** (forepart of the foot is brought down)

(2) **Uddhritagra** (Forepart of the feet is raised up)

(3) **Uddhrita** (Sole of the feet is raised from the ground)

(4) **Kunchanmadhya** (toes and heels touch the ground, middle part of the sole is bent)

(5) **Tirashchina** (sole of the feet is slanting)

**Tāḷahīnam**

Means lack of the sense of Rhythm or Laya.

**Tāla Prāṇa (Attributes)**

There are ten attributes (Prāna) of Tāla as follows :-

1. *Kala*
2. *Marga*
3. *Kriya*
4. *Anga*

5. *Graha (Chart)*
6. *Jaati*
7. *Kallai*
8. *Laya*
9. *Yati*
10. *Prastar*

*Kala* : measures the time interval of the beat and is concerned with definition the duration of the *shadangas* in absolute time.

*Marga :* means the way of rendering the tala by conforming to the duration of each beat and is relates to the rhythmic construction of a musical composition.

*Kriya :* means action. In the context of the *tala,* it refers to the various movements of the hand for maintaining the *tala*. It is the manner of counting the *shadangas* and *shodasangas*.

*Anga* : refers to the parts of the *tala,* each part being made up of one or more of the above *kriyas* the more widely prevalent *angas* are:

(i) *Anudruta :* consisting of just one beat represented by symbol U (half circle).

(ii) *Druta* : consisting of one beat and one *veechu* and represented by O (full circle).

(iii) *Laghu :* consisting of one beat and counting of fingers represented by **I** in notations.

Graha : signifies the point of the *tala* where the song would begin.

There are three types of *graha - sama, ateeta* and *anagata. Sama graha* (song and *tala* commence simultaneously). *Anagata graha* (song commences after tala cycle begins). *Ateeta graha/eduppu* (Song commences before *tala* cycle begins).

*Jaati* : While *anudruta* and *druta* are constant with one and two beats respectively, *laghu* is subject to variation depending on the *jaati* in which it is rendered. Five such *jaatis* (varieties) have been identified such as *tisra, chaturasra, khanda, misra and sankeerna,* representing 3, 4, 5, 7 and 9 beats respectively. While a beat is normally reckoned as having a unit duration, it is possible to vary the duration of each beat. This variable duration of the beat is referred to as '*gati*' which denotes the flow of music. **Gati** also follows the same classification as *jaati,* namely, *tisra gati, chaturasra gati, khanda gati, misra gati and sankeerna gati* representing 3, 4, 5, 7, and 9 unitary durations respectively. While *jaati* (variety) affects *laghu* alone, *gati* (duration of beat) applies to *laghu, druta* as well as *anudruta* or in other words, to the whole *tala*.

*Kallai :* signifies to the minor units figuring in the *tala akshara* and is a variant of the *laya* inasmuch as it refers to the tempo or speed of a particular song. A song in any *tala* of double *kallai* is of comparatively slow tempo while single *kallai* songs are racy.

*Laya :* signifies the speed or tempo of music. A composition is thus set to a particular *tala* but it needs to be rendered at a specified speed to bring out its spirit or essence. Three such speeds have been recognised, namely *chowka* (or *vilambita), madhya and durita* meaning slow, medium and fast.

*Yati :* is the manner of disposition of the several *angas* in *tala* and it signifies the type of the rhythmic pattern or design.

*Prastara :* any *tala anga* like *laghu* or *guru* can be split up into a number of *angas* of lesser magnitude. The *prastara* relates to the possible permutation and combination of such component *angas*.

**Taḷavam**

This means a player on the Kāhaḷa Vādyam. Also a musician (Vedic Index, Vol. II.). In the Purushamedha Prakayana of the *Taittiriya Brahmaṇa* (3rd Ashtaka and 4th Prashna), names of professional artists and musicians are mentioned whose services were called for in the sacrificial hall.

**Tamasika**

It means 'evil-minded, one of the three main types of character in Indian dance. Orther being Satvika (Godly) and Rajasika (Worldly).

**Tambala Vina**

Tambala or Tumbala Vina is a kind of stringed instrument *Āpasthamba Srauta Sūtra* mention Tambala or Tumbal Vina being played in the time of the Mahavrata ceremony.

**Tamrachuda Hasta**

This is a single hand gesture in which the index finger is curved up in the *mukula*.

This is used to denote : "cock, a crane, a crow, a camel, a child and a pen."

In Indian dance, it is also used to show falling down with a sound, beating time, leaf etc.

**Tana**

This is pentatonic and hexatonic versions of the Mūrcchanās.

**Tandava**

This vigorous dance combines Angahara-s, Rechaka-s and Pindibandha-s.

When Shiva was pleased to see the first dramatic representation of 'Amritamanthana' and also a Dima, he agreed to perform the *tandava* at the dusk time. An auspicious time was fixed and Shiva danced the cosmic dance "*tandava*", consisting of 108 *karanas* through *angaharas* and *rechakas* in Kailasa which was witnessed by Gods, Goddesses, *devas,* saints, *ganas, bhutas, yakshas, siddhars, sadhyas, amaras, vidyadharas, uragas and patagas.*

Shiva danced the *tandava* accompanied by Goddess Saraswati on veena, Lord Indra on flute, Lord Brahma on cymbals, Lord Vishnu on drum and Goddess Lakshmi rendering vocal music. The musical ensemble for Shiva's *tandava* consisted of mridangam, pataha, jhanjya, bhanda, bheri, dindima, gomukha, panava and dardura.

In the context of drama, Tandava or the manly dance. in an increasing intensity is performed on the stage in the Purvaranga part of a play and is called 'Vardhamāna'.

**Tandra**

It denotes 'Torpidity', an extra word used with reference to Mutable States/Vyabhichari Bhavas in acting.

**Tanmayibhava**

One pointed concentration of the spectator.

**Tantri**

It means 'stringed instruments'.

**Tanvantara**

This is the under elongation of the mātra - a defect to be avoided in performing the Karshana. .

**Tara bheda**

This means 'the movement of the eyeball and they are of nine types as follows:-

| | | |
|---|---|---|
| (1) | Bhramana | (circular movement) |
| (2) | Pātana | (lowering) |
| (3) | Chalana | (trembling) |
| (4) | Sampraveshana | (eyes are shrinking) |
| (5) | Vivartana | (moved to the side) |
| (6) | Samudvritta | (raised up) |
| (7) | Nishkrama | (widening eyes) |
| (8) | Prākrita | (natural position) |

**Tarduma (Tantri)**

This denotes the strings of the Vīṇa (harp or yāḷ) made of the nerves of animals.

**Tata**

This means 'Father'. The *Natyashastra* has prescribed a set of words for calling the different charactes according to their position. An old person is addressed as 'Tāta'. This is a mode of address in a Sanskrit drama.

**[see also Vatsa]**

**Tata (Music)**

Regular musical instruments are of four types, states *Natyashastra*. These are Tata (Stringed), Avanaddha (Covered), Ghana (Solid) and Susira (Hollow). Tata are those with strings.

Presently we have Chordophones or stringed instruments like the Veena, Violin, Sitar, Sarod, Surbahar, Sarangi, Tambura, Gotu Vadyam etc.

**Tathara**

In Indian dance, it represent the movement of belly.

**Tattva**

In the actual playing of the instruments, there are different methods. Three major styles are Tattva, Anugata and Ogha. Tattva is instrumentation that goes in advance piloting the coming theme.

**Tatvam**

It denotes slow dance (Amarakosha).

**Taurika**

In a dramatic performance, the 'Taurika' is the head of warriors and trumpeters, an expert in blowing all musical instruments.

**Tēna / Tenaka**

A vocalise on the auspicious word 'tena', one of the six aṅgas available for use in a prabandha (art song).

**Thalapushpaputa**

Prescribed by *Natyashastra*, this is the first and one of the 108 Karanas (cosmic Shiva Bharata poses). Here the left hand is in Pushpaputa hasta, one foot in Agratala sanchara, ie, the heel is raised and the leg rests on the first toe. One side is in Sannata ie, bent to one side.

**Theatre (Construction) see Pusya, Ranga etc.**

**Tiraskarṇī**

A hand-held stage curtain; magical art of disappearance.

**Trāsa**

It denotes 'Terror, Fright' etc. Trāsa or Terror is thirty second Mutable Stage/ Vyabhichari Bhava which according to Bharata should be represented on stage by contraction of limbs, trembling, paralysis, horripilation, chocking of voice and irrelevant speech.

**Trayasra Tāla**

A musical rhythm pattern of six time beats (mātrā-s).

**Trigata**

This is the second last item of purvaranga (preliminaries in a play) which is performed on the stage. In all there are twenty constituent parts of preliminaries. Trigata features conversation between the Sutradhara (the Stage-manager), the Vidusaka (the Jester) and a Pariparshvika in which Vidusaka speaks all kinds of nonsense. This is, therefore, the three men's talk in the prologues of Sanskrit plays.

**Trigunatmaka Prakṛti**

Three fundamental qualities pervading all aspects of the universe such as *Sattva* (awareness) *Rajas* (action) and *Tamas* (inertia).

**Tripataka Hasta**

A single hand gesture in which assume *Pataka* and bend the ring finger at the second phalange from the top.

This is used to express crown, tree, the *vajra* (weapon of Indra), and the bearer of *vajra* (Indra), the *ketaki* flower, a lamp, rising flames, a pigeon, patterns drawn on a leaf, an arrow, and turning round or change.

**Trishula Hasta**

This is a single hand gesture in which the three fingers are kept straight pointing upwards with the last finger and the thumb touching each other. This is used to express "a *'bel*-leaf, the idea of Trinity, a trident".

**Trivarga Sadahana**

Three goals of human existence (Artha, Kama, Dharma).

**[see also Purusartha, Sadhana etc]**

**Trotaka**

The tenth anga of the Garbhasamdhi is termed as 'Toṭaka or Trotaka' and this word connotes 'confused, excited speech'. One also hear of a dance called 'Troṭaka'.

**Trotaka (Uparupaka)**

This is one of the sub-classes of drama, a minor form (Uparupaka) which has five, seven, eight or nine acts in it.

A Trotaka deals with gods and men and in each act appears a Vidusaka Kalidasa's Vikramorvasiya is a Trotaka.

**Tryasra Purvaranga**

According to Bharata, there are twenty different constituent parts of a purvaranga (the first nine are presented off stage and the rest on the stage. They are the part of a regular Purvaranga or a chaturasra Purvaranga. The Tryasra Purvaranga is similar but shortened.

**Tulya-tarka (Inference from Similitude) see Vagyabhinaya**

**Tūṇabadma (vadma)**

This denotes a flute prayer. Tuṇava is intrepreted by Bhatta Bhaskara as a flute or Veṇu. Therefore, Tūṇabadma should be a player on the mukhavādya or wind instrument. Sayana generalises this term as referring to a player on a wind instrument.

'Tunavadma' is mentioned in the Purushamedha Prakayana of the *Taittiriya Brāhmana* (3rd Ashṭaka and 4th Prashana) a professional musicians whose service was called for in the sacrificial hall.

**Tūnava**

Bhatta Bhaskara describes Tūnava as the flute or Veṇu.

[See 'Tunabadma']

**Tūṇavam**

This is a kind of wind instrument, a type of flute. In the Vedic index the following references are found, where the instrument is referred to as a musical instrument of wood probably a flute. Taittiriya Samhita, Maitrayani Samhita, Kathaka Samhita, Panchavisma Brahamana and Taittiriya Brahmana also mention this.

Āpasthamba Shrantha Sutra mentions 'Tūṇavan' as musical instrument being played in the Mahavrata ceremony.

# U

**Ūdaharana (Parallelism) see Vagyabhinaya**

**Udara bheda see Prishtha and Udara bheda.**

**Udātta**

This is an acute accent in Vedic recitation.

Other than Rig and Sama - Vedic verses, even the prose part of the Yajurveda are in Sanskrit with Vedic accents called as Udātta, Anudatta and Svarita. These accents were the musical notes, used in Vedic chants.

**Udātta (Gunas) see Gunas**

**Udātta Prakriti Nayika**

A celestial woman, a princess or royal queen (as Heroines) are expected to be endowed with all the desirable qualities and will be of Udātta Prakriti.

**[see 'Nayika']**

**Udātta Svara**

An ascending note.

**Uddipana see Vibhāvas**

**Udgātri**

This denotes the singer of Rigvedic hymns.

**Udghaṭṭaḥ**

One of the five Mārga Tāla patterns, with a proportional structure of 2: 2: 2.

**Udgrāha**

This is the opening component of a prabandha (an art song), often an epigram or metrical couplet).

**[see 'Dhatus']**

**Udha Nayika see Paroḍhā Nayika**

**Ughrishtam**

Refers to 'Restricted pronounciation of words', one of the fourteen defects in singing.

**Ugratā**

It denotes 'Violence, Cruelty' etc. Ugrata or violence is the twentyseventh Mutable State/Vyabhichari Bhava which according to Bharata's *Natyashastra* should be represented on the stage by killing, arresting, beating and rebuking.

**Ullāpya**

This is a form of minor drama (Uparupaka) having one - act. According to *Sahityadarpana* it is full of fighting and *Asragita,* ie, back ground music played from behind the stage with reference to the plot.

**Unmāda**

It denotes 'Insanity, Madness, Extravagance' etc.

Unmāda or Insanity is the thirtieth Mutable State / Vyabhichari Bhava, which according to *Natyashastra*, should be represented by laughing, weeping, crying, irrelevant talk, lying down, sitting and engaging in such other abnormal activities.

**Upadista (Pointed Utterance) see Vagyabhinaya**

**Upagānam**

This denotes the accompaniment. In Taṇdya Mahā Brāhmana, it is mentioned that Udgātri recited the Sāman, while the wives of the priests provided the accompaniment (Upaganaam) on a pair of instrument called Apaghātila.

Upagānam refers to the accompaniment on the musical instruments during the recitation of the Sāmaveda.

**Upakaraṇa**

This denotes the 'Stage property, material implements'.

**Upama**

This is 'Simile' one of the four Alankaras (Figure of speech) available to a playwright. Bharata clasify Upama into five kinds, viz, Prashamsa (Praise), Ninda (Censure), Kalpita (Conceit), Sadshri (Uniqueness), Kimchit Sadrisi (Partial Likeness). *Natyashastra* gives examples of these five varities of Upama.

(1) **Prashamsa (Simile of Praise)**

The king was pleased to see that large-eyed lady just as the sages are pleased to see the success incarnate after it has been achieved with austerity.

(2) **Ninda (Simile of Censure)**

The woman clung to that rough looking person devoid of all good qualities just as a creeper clings round a thorny tree which has been scorched by the forest fire.

(3) **Kalpita (Simile of Conceit)**

Elephants exuding ichor and moving slowly with gracefulness look like mobile mountains.

(4) **Sadshri (Simile of Uniqueness)**

What you have done today to satisfy some one else's desire, is worthy of you and is comparable only to your (other) superhuman deeds.

(5) **Kimchit Sadrisi (Simile of Partial likeness)**

Here has come may lady friend whose face is like the full moon, eyes are like the petals of a blue lotus and the gait is like that of an elephant in rut.

**Upamukha**

A technical term referring to the blowing of the air through the mouth, of the instrument Pichchhora.

**[see 'Pichchhola']**

**Upanayaka**

It refers to a Secondary Hero of Sanskrit drama. Pithamarda, an associate of Hero in the context of love affairs in regarded as a Patākānāyaka (the Hero of the sub-plot) or Upanayaka (a Secondary Hero). An Upanayaka is just a little inferior to the Hero so far as the qualities and accomplishments are concerned.

However, a playwright may keep the role of Pithamarda and Upanayaka distinct. An excellent example of a pure Upanayaka or Patakanayaka is the character of Makaranda in Bhavabhuti's play 'Malatimadhava', who displays touching devotion to his friend, Madhava, the Nayaka and brilliant heroic qualities as well, worthy of a true Hero.

**[see also 'Pataka Nayaka, Pithamarda and Kamasachiva]**

**Upanga**

Upanga is the limbs of face, used for making gesture.

Upangas denotes facial and other minor features such as drishti; bhru; puta; tara; kapola; nasa; adhara; jihva; dashna; chibuka and hanu; vadana. They are, thus, eyebrows, nose, lips, cheeks, eyes and chin etc.

**[see 'Angikabhinaya']**

**Upapati**

Rasarnavasudhakara gives us a categorization of Nayaka

(The Hero) in the context of love into three types:- Pati, Upapati and Vaishika. Upapati or a Paramour is one who disregards the social etiquette and takes a woman to a love-tryst without the sanction of a lawful marriage. A lover-hero of this type usually fall under the division of Shaṭha.

**[see also 'Nayaka']**

**Uparasas**

There are three additional essences called Uparasas. These are :-

(I) Vātsalya (Parent's love for the child)

(II) Bhakti (Devotion)

(III) Gāna Rasa (Musical Aesthetics)

**Uparupakas**

Those drama which did not fit in with Bharata's description of 'Rupakas' (Ten varities of drama) were, probably treated and systematised, in course of time, as new genres of drama and they came to be known as 'Uparupakas', the further divisions and sub-divisions by the later theorists of the ten main forms which nevertheless, remained intact.

Notable minor types 'Uparupakas' are:-

Nāṭikā

Troṭaka

Goṣṭhī

Saṭṭaka

Nāṭyarāsaka

Prasthāna

Ullāpya

Kāvya

Preṅkhaṇa

Rāsaka

Saṁlāpaka

Śrīgadita

Śilpaka

Vilāsika / Vinayika / Durmallika

Durmallī

Prakaraṇikā

Hallīśa

Bhāṇikā

About Uparupakas, the later theories like *'Dasharupa'* elaborately discusses 'Natika' for the first time. The *Bhavaprakasha* furnishes twenty minor forms of drama. *The Sahitya darpana* deals with eighteen types of dramas as Uparupakas. In addition to ten Rupakas, the *Agnipurana* informs about seventeen minor genres.

Uparupaka denotes minor varities of drama with stress on dance, song, abhinaya with lesser emphasis on spoken words.

The *Bhavaprakasa* states that Rupakas are Rasatmaka, ie, dependent on Sentiment, while Uparupakas are Bhavatmaka, dependent on Emotion. The former is termed as Nātyabhedah, ie, species of Natya, while the latter is Nrityabhedah, ie, species of Nritya.

The most striking difference between Rupaka and Uparupaka is that an Uparupaka primarily stresses on Kayabhinaya (Bodily gestures) and music, which in Rupaka is secondary. Thus Uparupaka gives importance to Kayabhinaya while in Rupaka, emphasis is on Satvika temperament and other abhinayas.

**Upasamhara Samdhi see Nirvahana Samdhi**

**Upavartana**

This is a connecting tactic in the Gitakas, in which a final unit of text and melody is repeated at double speed.

**Upa Vīṇa**

Accompanying of the vocal music on the Vīṇa.

**Upohana**

A melodic incipit sung to meaningless syllables is called 'Upohana'.

**Urnanabha Hasta**

The only asamyuta hasta which is not mentioned in *Abhinaya Darpana* but given in *Natyashastra* is Urnanabha. Here assume *padmakosha* and bend all the fingers and the thumb towards the palm.

This is used to express "scratching the head secretly,skin disease, lion, tiger and such other animals and holding touchstone."

**Urubheda**

This refers to the movements of the thighs and are of five kinds:-

(1) **Kampana** (lowering and raising the thighs repeatedly)

(2) **Valana** (knees are brought in)

(3) **Stambhana** (keeping the thighs still and without moving)

(4) **Udvartana** (drawing the knees inward and then moving it)

(5) **Nivartana** (heels are drawn inside and knees are stretched outward)

**Utplavana Bheda**

Utplavana denotes 'leap' and Utplavana Bheda falls under 'Cheshtakrita' (Movements of the entire body) and the latter comes under Angikabhinaya. According to **Abhinaya darpanam**, there are five types of jumps They are :-

(1) **Alaga (not easy):** Jump from side to side with both the feet and place the hands in *Shikhara* at the waist.

(2) **Kartari (scissors):** Jump with the fore feet back and front, in crossing movement (like scissors) showing *Kartarimukha* and then placing the hands in *Shikhara* at the waist.

(3) **Ashva (Horse):** Jump with both the feet together in Sampada and the hands in Tripataka.

(4) **Motita (Crushing):** Jump on both sides alternately like scissors with hands in *Tripataka* stretched side ways.

(5) **Kripālaga (Intense compassion):** Jump with the heel of each foot alternately and hands in *Ardhachandra* at the waist.

### Utsāha

It refers to 'Zeal, Energy, Enthusiasm' etc.

Utsāha is the fifth permanent state (Sthayi Bhava) projected in acting by firmness on the face, spirited movements, leadership and the like. This is related to the superior class of nature. It is produced by means of joy, power, patience, valour and the like.

### Utsanga Hasta

This is a double hand gesture in which the two hands in *Mrigasirsha* face each other.

This is used to denote "embrace, shyness, displaying the limbs and teaching. This gesture also expresses touching the object beyond sight, act of anger, showing the armlets, etc. in Indian dance.

### Uṭshepiṇi

This is the technique employed in the singing of higher notes from Dvitīya to Krushṭa; corresponds to the upper tetrachord or Uttāranga of a scale; included in the āhvāraka svaras.

### Utsristikanka

Since the term 'Aṅka' is more used in the sense of "An Act". Anka when denotes one of the ten recognised varieties of Sanskrit drama is called Utsristikanka.

This is one of the major types of drama in one-act in which the plot is wellknown but it may sometimes be otherwise. It depicts ones' fall and the dramatis personae must be male other than those who are divine.

The predominant sentiment is Pathetic and treats of women's lamentations and despondent utterances at a time after battles and violent fightings have ceased to rage.

Duta Ghatotkaca of Bhasa is an example of Utsristikanta, because, as required in it, the one-act play describes the tradic death of Abhimanyu, which is full of pathos, and the impending deathof the Kurus.

**[see also 'Anka']**

**Utsvarita**

Passing from Chaturtha to Mandra, included in the Āvāntara svaras.

**Uttama Nāyaka see Jyestha Nāyaka**

**Uttama Nayika see Nayika and Uttama Prakriti Pramada**

**Uttama Prakriti Pramadā**

According to Bharata, a female character of soft nature, unimpetuous, speaking always with a smile, kindly in disposition, diligent in her obedience to elders, shy, modest, endowed with the natural qualities of loveliness, sweetness to all people, but also possessed of seriousness, depth and fortitude.

**Utthapana**

This denotes 'song on the setting up of the banner of Indra called 'Jarjara'. This is one of the twenty items of Purvaranga [Preliminaries of a play]. This is taken up on the stage. Here the Sutradhara emerges, followed by two aids 'Pariparshvika' who carry a water jug (Bhringara) and Indra's Banner (Jarjara). The Sutradhara strews flowers, brings in Indra's banner and cleanses himself with the water of the jug.

**[see also 'Purvaranga']**

# V

## Vachika Abhinaya

One of the four kinds of abhinaya, expressed through 'words'.

In four chapters from XIV to XVII, Bharata deals with Vachikabhinaya covering topics like phonetics, prosody, metres, figures of speech in the first three parts and only in the last chapter he explains 'Dramaic Speech (XVII) (Speech Language) highlights some special uses of language and intonation or more precisely 'voice-control'.

Dramatic speech represents spoken language and in a drama a speech language is of four types. Bharata classify it according to the social status of the character on the one hand and the part of the country to which that character belongs. They are:-

(I) **Atibhasa:** This is the grandiloquent language of gods and supermen.

(II) **Aryabhasa:** The refined speech of kind and aristocracy.

(III) **Jatibhasa:** The mother tongue of the ordinary people.

(IV) **Mlecchabhasa:** The corrupt language of the foreigners and the low-born.

*Natyashastra* also mentions the language of birds and beasts (chapter XVII, 25-29). It implies the imitation of the sounds emitted by them and this language could have a meaning only in a drama.

It addition, there could be other kinds of dialects not mentioned here but necessitated by the dramatic context, writes Bharata (XVII, 62).

Dramatic speech is neither prose, nor poetry, nor follows the gramatic rules, but represent spoken language of the character in a play.

It is pertinent to note that Bharata has also stresses on some special uses of language in a drama. He points out that the way in which characters address each other and this itself does communicate to the spectator the social standing and the mutual relation of the character (XVII, 64). Subsequently he enlist these words which are nothing but the mode of addresses to different characters on the stage.

While dealing with Dramatic speech, *Natyashastra* discusses about voice-control and discusses some intonations which has to be produced deliberately by the actor and this intonation is the part of the Vacikabhinaya. Bharata states that language is mostly used for conversation between two actual persons in a dramatic piece, but it may be necessary for a character to speak or converse to a person who is not on the stage. In such cases, intonation is required and therefore, Bharata provides some verses which he termed as 'Anuvamshya', ie handed down by tradition and which describe the nature of Kaku intonation.

He further mentions some vowels and consonants that if given a sepcial intonation convey a particular emotion. Even a pause would be significant in a dramatic speech (XVII, 120-126).

He stressed on the pecularities of the intonations of men and women which an actor must know.

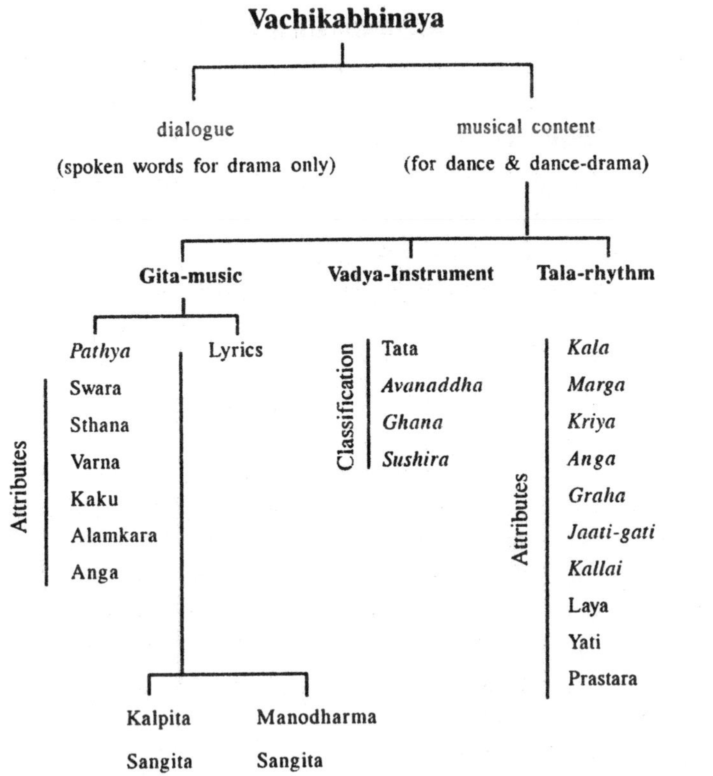


## Vādana

In the Aranyakas of the Rig Veda, Vādana refers to the plectrum of a harp.

Vadana Bheda

This means 'the movements of the mouth' and are of six varities :-

(1) **Vidhuta** (obliquely stretched)

Used to show 'refusal or showing hindrance'.

(2) **Vinivritta** (the mouth is with the pursed lips)

To express 'envy, anger, disrespect, a desire due to bashfulness.

(3) **Nirbhugna** (the lower jaw is lowered)

To denote 'looking into depth or being in deep thought'.

(4) **Bhugna** (slightly opened out)

To express, 'shame, discouragement, impatience, anxeity, consulting.

(5) **Vivritta** (the mouth is kept open)

To denote 'laughter, grief, fear'.

(6) **Udvahi** (lips are lifted up)

To show 'pride or disagreement'.

**Vādi**

It refers to 'Sonant'. Bharata's *Natyashastra* divides Svaras (Notes) into four varities namely, Vādi (Sonant), Samvādī (Consonant), Anuvādī (Assonant) and Vivādī (Dissonant) according to the number of Shrutis (Intervals) between them and ever since this has remained the accepted ramification.

According to *Sangitamakarandah* 'Vadi is the king of notes'. It is most significant note taken in the Rāga and is oft repeated than the rest of the notes. A predominant expression of the Raga, its character determines the mood and helps one to recognize a Rāga and indicates the time of singing it. The speaking note is called 'Vādi'.

According to traditional musical theory, there are three important notes in the Raga, namely, Graha, Amsha and Nyāsa. Sharangadeva describes Graha as the starting note, Amsha, the predominanat or the soul of the Raga and Nyāsa, the ending note. In his *Sangita Ratnakara*, he identifies the Amsha, the main note with the sonant 'Vadi'. Because it is most used during a performance, the Vādī (Sonant) is called Amsha (main note).

*Abhinavabharati* of Abhinavagupta expresses the same view "the Amsha svara is the same as the Vadi."

**Vadya**

Vādya denotes 'Instrumental music' and in a more restricted sense, drumming.

**Vādyakam**

Vādyakam or Vadyamanam denotes the instrumental music. The Vādyaḥ or Vadyam also refers to an 'Instrumental music, where as 'Vadyam' may also be a musical instrument. According to *Saṅgitadāmodara* 'Vadyam' is the sound of a musical instrument. 'Vadyam' plays a key part in the enactment of Sanskrit drama.

In chapter 29 of *Natyashastra*, Bharata has mentioned the proper instrumentation in dramatic performances.

In the actual playing of the instruments, there are different methods. Three major styles are Tattva, Anugata and Ogha. Tattva is instrumentation that goes in advance piloting the coming theme, Anugata is close accompaniment of the song; Ogha is the play of the instrument in a crescendo. Not only these but 19 other ways of instrumental playing are prescribed by Bharata, each with its emotional and contexual application. "The instruments are the very bed of the performance" concludes Bharata.

According to Bharata, when there are no Dhruvas, the occasion is called 'music', for example, in the second Act of the Malavikagnimitra where the heroine is dancing, music forms a part of the action of the play itself.

Each gait and bearing, the manner in which a character walks in being most important for producing the first impression of the character, mood and situation in the minds of the audience, Bharata devotes much attention to the fitting of suitable instrumental accompaniment to the movement. Bharata has spoken of pure drumming to accentuate action. The music in which there are no words or songs but only rhythm - syllables like Jhuntum, Dhen, Dhi, Dhan, Ti, Kita - what are now called Jati, Sol, Bol, which were played on the instruments only is called by Bharata 'Nirgitavadya'.

When a Dhruva song is taken off, its renderation should have its first round without the drum - accompaniment which should join up later (XXXII, 440), this is necessary as otherwise the audience may not hear properly the theme of Dhruva.

**[see also 'Atodya' and 'Nirgita Vadya']**

**Vagyabhinaya**

It refers to 'Diction' in a dramatic composition. This aspect has been discussed in much detail by Bharata in his *Natyashastra*. He has furnished thirty six significant points for the composition of a drama.

These thirty six points embellish and beautify a play, if used with discrimination, according to the sentiment introduced. Manmohan Ghosh's free English rendering of these Sanskrit verses are given below:-

(1) **Bhusana (Ornateness)**

It is providing a composition with many figures of speech and Gunas placed like ornaments.

(2) **Aksara - samghata (Compactness)**

It is the expression of a wonderful sense by means of a small number of syllables with double entendre.

(3) **Shobha (Brilliance)**

It is calling forth of a less known meaning alongwith the well-known one for the purpose of giving distinction to a case of double entendre (Shlesa).

(4) **Udaharana (Parallelism)**

When by a sentence expressing a similar situation a suggestion is made by clever people to accomplish some objects, it is Parallelism.

(5) **Hetu (Causation)**

When a brief and pleasing sentence by the force of its tactful use achieves the desired object, it is termed as Hetu (Causation).

(6) **Samshaya (Hesitation)**

Literally it means 'doubt' and when due to many considerations a sentence is brought to an end without fully communicating the essential theme in view, it is called 'Samshaya'.

(7) **Dristanta (Favourable Precedent)**

Literally it denotes 'example'. Dristanta is that which supporting the case in hand, is an expression of its reason and is pleasing to all people, is a Precedent Favourable to the speaker.

(8) **Prāpti (Discovery)**

Literally it denotes 'Attainment' when on seeing some indications the existence of something is assumed, it becomes an instance of Discovery.

(9) **Abhipraya (Fancy)**

Literally it means 'Belief'. When an idea interesting of people but hitherto non-existent, it conceived on the basis of similarity, it is fancy.

(10) **Nidarshana (Unfavourable Precedent)**

Literally it denotes 'Example'. When well known instances are mentioned for rejecting the contrary view, it is Unfavourable Precedent.

(11) **Nirukta (Convincing Explanation)**

Literally the term means Etymology. Words that are spoken in support of some unobjectionable statement made before, constitute 'Convincing Explanation'.

(12) **Siddhi (Persuation)**

Literally it denotes 'Success'. When the names of many relevant persons are mentioned with a view to accomplishing the object aimed at, it is Persuation.

(13) **Vishesana (Distinction)**

When after mentioning many well-known great objects, something is said to distinguish a thing from them it is Distinction.

(14) **Gunatipata (Accusation of Virtues)**

Literally the term means 'Opposition of virtues'. When virtues are mentioned with, sweet words of harsh import, which carry a contrary implication, it is 'Accusation of Virtues'.

(15) **Atishaya (Excellence)**

When after enumerating the qualities available in common men, one mentions some special qualities, it is Excellence.

(16) **Tulya-tarka (Inference from Similitude)**

Literally it means 'Reasoning from the comparables'. When an object not believable, is inferred from a metaphor or a simile, applied in a similar sense, it is 'Inference from Similitude'.

(17) **Padoccaya (Multiplex Prediction)**

The term literally means 'Collection of words'. When a number of words are used alongwith a number of other words to form different groups for the same purpose, it becomes Multiplex Prediction.

(18) **Dista (Apt Description)**

The term literally means 'Described'. When any object or incident directly seen or not, is described in harmony with locality, time or form related to it, it becomes an instance of Apt Description.

(19) **Upadista (Pointed Utterance)**

When one says something with a happy end on the basis of Shastras and thereby pleases the learned, it is a Pointed Utterance.

(20) **Vichara (Deliberation)**

That which establishes something not directly perceived and is in harmony with the meaning expressed earlier, and includes much elimination of errors (apoha) is called 'Deliberation'.

(21) **Viparyaya (Inversion)**

When due to seeing something, an alteration of Deliberation is made on account of a doubt, it is called 'Inversion'.

(22) **Bhramsha (Slip of Tongue)**

Manifold and sudden deviation of haughty and such other persons from the intended words to something else, is called 'Slip of Tongue'.

(23) **Anunaya (Mediation)**

The term 'Anunaya' literally means 'Imploring'. Words, which are used to please two persons with mutually opposed resolution and are aimed at accomplishing some object constitue 'Mediation'.

(24) **Māla (Series of Offers)**

Literally it means 'Garland'. When for the purpose of accomplishing a desired object, one suggests to a person his many needs (that may be met), it is an instance of 'Series of Offers'.

(25) **Daksinya (Clever Manner)**

When one attends another person with happy and pleased face, sweet speech and other agreeable movements, it is an instance of 'Clever Manners'.

(26) **Garhaṇa (Censure)**

If any one mentions some one's faults and explains them as merits, or decries one's merits and calls them faults, it is an instance of Censure.

(27) **Arthapatti (Presumption)**

When from a sweetly-worded mention of something, some other object is to be understood, it is Presumption.

(28) **Prasiddhi (Celebrity)**

That which is expressed with excellent words mentioning many well-known exploits, is 'Celebrity'.

(29) **Priccha (Interrogation)**

When with gesticulating words, one questions oneself or another and speeks something, it is Interrogation.

(30) **Sarupya (Identity)**

When from seeing, hearing or feeling something, one is excited by its likeness (with another), it is Identity.

(31) **Manoratha (Indirect Expression of Desire)**

Literally the term 'Manoratha' means 'Object of the mind'. Expressing one's secret desire of the heart by a pretence of referring to somebody else's condition, is called 'Indirect Expression of Desire'.

(32) **Lesha (Wit)**

Words which are spoken in a clever manner by expert disputants and which relate to accomplishment of similár objects, constitute wit.

(33) **Saṃksobha (Concealment)**

Literally it means 'Upsetting'. When being faultless one takes upn oneself various faults of another, or ascribes them to another blameless person, it is 'Concealment'.

(34) **Guna-kirtana (Enumeration of Merits)**

When merits of men who excel others in qualities in this world, are ascribed to one single person it is 'Enumeration of Merits'.

(35) **Anukta - siddhi (Semi-uttered Expression)**

Literally the term denotes 'Un-uttered achievement'. When from the mere commencement of a subject, the rest of it is comprehended without being actually expressed in words, it is 'Semi-uttered Expression'.

(36) **Priyokti (Compliment)**

The term 'Priyokti' literally means 'Pleasing utterance'. When words are uttered in a pleasant mood to honour an honourable person and to express joy for his acts, it is 'Compliment'.

**Vaishika**

*Rasarnavasudhakara* gives us a categorization of Nayaka (the Hero) in the context of love into three types : - Pati, Upapati and Vaishika. Vaishika is a handsome, comely youth, born of a noble family, well - bred, always finely dressed and perfumed, well-versed in sciences, intelligent, fearless and brave, not given to wretchedness, liberal-minded, patient, and a sweet-talker; diligence, cleverness, sweetness and charm are his qualities, he is willing to enjoy sensual pleasures in the company of a harlot or a courtesan.

**Vaivarnya**

This means "change of facial complexion" (Sixth Sattvika Bhava / Emotional State) which according to Bharata is enacted by an actor by changing the tint of face and this is done by the difficult and delicate process of putting pressure on the arteries and the nerves.

**Vajra**

Denotes a 'Thunderbolt', the weapon of Indra. Treated as one of the presiding deities of theatre, who according to Bharata should be worshipped with offerings and sacrifices.

**Vakra**

It means "crooked", with reference to a Scale or Rāga that doesnot follow a straight path in ascent or descent.

**Vakra (Instrument)**

This is kind of Vina which is said to be extremely zigzag, that is, its daṇḍi is inferred to be crooked. This was used in the time of the Mahāvrata ceremony. This was played by the Vina player at the command of the Sdhvāryu who were seated in a 'Sadomaṇḍapa' in the eastern side of hte Sacrificial hall states *Drahyaya Shrauta Sutra*. The instrument Vakra is also mentioned int he *Latyana Shrauta Sutra*.

**Vaksha bheda**

This denotes the movements of the chest. According to

Natyashastra its five varities are :-

Abhugna, Nirbhugna, Prakampita, Udvahita, Sama.

(1) **Abhugna:** In this, the chest is lowered, back is high and shoulders are slightly bent and kept loose. Abhugna is used to depict 'confusion, dispair, fainting, sorrow, fear, sickness, broken heart, touching cold objects, rain, and shame.

(2) **Nirbhugna :** Here the chest is held steady and motionless, with lowered back and raised shoulders. Used to depict 'stun, paralysis, resentment, surprise, asserting the truth, haughty, and valour.

(3) **Prakampita:** This is a continuous heaving motion of the chest to exhibit 'laughter, fits of convulsions, confusion, fear, hard work, sickness etc.

(4) **Udvahita:** In Udvahita, the chest is raised to show "deep breathing, viewing high placed objects and yawning."

(5) **Sama:** In Sama, all the limbs are in natural position. Used to portray the natural position of the limbs.

**Vakrapani**

This is the fifth constituent parts of Purvaranga (preliminaries of a play) taken up behind the curtain. It means the tuning of the wind instruments (Vadya).

**Vakyam**

Spoken words in a play.

**Valithorukam**

As presented by Bharata in his *Natyasastra*, this is the third and one of the 108 Karanas or cosmic Shiva Bharata Poses. Here the hands are in Sukathunda hasta and is held in and out. The thighs are a little apart with the knees bent.

**Vaṁsha**

The *Natyashastra* helds music, an indispensable adjunct

of Sanskrit drama. It informs about some musical instruments like Mridanga, Paṇava, Dardura, Dundubhi, Muraja, Jhallari, Paṭaha, Vaṁsha, Shaṅkha and Ḍakkinī.

**Vāṇa**

This instrument is mentioned in all the Shrauta Sutras, particularly in the *Lātyana Shrauta Sutra*, *Drāhyayana Shrauta Sutra and Āpasthamba Shrauta Sutra*.

According to the *Apastamba Srauta* Sutra, the daṇḍi is made of the Audumbara tree. It had three holes to each of which ten strings were tied. Therefore the instrument was one with hundred strings, Satatantu Vina (Āpāsthamba). The strings were made of a kind of grass called '*munji*' which is said to be soft and strong. As an alternative, *darbha grass* was also used as strings.

The Srauta of Drāhyāyana informs "the belly of the instrument over the resonator was of the hide of an ox. This part was known as the Mukhabilam.

The instrument is said to have had three holes. To the two holes on either side were attached thirty three strings, while in the middle one there were thirty four. After being tied to these three holes the other end (of the strings are said to have been terminated at the Mukhabilam. Before actually commencing to play, the strings were tightened and tuned. It was played with the sticks of Nāṇal or Nocchi with a natural bend at the end. The strings, instead of being struck or plucked were merely rubbed starting from near the daṇḍi with holes towards the Mukhabilam. The *Udgabr* first demonstrated this to and four playing of the instrument and then handed over the instrument to a *Bramin* who continued the playing throughout the Mahavrata ceremony.

**Vanaspati**

In Vājasaneyi Samhita, it is mentioned as a wooden drum.

**Vāṇici**

This is explained in the sense of musical instrument in a verse of the Rig Veda. (V. 75-4).

**Varāha Hasta**

This is a double hand gesture in which the hands in *mrigaseersha* should be placed one above the other with the thumbs and the little fingers stretched out.

It denotes "boar."

**Vardhamana Hasta**

This is a double hand gesture in which the two hands in *Hamsapaksha* are held opposite to each other.

This gesture is used to denote : "opening of ventilator or window."

**Vardhamāna (Purvaranga)**

This is one of the constituent parts of Purvaranga (preliminaries of a play, performed on the stage). Vardhamāna commences immediately after 'Nandi' or benediction. It features an increasing intensity of manly dance 'Tandava'. The ritual is termed as 'Vardhamānā'.

**Vardhamanaka**

Gandharva gita-s where the syllables, tempo and number of dancers gradually increase.

**Varjya**

A discarded Shruti (or the removal of a shruti in the process of composing a new Rāga) is called Varjya.

**Varjya Svara**

It means 'Abandoned note' and refers to 'Vivadi' or dissonant note, one of the four kinds of svaras (Notes).

**[see 'Vivadi']**

**Varna**

It denotes 'facial colour.

**[For details see 'Mukhąraga']**

**Varṇa**

This is a melodic contour (e.g. ascending or descending), melodic choices. It is 'Melodic movement' and refers to the act of singing and is of four kinds viz Sthāyī (level), Repetition of the same sound; Ārohī (ascent); Avarohī (descent); and Sañcārī (wandering or ascent and descent combined).

Varna is one of the attributes of musical rendering (Pathyaguna). Four types of accent or Varna are:-

Udātta, Anudatta, Svarita and Kampita (Acute, grave, circumflex and quivering respectively).

According to Lewis Rowell, Professor of music theory at Indiana University "To put the three terms Varna, Alankara and Gamaka into their proper perspective, it is useful to imagine the decorative dimension in Indian music as a hierarchy : If Varṇa represents the generalized shape of a given unit of melody, Alankara signifies the specific pattern of decoration within this general shape, and Gamaka refers to the transitive elements around and between the individual svaras - the microlevel of melodic structure. And in addition to this progression from contour to path to microstructure, we can also infer another progression : from ornaments as conceived to ornaments as performed; once again from the potential to the actual. The idea of varna is readily grasped by the mind and described in words, but thc microscopic subtleties of the Gamakas resist description and are best learned by demonstration and imitation.

The musicians of ancient India seem to have reached an consensus on the concept of Varṇa, and all the authors of our corpus of literature accept the standard set of four : the Sthāyī (stable) Sañcāri (wandering); Arohī (ascending); and Avarohī (descending) contours. A melodic unit, then might dwell upon or prolong a single tone, it might proceed in a steady upward or downward direction, or it might exhibit a pattern with frequent change of direction.

In the later history of musical ornamentation, both Varna and Alankara have developed into abstract melodic concepts, freely translatable betwen vocal and instrumental performance; and the size of the unit determining the Varṇa is a matter of instinct and convention. It is, one can say, is melodic gesture or event.

**Varna Hasta**

It denotes Hastas for colour. They are :-

(1) **Kori** - white ... *Arala, tripataka, pataka, hamsapaksha or chatura* facing upward.

(2) **Pita** - yellow ... *Arala, tripataka, pataka, hamsapaksha or chatura* facing obliquely.

(3) **Nila** - blue ... *Pataka, arala, tripataka, hamsapaksha or chatura* facing downwards.

(4) **Ched** - red ... *Tamrachooda* facing obliquely towards the sides.

**Varṇikā**

It refers to the mask or dress of an actor.

**Varsavara**

It refers to the 'Eunuchs' who figures in the Sanskrit drama and depicted as serving the King in his Harem (Antahpura). Kañcuka, the Royal Chamberlain and the Varṣavara are said by Bharata to be employed in the harem and given the charge of looking after the young girls and princesses.

**[see also 'Kancuki']**

**Varthitam**

As discussed in the *Natyasastra*, this is the second and one of the 108 Karanas (Cosmic Shiva Bharata Poses). Here both hands is held with the palms outward in front of the thighs. The hands are crossed at the wrist as in Svasthika over each other, then they are separated over the chest, raised and placed on the thighs.

**Varuna**

Encompasser of the world, Name of an Aditya, chief among the Vedic gods, he specially presides over the waters, the night and the west.

He is omniscient, punishes sin and is prayed to for forgiveness; he is also the sender of disease; often associated with Mitra and Indra.

In classical Sanskrit (Post - Vedic), he is the god of the waters or ocean and regent of the west.

He is the god of truth and retribution, and cosmic order; as said, king of gods; subsequently an Aditya; god of the waters, one of the presiding deities of the theatre, who should be worshipped with offerings and sacrifices, states Bharata.

Varuna (Rain) controls the interior of the playhouse or auditorium.

**Vasakasajja Nayika**

According to *Natyashastra*, there is well known classification of Heroine into eight types (ie, Heroine - in love) basing it on the amorous relationship of the Heroine with Hero and depending on the variety of treatment and attention bestowed upon her by her lover. The Vasakasajja Nayika is one who is anxious and ready to welcome the lover, defines *Dasarupaka*.

**[see also 'Nayika']**

**Vastu**

This denotes 'Story' or 'Plot' of a play and according to Sanskrit dramatic theory, Neta (Hero), Vastu (Story) and Rasa

(Artistic enjoyment / sentiment) constitue the three essential ingredients of a dramatic composition and further, according tothe difference in these respects the ten varieties (Daśarūpakas) are to be recognised.

**[see also : Adhikarika Vritta, Prasangika and Itivritta]**

**Vastu (Music)**

In music, it denotes a large formal section in a Gītaka; and also a synonym for Prabandha (with reference to its formal structure).

**Vasuki**

One of the three great serpents who is supposed to preside in the knot of the flag-staff of Indra (Jarjara), the setting up of which is regarded as the most important of the sacred rites on the stage.

**Vatsa**

In chapter XIX of *Natyashastra*, Bharata devoted on Modes of Address and Intonation. Vatsa denotes 'Child'. Bharata has prescribed a set of words for calling the different charcters according to their position. A pupil or son was addressed as 'Vatsa' 'Putraka' (son), Tātā (a term of endearment) or by the name of his gotra by father or preceptor.

**Vayasya**

This is a mode of address prescribed in *Natyashastra* in which a jester should address the king as 'friend' (Vayasya) and vice-versa.

**Vedas**

The term Veda is derived from the Sanskrit root *vid*, to know.

Veda means 'sacred knowledge, revelation. Vedas are the most sacred book of the Hindu. Each Veda (Rig, Sāma, Yajur and Artharva) has its own Brahmana or Brahmanas.

The Vedas are called Samhitas because they are collections or anthologies of hymns and mantras. They contain secret knowledge - knowledge of the highest spiritual truth of which the human mind is capable and its relationship with the world and the individual and collective life in the world and on the earth.

It is pertinent to add here that Bharatas monumental work on dramatics called '*Natyashastra*' is considered as the -Veda (Fifth Veda) or Natya Veda. *Natyashastra* laid down the rules for the three arts - drama, music and dancing. However Bharata devoted only five chapters on music, as music was considered an adjunct of drama. This is, therefore, primarily a work on dramatic art having 32 chapters. in which namely, 28 to 32 chapters are devoted to the then current form of music.

To trace the history of the music tradition in India, one has to look back to our vedic past (4500 B.C. to 1000 B.C.)

The hymns of the Rigveda, the oldest religious text in the world were composed between 1500 and 900 B.C. or even earlier as the date of the Rig Veda is a matter of controversy.

Samaveda came later (between 1800 to 1000 B.C.) which is a collection of hymns taken from the Rigveda to be employed for chanting on occasions such as sacrifies, so essential in Vedic rituals, later developed into a highly secular art.

The rules for chanting the hymns are prescribed in the Sama Sutra, directly the way of modulation and intonation, etc of letters, syllables and tones.

A scale of four notes called 'Svaratantra' came into being. The ancient Aryans had their music confined to four notes. For the first time, an account of the seven notes was found in the Manduki Siksha of the Atharva Veda.

This hymns was sung by three classes of Brahmans named Hotris, the Udagatra and the Adhabharya. The Hotris used to recite the hymns, the Udagatris had to chant the hymns and the Adhabharyas used to perform the sacrificial rites and offered oblations in fire. **[see 'Natyaveda' for Theatre]**

**Vedika**

Denotes a decorative arrangement at the bottom of a wall, door, window etc and also at the front vertical face of the Rangapitha; mentioned in Bharata's *Natyashastra* (2.77). *Natyashastra* in its stanza 2.98, has specified that the Rangpitha should be eight hastas broad and be adorned like a Vedika. The Adornment of the Rangapitha, according to Bharata, meant that its vertical front side should have mouldings like the Vedika. According to a scholar, a step at a lower level than the Rangapitha is provided around it and this step is called the Vedika, while few opine that Vedika refers to a Varandah. But the opposite school argues that if a Varandah around the Rangapitha then how to explain the additional Varandahs (Mattavaranis) provided on both the sides of the Rangapitha.

**Venu**

It is described as a reed of bamboo in the Aharva Veda. In later works like *Taittiriya Samhita* and *Kāthaka Samhita* also mention about Venu. In the *Taittiriya Samhita* it is described as Susīra ie hollow (V. I. I. 4).

**Vepathu**

This means "Trembling, Tremor, Shivering", etc (Fifth Sattvika Bhava / Emotional State), which according to Bharata should be exhibited on the stage by shivering, trembling and shaking of the body.

**Vesakara**

The *Natyashastra* refers to some Acharyas who are expert in preparing materials for the stage. There are many types of artisan seems to have been necessary in the presentation of plays. Vesakara is one who prepares dresses for the actors, as laid down in the *Natyashastra*.

**Vibhasas**

This denote the Sub-dialects of Prakrita, used in Sanskrit drama. Bharata mentions about Shakari, Abhiri, Chandali, Shabari, Dravidi, Auḍri and Vanaukasi as 'Vibhasas'.

**Vibhavas**

Vibhava is stimuli in the form of dramatis personae placed in different situations in the plot for rasa (sentiment) evocation.

It denotes determinants that help the development of a feeling into a sentiment. They are of two kinds, viz Ālamhana (supporting) and Uddīpana (excitant) The Anubhāvas or consequents are the reactions to these determinants. Therefore, Vibhavas Anubhavas and Vyabhicharibhavas are indispensable for the development of a permanent mood into its fullness as 'Rasa'.

**Vibodha**

It denotes 'Awakening, Perception' etc.

Vibodha or 'Awakening is the twenty - fourth Mutable State / Vyabhichari Bhava which according to Bharata should be represented by yawning, rubbing the eyes, leaving the bend and so on.

**Vicchinna**

In music, it is used to denote 'abrupt passing to the next note; one of the defects to be avoided in performing Karshaṇa.

**Vichara (Deliberation) see Vagyabhinaya**

**Vidārī**

In rhythmic system, Vidārī is pause or cadence, also a line or phrase ending with such a pause or cadence.

Thus it connotes two things :-

(a) a pause or melodic cadence;

(b) a unit ending with a prescribed pause or cadence.

**Vidushaka**

Denotes a 'Jester' or Clown of a Sanskrit drama. A typical character, usually a disreputable and illiterate Brahmin with an insatiable appetite food, bald and deformed, with staring eyes, and protruding teeth. He speaks in Prakrit, the vernacular then in vogue (in the ancient time) among the low-class characters, as Sanskrit being reserved for kings, nobles and divine characters.

A modern scholar has touched upon the various shades of this typical character in the following words :-

"The most familiar type of Vidūṣaka is a Brahmin. The Vīdūṣaka has the ability to make cultured people laugh in matters of money and women. He is irreproachable and liked by all. He instigates jealousies and quarrels, he is witty, and is able to pacify the hero or the heroine to some extent. He also stimulates love and enjoyment between the king and his beloved. He is, therefore, invariably a companion of the hero, and assists him in his love affairs. The Vidūṣaka, who causes, mainly, laughter is sometimes an intelligent critics also. It is obvious from his functions that he is rather an important person in a drama. He can do and undo things. He sometimes provokes, unwittingly or otherwise, a tiff between the hero and the heroine, and sometimes brings about reconciliation between them. Through his love and loyalty for the hero, he sometimes helps him in solving his problems, but sometimes in doing so, his clumsiness results only in accentuating the troubles of his friend, as in *Mṛcchkaṭikam.* This character, therefore, sometimes creates and accentuates conflict, though more often than not he is hardly inside the conflict".

Vidusaka is a significant dramatic character, who appears in four roles in association with the four kind of heroes described in Bharata's dramatic theory.

(1) When associated with a Dhiroddhata celestial hero, the Vidusaka emerges as an ascetic or a Muni, for e.g., Nārada.

(2) When he is a companion of a Dhiralalita Royal hero, he is a Brahmin.

(3) When depicted alongwith a Dhiroḍatta minister or army chief, he will be a Royal servant.

(4) With a Dhiraprashanta merchant or a Brahmin preceptor, the Vidusaka is represented on the stage as a pupil, as shown in Bodhyayana's play 'Bhagavadajjukiya'.

As the surviving dramatic patterns are mostly Natakas with Royal heroes and the late prahasanas, we have mostly 'Dvija' and 'Shisya' varieties of Vidusakas, while Liṅgi and Rajajivi types are almost missing.

The impression that we get about the Vidusaka from the classical plays is that they are rather biased in favour of the Brahmin Vidusaka, a common type employed and in the later period, rather stale and stereo typed humour.

According to *Sahityadarpana*, the Vidusaka is a character of the middling rank. But in the context of drama, the Vidusaka in *Bhāṇa* is considered to be low character (nicha patra).

*Daśarupaka* describes the Vidusaka as causing laughter. *Bhavaprakashana* and *Rasarnavasudhakara* state that the Vidusaka produces laughter with his distroted or defective or ugly body, his funny costume and his consistent, witty and humorous talk.

*Sahityadarpana* adds that Vidusaka is fond of instigating quarrels and knows his dramatic business quite well.

On the whole, he is the humorous companion and confidential friend of the hero in a play, who excited mirth by his quaint dress, speeches, gestures, appearances etc. and by allowing himself to be made the butt of ridicule by almost everybody.

This character falls under the head of 'Kamasachiva' of the hero, ie, an associate in the context of love matters.

**[see also 'Adhama' and 'Kamasachiva']**

**Vidyadhara**

Bearer of wisdom, mythical figures who resemble men, have magic powers and change forms at will; usually move in pairs and shower flowers over the valiant heroes from the sky, often represented in Sanskrit drama.

**Vidyut**

Vidyut is 'Lightning', one of the presiding deities of theatre, states Bharata, who should be worshipped with offerings and sacrifices.

**Vighna**

It refers to an obstacle the hero must ones come in order to achieve his derired objective.

**Vikṣepa**

This is one of the four silent Tāla gestures (right hand cast to the right).

**Vilasa**

Bharata in his *Natyashastra* uses such words like Vilasa, Sukha and Vinoda, in order to suggest entertainment. According to him, *Natyashastra* emerged out of the need for entertainment. But at the sametime he realized the seductive power of dramatic art and laid equal emphasis on both entertainment and instruction.

**Vilasika**

Also known as 'Vinayika' and 'Duramallika', Vilasika is a minor form of drama (Uparupaka) having just one-act.

**Vimarsha see Avamarsha - Samdhi**

**Vīṇā**

This is a stringed instrument.

The Vina, an ancient musical instrument, is associated with Saraswati, the Goddess of learning and music who is invariably depicted playing a Vina. This is one of the oldest stringed instruments of the past and was in vogue even in Vedic age for the fulfillment of chants of sacred hymns of the Vedas. It is a self-contained instrument having in itself Svara, Raga and Tala.

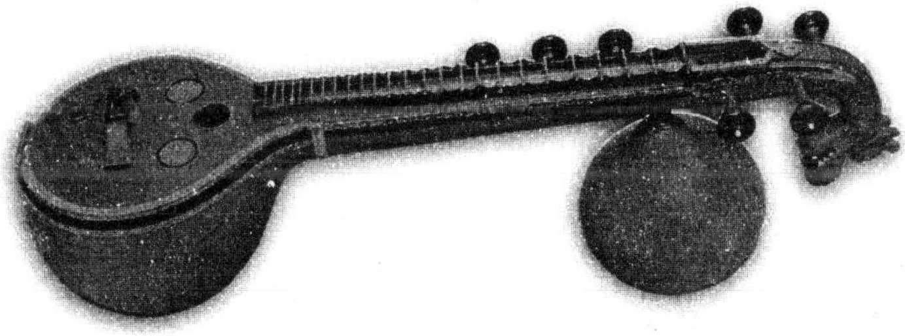

The Ancient musicians held that the primry instrument that products 'Dhvani' being the human body. The human body which is created by God is called Daiva Vīṇa, whereas the musical instrument, Viṇa is the creation of man which is held and played by the musician. This manushivina is called '*Kāshṭ avīṇā*'.

The head of the human body is compared to the gourd of the Vīṇa which is supported by the left shoulder of the player.

The Udaram or stomach of the Daiva Viṇa is similar to the Ambhaṇa (resonator) of the Mānushi Viṇa which is the curved interior part of the Vīṇa daṇḍam. The tongue (Jihvā) of men (Daiva Vina) is akin to the Vādana of the manmade Vina. Just as the tongue forces the production of sound in the human body, so also the Vādana, which is kōṇa or plectrum resembling the tongue strikes the strings to produce sound on the Manushi vina.

The fingers of different length of human body are comparable to the strings (Tantri) of different lengths of the Vīṇā. Svaras can be produced by both the Daivavina and Manushi Vina. Just as the Svaras are produced by the air from the Mūlādhāra (and touches different parts of organs of the human body) so also the svaras are produced on the Vīṇa when the strings are stimulated (sparsa). Shabda or Dhvani (sound) is common to both. The nerves (Tardma) of the body are tied firmly to the joints in the body. Similarly the nerves (Tardma) of string are tied to the (two ends) of the Viṇa. The human body is covered with a skin Sharmaṇi full of hair. So also the Viṇa is covered with the hairy skin of a tiger.

In India many stringed musical instruments were known as Veena such as Shapta-tantri Vina, Chitra Vina, Rudra Vina, Kachhapi Vina, Vipanchi Vina etc.

*Sangita Ratnakara* furnishes ten varities of Vina and its species prevalent in India from 11-13th cent. A.D. These are:-

1. Eka - tantri
2. Nakula
3. Tri - tantri
4. Chitra
5. Vipanchi
6. Matta - kokila
7. Alapini
8. Kinnari
9. Pinaki
10. Nishanka - Vina

Someshvaradeva's *Manasollasa* provides details of craftsmanship of string instruments like the Ekatantri Vina (verses 586 - 613), Kinnari Vina (verses 666 - 701), and Mridanga, a percussion instrument (verses 687 - 701). The criteria to be adopted for the selection of raw materials - wood, hide, etc are described in the *Sangitaratnaka* (Chapter VI, verses 1158 - 1163).

Today's South Indian Vina has seven strings and 22 fixed frets. It has these strings to play the Raga, it has the drone and the strings are so placed that Tala can also be played on them.

**Vinadri**

This is one of the tonal qualities mentioned in the '*Chandogya Upanishad*'.

In the musical field, the term was used to denote a voice resembling that of an ox (rishabha).

**Vinata**

Means 'passing from prathama svara to dvitiya svara; the thumb merely touching the first parva of the index finger - a gīti - upāya. One of the Āvāntara Svaras.

**Vīnāvāda**

In the Purushamedha Prakayana of the *Taittiriya Brahmaṇa* (3rd Ashtaka and 4th Prashana), names of professional artists and musicians are given whose services were required in the sacrificial hall. Vīnavāda is one of them. Vinavāda denotes an expert player on the Vīṇa.

**Vīṇavada Gaṇaka**

Refers to expert Vina players with their disciples.

**[see 'Vinavada']**

**Vinayika see Vilasika**

**Vinoda see Vilasa**

**Viparyaya (Inversion) see Vagyabhinaya**

**Vipralabdha Nayika**

This denotes one of the eight varities of Heroine-in-love, as depicted in Bharata's *Natyashastra*. *Dasarupaka*, another ancient treatise describes her as one whose lover has not come to her even though she has sent a message. In this case there is a vogue presupposition of the other woman which brings in, jealousy. It is, therefore, less poignant, yet, the lovers failure to respond makes her no doubt unhappy, and gives rise to many speculations.

**[see also 'Nayika']**

**Vipralambha Shringara see Shringararasa**

**Viprayoga see Shringara rasa**

**Vira Rasa**

Vira means 'Chivalry, Heroic, Mighty' etc. Vira rasa is one of the navarasa (Nine Ruptures/Rasas).

Chivalry or Heroic sentiment is represented on the stage by firmness, patience, heroism, pride, zeal, valour and wit.

The commentary on *Dasarupaka* categorizes the heroic into three varities. A hero can be a (1) *Dayavira* (Jimutavahana in 'Nagananda') Kavyanusasana regards him Dharmavira.

(2) *Yuddhavira*

(3) *Dānāvīra* (Karna's sacrifice of his armour and ear rings in Karṇabhāra).

The Vyabhichari bhavas or Transient feelings are Fortitude (Dhriti), Remembrance (Smriti), Arrogance (Garva), Dignity, Strength etc.

Sthayibhava in Virarasa is Utsāha (Energy), this is obvious because Slothfulness or lassitude can never produce heroic behaviour.

Vibhāvas in this sentiment are discipline, prowess, strength, valour etc.

| | | |
|---|---|---|
| Varna | : | Gaura (Wheatish brown) |
| Mukharaga | : | Rakta (Reg) |
| Hasta | : | Chandrakala |
| Svaras | : | Shadja, Rishabha |

Raga : The suitable Ragas to Vira Rasa are Nātakuranji, Devagāndhāri, Ārabhi, Gaula, Nāta, Reethigaula, Kedāra, Begade, Gambira nāta etc. Ghana Ragas, among others depict this Vira Rasa in effective manner.

Presiding deity : Indra.

**Virasam**

This refers to the lack of concentration while singing. Virasam is a defect in singing.

**Virahotkanthita Nayika**

There is a categorisation of Heroine into eight types, according traditional dramatic theory '*Natyashastra*'. This is based on the amorous relationship of the Heroine with the Hero and depends on the variety of treatment and attention bestowed upon her by her lover. Virahotkanthita Nayika is "one of these and *Dasarupaka* describes her as one who is separated from her lover and is anxious to meet him." The Virahotkanthita Nayika, at this stage, is undoubtedly unhappy and the cause of separation may be due to various reasons like circumstances, fate, curse, elderly persons and so on.

**Vishalishṭam**

This is a defect in singing. It means 'separating the words in irregular places'.

**Vishamāhatam**

In the domain of music, it connotes two things :-

(a) Confused utterances of the mātras, hrsva, dīrgha, etc., one of the fourteen defects in singing.

(b) Shaking of the first svara in order to reach the next svara - also a defect in performing Karshaṇa.

**[see 'Nayika']**

**Virūpā**

The *Natyashastra* admits of three modes of representation of dramatis personae. In Sanskrit drama, the roles were of three different qualities, namely, Anurupā, Virūpa and Rūpanusarini. In Virupa variety, a child portrays the role of an old man and an old man portrays the role of a child. Therefore, the characters of the old may be taken up by the young and the vice versa.

**Visama see Dosas**

**Visandhi see Dosas**

**Vishada**

It denotes 'Dejection, Depression, Despair' etc.

Vishada is the nineteenth Mutable State/Vyabhichari Bhava which Bharata states should be represented in acting by searching for help, worrying about means, weakness, senselessness, deep breathing and so on.

**Visha lishṭam**

This is a defect in singing. It means 'Acparating the words in irregular places.'

**Vishamāhatam**

In the darrom of music, it connotes two thonp:-

(a) Confused ufferances of the mātras, hrsva, dirgha, etc., one of the fourfeen defceb in singing.

(b) Shaking of the frist svara in order to reach the next svari - also a defect in performating Karshaṇa.

**Vishesana (Distinction) see Vagyabhinaya**

**Vishnu**

"Striding widely over the Peaks of the Earth", the Preserver of the cosmos; the second god in the trinity with Brahma the Creator and Shiva, who is assigned the role of the Destroyer. He is the second of triad, the Preserver, husband of Lakshmi or Sri, and Sarasvati, father of the god of love, rests on the serpent Sesha and has Garuda for his vehicle, descends to earth in several Avatars.

Vishnu is the God of love (Sringara rasa), States *Natya-shastra* (6, 44).

One of the presiding deities of theatre, according to Bharata and should be worshipped with offerings and sacrifices.

**Viskambhaka**

Linking supporting scenes in the beginning of an act is called 'Viskambhaka'.

**[see 'Arthopakshepakas']**

**Vismaya**

It means 'Surprise, Astonishment'.

Vismaya is a sthayi bhava, shown by an actor by the wide opening of eyes, looking steadily without winking, movements of eyebrows, horripilation, tremor of head, commenting appreciation and the like.

Vismay, as a permanent state is produced by means of sudden appearance, magic feats, extraordinary human acts, excellent paintings, art and crafts, etc.

**Visvakarman**

"The all maker", ie, Prajapati or Tvaṣṭr as the creator *per artem;* subsequently the master architect of the gods.

Vishvakarma appears in Rigveda, presiding deity of all craftsmen.

He is the divine architect who extended his support when the new veda of the dramatic art '*Natyaveda*' was forged by Brahma. Visvakarma was commissioned to build a playhouse for the enactment of the new art.

**[see also 'Natyaveda']**

**Visvaram**

When one is not conforming to the rules of singing the svaras in correct places, i.e., singing out of sruti, it is called 'Visvaram'.

**Vita**

A character in Sanskrit play, a gallant parasite, a rake, an expert in the ways of the courtesans.

In dramatic treatise, Vita is technically described as ekavidya, that is wellversed in one of the fine arts, music, dance or poetry. This dramatic character is also exceptionally gifted in the arts of love and falls under the category of Kama sachiva, ie, an associate of hero in love matters.

This 'rake' is a typical character who used to assist the hero in his less reputable adventures. A thoroughly disreputable character in Bhāṇa type of play, who walks through the less respectable parts of the town holding imaginary conversatioons with the people he meets.

According to *Sahityadarpana*, Viṭa is proficient in one of the arts; an expert in dealing with courtesans, knowing all their ways and etiquettes; a lover of gambling and (rather surprisingly) not interested in sexual pleasures; he is an eloquent speaker, very much prized in literary assemblies and clubs; he is a sweet-talker and has a sweet temper too. According to *Sahityadarpana,* the Vita is a character of the middling rank. But in the context of drama, the Vita in Bhāna is considered to be low character (nicha patra).

*Nataka-Laksana-Ratnakosha* states that a Vita is a friend of the courtesans. It implies that this character is very intelligent also, and is befriended even by a king.

Vita is also hero of the Bhāna type of drama which gives absorbing accounts of his romantic escapades, his love intrigues, his fine culture and wit, and his bohemian life style.

*Bhavaprakashana* describes Vita as a courteous person, a poet, a very capable debator and, on the whole, very versatile.

**[see also 'Adhama']**

**Vitarka**

It denotes 'Deliberation, Conjecture' etc.

Vitarka or "Deliberation" is the thirty third Mutable State / Vyabhichari Bhava which according to Bharata should be represented on the stage by discussion, settling problems and keeping up deliberation.

**Vithi**

This is one of the ten major types of drama (Rupakas). Like Bhāna, it is also a one-act piece. The Vithi was acted by two actors. The *Sahitya darpana* mentions "According to the opinion of an anonymous authority, three actors may also participate, one portraying the role of a person of high social standing (Uttama), another of the middle order (Madhyama) and a third one of the low-class (Adhama). In all cases the deliberations are with imaginary persons, ie, Ākāśabhāṣita.

This is therefore one of the ten recognised forms of drama, mentioned in the classical dramatic treatise. The story is conceived by the playwright; one or two characters; the dominant sentiment is Śringara (Love), having just one act.

**Vithi see Prastavana**

**Vivadi**

It means 'Dissonant'. Bharata's *Natyashastra* divides Svaras (Notes) into four varities, namely, Vādī (Sonant), Samvādī (consonant), Anuvādī (Assonant) and Vivādī (Dissonant), according to the number of Shrutis (Intervals) between them and ever since this has remained the accepted ramification.

Vivadi notes are like enemies. The speaking note is called Vādī, the note which converses with it is Samvadi, that which increases the beauty of the Raga is Anuvadi, while one which clashes with it is Vivadi. This Vivadi is not natural to a Raga but such note occurs in it sometimes only accidently. It is difficult to use a Vivadi note in a Rāga without marring its beauty and hence it is left out of the Raga and is known as 'Varjya Svara', ie, abandoned note.

**Vrīḍā**

It means 'Bashfulness, shame' etc.

Vrīḍa or 'Bashfulness' is the thirteenth Mutable State / Vyabhichari Bhava and according to Bharata, Bashfulness should be represented on the stage by covering the face, thinking, bowing down the head, writing on the ground, touching the clothes and the ring and biting nails and so on.

**Vrishchikalata**

"Scorpion-legged;" a cadence of musement whole one lcy B bent with the calf folded in and the calf folded in and the other back or sideways.

**Vritta natyamandapa**

*Bhavaprakashana* has mentioned about three theatre-pendals these are square, trinagular and circular. The last Vritta natyamandapa or mandapa is a new addition to Bharata's prescription.

This is a circular type of theatre. The *Bhavaprakashana* mentions Vritta in place of Vikrista play-house, but gives no structural details are provided in it.

**[see 'Ranga']**

**Vrittanta see Itivritta**

**Vrittis**

This is one of the many misused Sanskrit words. In Sanskrit dramaturgies and commentaries, Vritti is recognised in a technical sense. Broadly it denotes 'A style of production' Bharata while delineating ten genres of drama, gives the reason for this kind of categorisation and the basis on which they are recognised. The bases or the mother-sources he calls 'Vrittis' (XVIII.4).

Chapter XXII of *Natyashastra* explains four types of Vritti, ie, styles of expression.

According to Bharata, drama as the fifth Veda originated out of the four Vedas, the words (prose and poetry) (Bharati Vritti) were taken from Rigveda, ie, Music from Sāmaveda (Sāttvati Vritti, ie, singing and dancing) Acting from the Yajurveda and Rasa from Atharvaveda (Ārabhati Vritti, ie, Final enjoyment or entertaining activities) Drama was, therefore, born out of imitation, singing, dancing and words.

He furthers states that Bharati Vritti was derieved from Rigveda, Sāttvati from Yajurveda, Kaisiki from Samaveda and Arabhati from Atharvaveda.

Vritti or style according to classical theories of drama are of four types:-

(1) Bharativritti (Eloquent style)

(2) Sāttvati (Grandiose style)

(3) Kaishiki (Gay style)

(4) Arabhati (Horrific style)

In one of the verses in Chapter VI of *Natyashastra* Bharata has furnished eleven elements of Drama which can be collectively called the *'Digest of Natyashastra*. These significant dramatic components are :-

Rasa (Sentiment)

Bhava (Emotion)

Abhinaya (Acting)

Dharmi (Modes of representation)

Vritti (Styles of expression)

Pravritti (Local usages)

Siddhi (Success of production)

Svara (Note)

Atodya (Musical instruments)

Gana (Song)

Ranga (Theatre)

Vritti is, therefore, a significant domain of Sanskrit drama.

All Sanskrit dramatic treatises dealtwith all possiblities of situations - grave and gay, light and serious which be represented in a dramatic composition and therefore, proceeded to provide for all such situations even from the point of view of *the manner of its presentation.*

Bharativritti, one of the four Vrittis can be found in the preliminaries to a drama having four varieties, Prarochana, Prahasana, Vithi and Amukha. Of these Laudation or Prarochana can occur only at the beginning of a play, a part of the Amukha, but Pahasana and Vithi can spread over the whole body of the play.

The Sattvati (mental action) is accompanied by straight forwardness, a challenge, joy, fortitude and Raudra, Vira and Santa rasas. An elevated or exuberance of spirit or mental activity (condition) can be seen represented through an enthusiastic type of 'Service to the elders', liberality (Tyaga) or bravery (Saurya) etc.

Kaishiki is most popular Vritti. This denotes the gay style - graceful, suitable for the delineation of the delicacies of Śringara rasa. According to *Natya Darpana* in its commentary, the word 'Kaishiki' comes from Kesha. Women have lovely hair and breasts, and because these are prominent in this Vritti, it is termed as 'Kaishiki'. Bharata's *Natyashastra* defines it as variegated with beautiful dresses, charming with delicate women and full of dance and music to help the development of the sentiment of love which is its main purpose. *Dasarupaka* describes it as comprising of gestures portraying love; full of songs, dances and delicate with love sports. This Vritti deals with love and eventually all its sub-divisions also reveal the different tender aspects of love.

Arabhati Vritti refers to the 'Horrific style' and this fourth Vritti whose very nature is violent. Natyashastra states that it is full of characters who are haughty, vainglorious and puffed up. They are rash, reckless, and even resort to fraud and lies. *Dasarupaka* explains that Arabhati shows behaviour of characters angry, excited and involved in fights on battle field. It is through this Vritti that representation of supernatural, horrible events or illusions etc are carried out on the stage.

In short, Vritti is the mental disposition of a particular personages in particular situations. Bharativritti is broughtout is words; Sātvatī is disclosed in conduct; Kaishiki consists of words and acts of mildness and delicacy and Arabhati comprises of vigorous, strong or even violent words and actions.

Apart from the four modes of dramatic expression, it also denotes :-

(2) Poetic and / or Musical style

(3) The Tempo of Recitation.

**Vyabhicari Bhava**

This is the transitory states employed in the development of the Rasa and are thirty-three in number, viz.

(1) Nirveda (Despondency)

(2) Glāni (Weakness-languishing)

(3) Shanka (Apprehension)

(4) Asūyā (Envy - Jealousy)

(5) Mada (Intoxication)

(6) Shrama (Weariness - fatigue)

(7) Alasya (Indolence - lassitude)

(8) Dainya (Depression - wretchedness)

(9) Chinta (Anxiety)

(10) Moha (Distraction - delusion)

(11) Smriti (Recollection - remembrance)

(12) Dhriti (Contentment)

(13) Vriḍā (Shame)

(14) Chapalatā (Unsteadiness - inconstancy)

(15) Harsa (Joy)

(16) Āvega (Agitation)

(17) Garva (Arrogance)

(18) Jaḍata (Stupor)

(19) Viṣāda (Despair - depression)

(20) Autsukya (Longing)

(21) Nidrā (Sleep)

(22) Apasmāra (Epilepsy)

(23) Sūpta (Dreaming)

(24) Vibodha (Awakening)

(25) Amarsa (Indignation)

(26) Avahitta (Dissimulation)

(27) Ugratā (Severing)

(28) Mati (Thought)

(29) Vyādhi (Sickness)

(30) Unmāḍa (Insanity)

(31) Maraṇa (Pangs of death)

(32) Trāsa (Terror)

(33) Vitarka (Deliberation)

The Vibhavas, Anubhavas and Vyabhicaribhavas are indispensable for the development of a permanent mood into its fullness as 'Rasa'.

**Vyādhi**

It denotes 'Disorder, sickness, Extravagance' etc.

Vyādhi or 'Disorder' is the twenty-ninth Mutable State / Vyabhichari Bhava which according to Bharata, should be shown on the stage by distorting the face, dullness of the body, heavy breathing, crying, trembling, etc.

**Vyaghra Hasta**

This is a single hand gesture in which the fingers are kept apart in a curved position.

This is used to denote "a tiger, frog, monkey and an oyster (mother of pearl)."

**Vyajima see Pusta**

**Vyakula**

In music, it means singing without uniformity.

**Vyanjanadhatus see Dhātu**

**Vyayoga**

This is one of the ten recognised forms of drama, as stated in the traditional Sanskrit Treatise. The story is well known;

the Hero is a royal sage but not a divine being; rasa (sentiment) could be any except hasya or sringara; having just one act.

Vyayoga belongs to old popular stage and derieves its name from the fact that in it many men disagree with one another (Vyāyujyante).

This is a 'Rupaka' in one-act in which female has no role. The plot does not last for more than one day. It abounds in fighting and dissention.

The drama 'Kiratarjuniya' is a Vyayoga.

# Y

**Yajna**

In the context of drama, the term denotes 'Offering' Bharata at the end of *Natyashastra* says "The drama is offering (Yajna) to the gods, superior to the ordinary sacrificial offering, and pleasing to their eyes.

**Yakṣa**

A class of demi-gods, attendants of Kubera. King of Yaksas is 'Kubera', the ugly body, god of riches. They are not only represented in a Sanskrit drama, but are also the presiding deities of theatre, according to Bharata, who should be worshipped with offerings and sacrifices.

**Yaksin**

It refers to female Yaksha.

**Yaksinya**

At one place, Bharata has mentioned them as one of the presiding deities of theatre who should be worshipped with offerings and sacrifices.

**Yama**

In Veda, Yama is the god who rules over the departed fathers in heaven. In classical (post - vedic) Sanskrit, he is regarded as the god of death, presiding in the lower regions (his name being supposed to mean subduer or punisher).

Yama is the god of the dead. The Rod of Yama is regarded as one of the presiding deities of the theatre and should be worshipped with offerings and sacrifices, says Bharata.

According to *Natyashastra* (6, 44), Yama is the God of Pathos (Karuna rasa).

**Yama (Music)**

This is a kind of embellishment or grace, used in the pronounciation of the Vedic accents and the Svaras of Lankiganam'.

**Yamaka**

This is one of the four figures of speech (Alankaras) mentioned by Bharata which is available to a playwright. Yamaka is Alliteration, repetition of words or syllables similar in sound, Manmohan Ghosh translates this term as 'Twin'. According to *Natyashastra,* Yamaka is an embellishment born out of 'repetition of words at the beginning of the feet and other places. There are ten varities and while explaining them with illustrations, what we find is that the beauty of expression lies in repetition whether of a syllable or of a word, sometimes at the beginning, sometimes in the middle and sometimes at the end of the foot, or of all the feet.

**Yamanika see Javanika**

**Yati**

In music, it means the progression of tempo, ie, even, accelerating, decelerating.

In rhythmic system, Yati is the principle of regulation and rhythmic control; also, in a more specialized sense, temporal flow (whether even, accelerating, or decelerating).

**Yatna see Pratimukha - Samdhi**

**Yavanika see Javanika**

**Yonyantri-bhasa see Bhasavidhanam**

# References


Ahobaḷa Pandit. Sangitaparijata / ed. by Kalindaji. - Hathras : Sangit Karyalaya, 1941.

Amarakosa : gems from the treasure house of Sanskrit words / tr. into English by C.D. Deshmukh. - New Delhi : Uppal Publishing House, 1981.

Bharata. Natyashastra / ed. by Manmohan Ghosh. - Calcutta : The Asiatic Society, 1950-61.

.- Calcutta; Manisha Granthalaya, 1967.

.- / ed. & tr. by N.P. Unni - Delhi : Nag Publishers, 1998.

Bhide, Vidyadhar Vaman. A Concise Sanskrit - English dictionary. - Delhi : Gian Publishing House, 1986.

Dalal, Minakshi L. Conflict in Sanskrit drama. - Bombay : Somaiya Publications, 1973.

Dhananjaya. Dasharupaka / tr. into English by George C.O. Haas. - Delhi : Motilal Banarsidass, 1966.

Gupta, Chandra Bhan. The Indian Theatre: its origin and development upto the present day. - Banaras : Motilal Banarsidass, 1954.

India 2001 : Reference encyclopaedia .- Bangalore : Indmark Publishing, 1995.

Keith, A. Berriedale. The Sanskrit drama in its origin, development, theory and practice .- London : Oxford University Press, 1954.

Kulkarni, R.P. The Theatre according to the Natyashastra of Bharata. - Delhi : Kanishka Publishers, 1994.

Manasara Shilpashastra / ed. by P.K. Acharya. - London : Oxford University Press, 1933.

Matangamuni. Brihaddeshi / ed by K. Sambashiva Shastr. - Trivandrum : [s.n.], 1928.

[Trivandrum Sanskrit Series; No. XCIV.]

Nandikeshwara. Abhinaya darpanam / ed. by Manomohan Ghosh.- Calcutta : Metropolitan Printing & Publishing House, 1934.

The Mirror of gesture / tr. into English by Ananda Coomaraswamy and Gopala Krishnayya Duggirala. - Cambridge : Harvard University Press, 1917.

Naradamuni. Sangita - Makaranda / ed. by Mangesha Rama Krishna Telang - Baroda : [s.n.], 1920.

[Gaekwad Oriental Series; No. XVI].

Premalatha, V. Music through the ages. - Delhi : Sundeep Prakashan, 1985.

Raghavan, V. Sanskrit, rama : its aesthetics and production. - Madras : Sarada Raghavan, 1993.

Ramachandra and Gunachandra. Natyadarpana / ed. with introd. in English and indices by G.K. Shrigondekar - Baroda : Oriental Institute, 1929. (Gaekwad's Oriental series; No. 48).

Rangacharya, Adya. Introduction to Bharata's Natyashastra New Delhi : Munshi Ram Manohar Lal, 1998.

Rasa-bhava darshan. Delhi - Clarion Books, 1997.

[A joint venture of Sajjan, B.V. Mishra and O.P. Sharma].

Rowell, Lewis. Music and musical thought in early India. - New Delhi : Munshiram Manoharlal, 1998.

Sagaranandin. Nataka - Laksana - Ratnakosha with Hindi comm. *Prabhā* by Babulal Shukla Shastri. - Varanasi : Chowkhambha Sanskrit Series Office, 1972.

Saroja Vaidyanathan. Bharatanatyam : an indepth study .- New Delhi : Ganesa Natyalaya, 1996.

Sharadatanaya Bhavaprakashana / ed. with introd. & indices by Yadugiri Yatiraja Swami of Melcot and K.S. Ramaswami Shastri. - Baroda : Oriental Institute, 1968.

(Gaekwad's Oriental Series; No. 45)

Sharangadeva. Sangitaratnakara with Kallinātha commentary I and II / ed. by Mangesha Ramakrishna Telang. - Bombay : [s.n.], 1896-97.

(Anandashram Sanskrit Granthavali; No. 35).

Shrikumara. Shilparatna / ed. by Ganapati Shastri. - Trivandrum : [s.n.], 1922 (Trivandrum Sanskrit Series; No. LXXV).

Shri Parshvadeva. Sangitasamayasara / ed. by T. Ganapati Shastri. - Trivandrum : [s.n.], 1925.

(Trivandrum Sanskrit Series; No. LXXXVII).

Singal, R.L. Aristotle and Bharata: a comparative study of their theories of drama. - Chandigarh : The author, 1977.

Singha Bhupala. Rasarnavasudhakara / ed. by Ramji Upadhyaya. - Saugar : Saugar University, 1969.

-. / ed. by T. Ganapati Shastri. - Trivandrum : [s.n.], 1916. (Trivandrum Sanskrit Series; No. L).

Vatsyayan, Kapila. The square and the circle of the Indian arts:- 2nd ed.—New Delhi: Abhinav Publications, 1997.

Vishvanatha. Sahityadarpana, with *'Lakshmi vyakhya'* by Krishnamohan Shastri. - Varanasi : Chowkhambha Sanskrit Series Office, 1967.

❑❑❑